Surgical Emergencies in the Newborn

Surgical Emergencies in the Newborn

J. ALEX HALLER, Jr., M.D.

Robert Garrett Professor of Surgery, The Johns Hopkins University; Children's Surgeon-in-Charge, The Johns Hopkins Hospital, Baltimore, Maryland

JAMES L. TALBERT, M.D.

Professor of Surgery and Pediatrics; Chief, Division of Pediatric Surgery, University of Florida College of Medicine, Gainesville, Florida

ILLUSTRATED

LEA & FEBIGER • PHILADELPHIA 1972

ISBN 0-8121-0312-2

Published in Great Britain by Henry Kimpton Publishers, London

Library of Congress Catalog Card Number: 79-135685

PRINTED IN THE UNITED STATES OF AMERICA

Preface

Pediatric surgery has evolved as a specialty within the province of general surgery owing to the unique nature of the congenital anomalies seen in newborn infants and to an increasing awareness that physiologic responses of a baby are both quantitatively and qualitatively different from those of an adult. Congenital anomalies that are incompatible with life, unless they are corrected, constitute the primary justification for this new specialty because they demand experienced judgment in early diagnosis and expeditious management, as well as highly refined operative technique and postoperative care. The purpose of this book is to focus on early diagnosis of major congenital abnormalities and to outline operative and postoperative management for those conditions that constitute surgical emergencies in the newborn.

For our purposes the congenital anomalies that require immediate operation can be divided arbitrarily into four groups: those characterized by acute respiratory difficulty, those that result in bilious vomiting, those that have significant skin defects, and those with large tumor masses. Almost all congenital anomalies that cause serious difficulty in newborn infants fall into one of these groups. In other words, if a baby has no obvious gross deformity and has neither respiratory distress nor continuing bilious vomiting, he probably does not require early surgical intervention.

Respiratory distress, the most urgent and alarming symptom, can be brought about by any congenital anomaly that causes significant obstruction to ventilation. Conditions of parenchymal origin, such as newborn pneumonitis, immaturity, and hyaline membrane disease, cannot be treated surgically, although some diseases of surgical significance are accompanied by parenchymal damage. These conditions are mainly congenital heart abnormalities that have associated respiratory distress, either on the basis of inadequate pulmonary arterial blood flow (the cyanotic congenital heart group) or from increased blood flow to the lungs that causes flooding of the parenchyma (the acyanotic congenital heart group).

Vomiting in a newborn infant is more a rule than an exception, but vomiting of bile-stained material in a full-term infant is strongly suggestive of mechanical intestinal obstruction below the ampulla of Vater. Normal full-term infants rarely vomit bile, although some premature infants may vomit bile-colored material as a result of an incompetent pyloric sphincter. Abdominal distention and evidence of abdominal discomfort may be absent, depending upon the level of intestinal obstruction, but recurrent vomiting which contains bile is the sine qua non of mechanical intestinal obstruction in the newborn and is an indication for early operative intervention.

No classification, however arbitrary, is complete without a miscellaneous group in which are included abnormalities that are grossly apparent. Any congenital abnormality which consists of a skin defect of the abdomen (omphalocele, sacrococcygeal teratoma) or of the spine (meningomyelocele) obviously represents a surgical emergency in the newborn. The immediate threat to the baby in such conditions is secondary infection and generalized sepsis. Large tumor masses represent another indication for emergency operation in the newborn and may be extrarenal or renal in origin. Finally, a much smaller group of emergencies result from birth trauma with its visible effects. These abnormalities are grossly obvious and usually do not

v

require refined diagnostic techniques. Their operative management demands a high degree of operative skill and judgment.

Postoperative management of a newborn infant is as important as operative skill for eventual recovery. Indeed, there are probably more lethal complications related to postoperative treatment than to intraoperative technique! More well trained surgeons are likely to be deficient in experience in postoperative care of infants than in operative management of the congenital anomalies. For this reason, we have included a detailed discussion of newer techniques of postoperative monitoring and have outlined a plan for intensive care of

newborn infants. Early definitive diagnosis of life threatening congenital anomalies, coupled with precise, delicate operative repair, will greatly improve a baby's chance for survival. When this excellent surgical management is then followed by carefully monitored postoperative fluid and electrolyte replacement and respiratory care, giant strides will be taken in overcoming the high mortality associated with newborn surgical emergencies. There are few greater challenges in surgery today.

Baltimore, Maryland   J. ALEX HALLER, JR., M.D.

Gainesville, Florida   JAMES L. TALBERT, M.D.

Acknowledgments

The authors wish to express their gratitude to the late Doctor Alfred Blalock; to Doctor George D. Zuidema, Doctor Blalock's successor as Chairman of the Department of Surgery at The Hopkins; Doctor David C. Sabiston, the first Chief of Children's Surgery at The Hopkins; and Doctor Marcus M. Ravitch, the incomparable surgical scholar and Pediatric Surgeon. Through their guidance and support, and through their leadership in development of the new Children's Medical and Surgical Center at The Hopkins, each of these men has provided an essential contribution to this book.

The senior author is especially indebted to Doctor Robert E. Gross, Ladd Professor of Pediatric Surgery at The Children's Hospital in Boston, and Doctor Hugh B. Lynn, Chief of Pediatric Surgery at the Mayo Clinic, for their inspirational stimulus in his choosing a career in Pediatric Surgery.

We also wish to acknowledge the assistance of our many associates at The Johns Hopkins Hospital and the University of Florida College of Medicine in preparing this manuscript. We are indebted to Doctor John J. White and Doctor Louise Schnaufer, our present and former pediatric colleagues in Baltimore, and to Doctor Edward R. Woodward and Doctor Gerold L. Schiebler, Professors and Chairmen of the Departments of Surgery and Pediatrics at the University of Florida, for their helpful comments and suggestions. We greatly appreciate the individual contributions of Doctor Richard Rowe and Doctor L. Jerome Krovetz of the Division of Pediatric Cardiology of The Hopkins in the preparation of Chapter 6; Doctor Donald V. Eitzman of The Division of Neonatology of the University of Florida, in the preparation of Chapters 2 and 3; and Doctor William H. Donnelly, of The Division of Pediatric Pathology of the University of Florida, in the preparation of Chapter 10. Doctor John Dorst, Chief of Pediatric Radiology at The Hopkins, and Doctor Alvin H. Felman, Chief of Pediatric Radiology at the University of Florida, gave invaluable advice in the selection of roentgenograms. As usual, Mr. Leon Schlossberg, Instructor of Art as Applied to Medicine at The Hopkins, has captured the essence of the operative procedures with many original illustrations.

Finally, we dedicate this book to our wives and children, who allowed us to impose upon them so that we might contribute in a small way to the surgical management of life-threatening emergencies in babies.

Contents

1

The Physiologic Challenge

Adaptation to extrauterine life confronts the newborn infant with a series of challenges that are magnified significantly by any condition requiring emergency operation. The five areas of immediate concern are those relating to respiratory, circulatory, fluid and electrolyte, metabolic, and immunologic mechanisms. In each instance, immaturity of physiologic function, combined with anatomic restrictions of tiny structures, demands specialized knowledge and techniques for successful preoperative, operative, and postoperative management.

Respiratory Function

Normal initiation of respiration may be impeded by prematurity, which is frequently complicated by congenital anomalies, sepsis, meconium aspiration, mucous plugs, and a variety of intra- and extrathoracic obstructions to the airway. Immaturity of central nervous system respiratory control is frequently reflected in intermittent spells of apnea, particularly in premature or debilitated infants. Anatomic size also limits respiratory reserve at this age. In the first week of life the vital capacity in a full-term infant is approximately 140 ml. and the tidal volume is 15 ml. The trachea may be only 4 cm. in length and 6 mm. in diameter. These factors, combined with weak thoracic musculature, flexible rib cage, and narrow bronchial passages, all affect ventilatory exchange and removal of tracheobronchial secretions.

Cardiovascular Function

The circulatory adjustments that are required for successful extrauterine survival include interruption of the placental circulation with closure of the umbilical arteries and vein, and rerouting of venous blood flow through the pulmonary arteries with closure of the foramen ovale and ductus arteriosus. Incompleteness of these events, with persistent function of fetal structures, can produce serious hemodynamic disturbances in the newborn, i.e., patent ductus arteriosus or interatrial septal defect.

Although the circulating blood volume of a newborn infant is relatively greater (108 ml./kg. body weight in premature infants and 85 ml./kg. body weight in full-term infants) than it will be later in life, his very small vascular pool emphasizes a need for caution. The loss of 20 ml. of blood (the amount absorbed by a single surgical sponge) in a full-term 5-lb. infant is comparable to a 500 ml. loss in a 150-lb. adult. Small amounts of blood in the vomitus or stool of an infant may represent a cause for alarm. Normally, the hematocrit is high in the first few days of life (50 to 70 per cent), and lower levels, which would be acceptable in older infants, may signify blood loss and anemia.

Fluid and Electrolyte Regulation

A newborn infant has a relatively greater proportion of total body water to lean body mass (82 per cent) than the adult (73 per cent). The extracellular fluid compartment is increased in the newborn infant, the relationship of extracellular to intracellular water being 46 per cent to 54 per cent. That of ECF to ICF in the adult is 40 per cent to 60 per cent. This proportionate increase in readily available fluid provides the neonate with a reserve that can sustain him during stressful situations in the first few days of life. Early diagnosis and correction

1

of any abnormalities allow the surgeon and pediatrician to benefit from this natural protective mechanism. Physiologically, a normal newborn appears optimally prepared to withstand the rigors of birth. There is a "golden period" of two to three days during which he can survive on his increased fluid volume and accumulated caloric reserves, anticipating the time when normal gastrointestinal alimentation will be instituted.

Concomitantly, the unique physiology of the neonate may confront the physician with a variety of unusual challenges. In a single day, the water excretion of an infant approaches 50 per cent of his ECF, whereas in a similar period, the adult excretes only 14 per cent of his ECF. Although the infant possesses a proportionately greater reservoir of fluid, at the same time he is much more sensitive to water loss.

The relative physiologic maturity of the individual baby plays an important role in each circumstance. Renal immaturity in the newborn, particularly in premature babies, is reflected in an inability to concentrate and conserve fluid and electrolytes. The glomerular filtration rate is decreased, and tubular re-absorption of fluid and electrolytes is diminished. This combination of factors restricts the neonate's ability to respond to conditions of stress and increased metabolic demand. As a result, urinary specific gravity may remain low (frequently resulting in a maximum specific gravity of approximately 1.015 in the premature versus a specific gravity of 1.035 in the older child), in spite of serious deficiencies in fluid intake. At the same time, congestive failure can ensue rapidly when overhydration occurs, since the decreased glomerular filtration rate limits renal excretion. The more mature the infant, the more likely he is to behave as an older child and show the usual antidiuretic response, which is initiated by surgical stress and limits urinary output immediately following a major abdominal or thoracic operation.

Maturation of other organ systems may also influence the regulation of fluid and electrolyte balance. In the first few days of life, the relative volume of gastric secretion is comparable to that of an adult, with a decrease to significantly lower levels in subsequent weeks. Failure to recognize this natural phenomenon can lead to gross inaccuracies in the calculation of fluid and electrolyte replacement of gastrointestinal losses.

Metabolism

Thermal Control. Caloric reserves available to a newborn infant, particularly the premature infant, are proportionately limited. Stores of insulating subcutaneous fat may be minimal, and thermal regulatory mecha-

nisms may be relatively immature. As a result, an infant's response to environmental changes can be extremely labile, particularly when he is exposed to cold temperatures. These natural limitations of a baby are compounded by an increase in his body surface area relative to his weight. Frequently, the thermal regulatory mechanism of the premature or debilitated infant proves inadequate to compensate for changes in environmental temperature. Temperature changes may be induced by intravenous administration of cold solutions or blood, exposure in air-conditioned rooms, induction of anesthesia, or application of highly volatile surgical prep solutions in the operating room. A warm-water heating pad in the operating room and heated Isolettes or cradle warmers in the intensive care unit are mandatory for successful management of these babies.

Unusual Drug Reactions. A subject of particular importance in the surgical management of newborn infants is drug therapy. Any physician caring for babies must have a thorough knowledge of possible drug idiosyncrasies as well as proper dosages for this age group. Aminophyllin, chloramphenicol, vitamin K, sulfonamides, tetracycline, muscle relaxants, novobiocin, and atropine are particularly hazardous for the newborn if administered improperly. Aminophyllin is very toxic and should be avoided. It is well known that chloramphenicol has been implicated in the production of aplastic anemia in children, but in neonates, it may also be responsible for a picture of acute vascular collapse, which has been descriptively labeled the "gray baby syndrome." Vitamin K toxicity may be reflected in hyperbilirubinemia. This complication is related to the administration of the water-soluble derivatives of menadione (HyKinone, SynKavite) and may be prevented either by the limitation of dosage to 1 mg. or by the substitution of vitamin K_1 (Mephyton, Konakion). The administration of sulfonamides has been associated with an unusual incidence of kernicterus in premature infants. Tetracyclines cause temporary inhibition of bone growth in premature infants and permanent hypoplasia and staining of dental enamel. Abnormally low levels of pseudocholinesterase have been found in very young infants and unusual sensitivity to d-tubocurarine has been identified. Novobiocin may interfere with biliary excretion of bilirubin through enzyme inhibition. Overdosage of atropine may result in central nervous system toxicity in newborns.

The necessity for adjusting medication dosages in infants to the variables of weight and surface area is immediately apparent. However, other factors such as alterations in rate of absorption, impaired hepatic and renal excretion, differences in distribution, and, finally variables in metabolism and detoxification are equally important in newborn and premature infants. It is recommended that any group caring for an injured child include a physician who is conversant in these important variables.

Immune Response

Infection represents a peculiar threat to the newborn infant. There appears to be a decrease in the phagocytic capacity of white blood cells as well as a diminished capability for immunoglobulin synthesis. Gamma globulin levels are significantly lower in premature than in full-term infants, and a further "physiologic" decrease occurs during the first few months of life. Infections encountered most frequently in these babies include pneumonia, peritonitis, septicemia, meningitis, and enterocolitis. Pneumonia may develop soon after birth as a result of aspiration of amniotic fluid or vaginal secretions during delivery, or aspiration of vomitus during resuscitative efforts following birth. Organisms that are seen most frequently include Staphylococcus aureus, coliform bacteria, Klebsiella, Pseudomonas, Proteus, and Salmonella. By far the most serious infections, and the most difficult to identify and treat, are the gram-negative septicemias. The newborn infant has few maternal antibodies to assist his own immature system in combating these organisms. For this reason an antimicrobial agent effective against gram-negative bacilli should be part of any regimen in the treatment of sepsis in the newborn, and especially in the premature infant.

Diagnosis of infection can prove particularly difficult in infants. Although a baby may respond with an anticipated elevation in temperature, it is not unusual, particularly in a premature infant, to find that lethargy and hypothermia are followed by jaundice, metabolic acidosis, and circulatory collapse. These signs are often the first indicators of occult sepsis. Most of the infections that develop after the first few hours of life result from environmental contamination. Every effort must be directed toward maintenance of clean surroundings. Frequent hand washing by physicians and nursing personnel caring for these tiny patients, and isolation technique requiring that a gown be worn, are important parts of overall management to prevent infection.

In summary, adaptation of a newborn infant to extrauterine life involves a series of physiologic responses, which must be appreciated by the physician who supervises the management of any neonatal surgical emergency. The immaturity of these processes in a premature infant warrants particular attention. The seriously ill, postoperative newborn infant often resembles a premature infant in his physiologic response to stress.

REFERENCES

Cooke, R. E., and Levin, S.: The Biologic Basis of Pediatric Practice. New York, McGraw-Hill Book Company, 1968.

Crelin, E. S.: Anatomy of the Newborn. Philadelphia, Lea & Febiger, 1969.

Dawes, G. S.: Foetal and Neonatal Physiology, Chicago, Year Book Medical Publishers, Inc., 1968.

Done, A. K.: Developmental pharmacology. Clin. Pharmacol. Ther., 5:432, 1964.

Nyhan, W. L., and Lampert, F.: Response of the fetus and newborn to drugs. Anesthesiology, 26:487, 1965.

Rashkind, W. J., Waldhausen, J. A., Downes, J. J., and Johnson, D. G.: Neonatal Respiratory Distress. Philadelphia, Lea & Febiger. In preparation.

2

Preoperative and Postoperative Care

The most important element in the successful management of a seriously ill newborn infant is continuous, careful surveillance by an experienced medical team. Unlike the surgeon, who treats adults, for whom routine visits twice daily often represent acceptable physician care, the pediatric surgeon must be prepared to re-evaluate a sick infant at minimum intervals of four to six hours. A trained, experienced nurse must be present at all times to ensure proper administration of treatment and interpretation of response. In few other areas of modern medicine does the nurse play as important a role as in the care of the neonatal surgical patient. Close cooperation between the physician and nurse is crucial to success. A full explanation of the patient's illness and projected therapy significantly enhances the nurse's ability to provide the level of support that the physician desires—and the patient requires!

Evolution of the concept of high-risk intensive care nurseries for the management of medical and surgical emergencies in the newborn has facilitated treatment of these babies. The pediatrician and surgeon may be qualified by training and experience to provide definitive care for the sick newborn, but in the absence of trained nursing personnel and specialized facilities and equipment, ideal care may prove impractical—if not impossible. The commitment required of any busy practitioner under such circumstances can be prohibitive. An important judgment must be made at this point by the primary physician. It is essential that he determine as soon as possible whether adequate care can be rendered with available facilities and personnel, or whether initial efforts should be directed toward early diagnosis and resuscitation, to be followed by rapid transfer to a specialized unit which is organized and equipped to handle the problems of the newborn infant on a day-to-day basis.

Preoperative Evaluation

Important determinants of potential difficulty in managing any neonatal surgical emergency are the relative maturity and size of the infant. In infants who are born prematurely (less than 37 weeks gestation) or have a low birth weight for gestational age, risk of neonatal morbidity and mortality is increased, even in the absence of serious complicating anomalies. Factors of immature physiologic and biologic function, as well as restrictions in size, must be considered in the care of such patients. The incidence of congenital anomalies is increased with prematurity, being 25 per cent in live-born infants with birth weights less than 1500 Gm., and 12 per cent in those with birth weights between 1500 and 2500 Gm.

Careful inspection of the placenta may prove helpful in suggesting other anomalies. Approximately one-third of infants with a single umbilical artery are found to have associated abnormalities, frequently multiple. These include trisomy of chromosome 18 and defects of the genitourinary and gastrointestinal tracts, the skeleton, the cardiovascular system, and the central nervous system. Approximately 50 per cent of the babies with esophageal atresia have serious associated anomalies (especially cardiac). The increased incidence of duodenal atresia and cardiac anomalies in mongoloid infants is well recognized. All forms of intestinal atresia are associated with an increased incidence of premature birth and with other congenital anomalies, particularly those involving the heart, spine, and urinary tract. Jejunal atresia may be associated with meconium ileus, intestinal malrotation, and volvulus. Malrotation of the intestine may also accompany omphalocele, diaphragmatic hernia, or asplenia. In some conditions, such as cystic fibrosis and meconium ileus, a history of affected siblings may prove helpful in defining the disease.

Preoperative evaluation of the infant also should include assessments of physiologic function and general activity. Pneumonia and respiratory distress should be alleviated by preoperative therapy whenever feasible. Over 90 per cent of infants pass urine and a meconium stool by 24 hours of age; failure to do so merits investigation. Lethargy may signify sepsis, which requires immediate treatment; premature infants are particularly prone to develop serious infections. The onset of jaundice after the second or third day of life is especially suggestive of septicemia. Icterus during the first 24 hours of life represents erythroblastosis fetalis until proved otherwise. Jaundice appearing later may be "physiologic" or may result from a variety of causes, including biliary atresia and neonatal hepatitis, as well as sepsis. Biliary obstruction almost never requires surgical intervention in the newborn period, but progressive hyperbilirubinemia from erythroblastosis fetalis may necessitate immediate exchange transfusion, prior to or following surgical correction of a life-threatening congenital anomaly.

Environmental Control

The importance of temperature regulation of the newborn has been emphasized. This requirement is best achieved in the controlled environment of a heated Isolette, avoiding extremes of either hyper- or hypothermia, with optimal maintenance of surface body temperature at 36°C. A clean Isolette provides the additional advantage of sheltering the susceptible neonate from infection. Maintenance of relative humidity between 60 and 70 per cent assists in stabilizing body temperature while preventing excessive drying of respiratory passages. Additional humidity occasionally may be required in the presence of excessively viscid tracheobronchial secretions, as may be associated with congenital tracheoesophageal fistula. Increased humidity from a heated or ultrasonic nebulizer is particularly helpful in the immediate postoperative period, following tracheal intubation and general anesthesia, or when the nasopharynx is bypassed with a nasotracheal tube or tracheostomy. Routine use of these humidifying devices, however, carries with it an increased risk of contamination and infection.

Oxygen should be added to the environment only when required for relief of cyanosis or dyspnea. When oxygen supplementation is needed, concentrations should be maintained at a level of less than 40 per cent whenever feasible, to avoid the complications of chronic oxygen toxicity (i.e., retrolental fibroplasia and pulmonary edema). Blood gas sampling should be carried out concomitantly, since oxygen toxicity is related more to circulating arterial pO_2 than to environmental concentrations. By means of this monitoring technique, inspired oxygen can be adjusted to maintain the pO_2 at a level of less than 100 mm. Hg.

Positioning of the child can also play an important role. Babies should *never* be "spread eagled" flat on their back by restraints that extend all four extremities. Ideally, they should be turned hourly from side to side and, when feasible, even allowed to assume the prone position in order to achieve optimal clearance of tracheobronchial secretions, to maintain respiratory exchange, and to avoid aspiration pneumonia. An infant with a congenital tracheoesophageal fistula should be placed in the semi-upright Fowler's position to minimize gastric reflux through the fistula into the tracheobronchial tree until a gastrostomy can be performed. A major hazard in the active newborn infant is his vigorous "grasp reflex," which will consistently result in forceful tugging of whatever tube lies within reach. To avoid potential disasters, while preserving the maximum of natural movement, a reasonable compromise is achieved by wrapping the baby's fingers and hands in a bulky mitten (resembling a miniature boxing glove).

Finally, ready access to the sick infant must be available at all times. Connections with intravenous tubes, drainage tubes, and ancillary equipment should be arranged in the Isolette in such a manner that the patient can be quickly and completely exposed at a moment's notice. There is no more frustrating situation than that presented by a critically ill infant who requires instant attention, but who is encompassed by a maze of tangled tubes and plastic walls.

Fluid and Electrolyte Therapy

Maintenance of an accurate balance of fluids and colloids requires particular attention in a seriously ill newborn infant. The margin for error is small, and the baby is poorly prepared to tolerate mistakes in replacement therapy.

Almost invariably, fluids must be administered intravenously. Oral feedings are rarely feasible in newborn surgical emergencies, and the potential contribution of hypodermoclysis is limited. To ensure a reliable route for fluid and drug therapy, both during and following operation, a venous cutdown is preferred. Central venous cannulation is indicated when a need for central venous pressure monitoring or long-term parenteral feeding is anticipated. Pediatric drip sets or constant infusion pumps should be utilized for exact regulation of flow. Reservoir filling should be limited to 50 ml. at a time, to guard against sudden, accidental overhydration.

Deficit Therapy. Adequate preoperative stabilization of the critically ill infant involves re-expansion of intravascular volume and restoration of electrolyte balance. In a few neonatal surgical emergencies, such as congenital diaphragmatic hernia, immediate surgical correction is mandatory. In most instances, however, time spent in preoperative preparation of the patient provides important benefits both during and following the surgical procedure.

The immediate objectives of preoperative fluid therapy should be adequate expansion of intravascular volume and correction of gross discrepancies in serum electrolytes and pH. Complete correction of all abnormalities, with total restoration of body fluid and electrolyte deficits, may require days rather than hours, but the aforementioned objectives can be satisfied by intensive treatment within a maximum period of four to six hours. As indicated previously, the patient's vital signs and clinical response are the ultimate test of satisfactory replacement, but important assistance can be gained through utilization of the monitoring routines described in Chapter 3.

The full-term newborn infant has an excess of body water (10 per cent of total body weight), which is normally excreted during the first few days of life (Fink and Cheek, 1960). In the presence of abnormal losses, however, such as those associated with intestinal obstruction and vomiting, peritonitis, ruptured omphalocele, or leaking meningomyelocele, deficits in total body water rapidly ensue. The maximum fluid loss that can be tolerated at this age is equivalent to 15 to 20 per cent of total body weight. Since the potential degree of dehydration is restricted by this limit, the relative fluid deficit can be estimated on the basis of physical signs and laboratory results. Severe dehydration occurs with fluid losses equivalent to 10 to 15 per cent of total body weight. Capillary and venous filling, fontanelle tension, skin turgor, and mucous membrane moisture should be noted. Observations of vital signs, hematocrit, serum proteins, electrolyte and urea nitrogen levels, blood gases and pH, and urinary output and specific gravity contribute to this assessment.

Replacement of the fluid deficit can be initiated with a balanced electrolyte solution such as Ringer's lactate. Subsequent modifications are dictated by clinical response and monitoring results. Serial recordings of central venous pressure are particularly helpful in situations requiring rapid intravascular expansion. Initial readings of central venous pressure are relatively meaningless in such circumstances, unless they are sufficiently high (exceeding 15 to 20 cm. water) to suggest right heart failure.

Filling of the vascular space is comparable to expansion of an inner tube. In the early stages, pressure changes are minimal. As expansion nears completion, however, pressure responses are magnified. Similarly, as adequate filling of the vascular system is achieved, central venous pressure begins to rise. Although recordings of central venous pressure may not prove as helpful in assessing the initial state of hydration, serial determinations are invaluable for monitoring subsequent adequacy of fluid and colloid replacement.

A satisfactory circulating blood volume is the most important element in determining whether a surgical procedure can be undertaken safely. In situations requiring immediate restitution of vascular volume, whole blood or plasma infusion may be required. Because of the relatively high hematocrit usually present in the newborn infant, plasma may prove preferable. In the absence of cardiac failure, an infant will tolerate rapid administration of 20 to 25 ml./kg. whole blood or plasma without ill effect. A minimum deficit of 25 per cent circulating blood volume is present in acute hypovolemic shock. In situations necessitating specific restrictions in electrolyte administration (as encountered with hyperkalemia), a plasma equivalent can be achieved by the addition of salt-poor albumin to the appropriate infusate solution.

Maintenance Fluids. In the absence of unusual losses, a full-term newborn infant may require no maintenance fluids for the first two days of life. The appropriateness of this approach, however, has been questioned with regard to the premature infant. These tiny patients, with their immature physiology and limited metabolic reserve, are particularly susceptible to hypoglycemia. Accordingly, fluid maintenance with 10 per cent glucose and water in a dosage of 50 ml./kg./day may be advisable in premature infants during the immediate neonatal period. After the first few days of life, when body water has equilibrated, maintenance fluid requirements increase. Initially, when basal metabolism is low and activity is minimal, approximately 70 ml. water/kg./day is required. Over the next few weeks, as metabolic activity increases, basic water needs rise to approximately 100 ml./kg./day (Darrow, 1959).

Additional water should be administered for elevations in body temperature (10 per cent for each degree Centigrade increase in temperature), but careful regulation of environmental temperature through utilization of an Isolette should obviate this need. Approximately 3 mEq. sodium and 2 mEq. potassium are required for each 100 ml. basic fluid administered. A solution of 5 or 10 per cent glucose, containing 30 mEq. sodium and chloride and 20 mEq. potassium per liter, usually satisfies maintenance requirements. During the 24 hours immediately following operation (a somewhat shorter period in the premature infant), basic fluid requirements are decreased by the normal physiologic response to stress, and no maintenance sodium or potassium may be required.

Replacement of Losses. Variables that may be particularly difficult to assess in the postoperative infant are the so-called "hidden losses" incurred by sequestration of fluids in traumatized tissues, intestines, and body cavities. With peritonitis, for example, fluid losses may approximate those experienced with a major body surface burn. In such circumstances, reliance on standard formulas for calculating maintenance fluid requirements leads to gross inaccuracies. On the other hand, overhydration frequently has resulted in the past because of a failure to appreciate the physiologic and anatomic limitations of these tiny patients.

It is in this exact circumstance, following major abdominal or thoracic procedures, that adaptation of the monitoring routine outlined in Chapter 3 may prove most useful. Measurements should be tabulated in an hourly flow chart (Table 2-1).

TABLE 2-1. Postoperative Monitoring Routine for Newborn Infants

I. At frequent intervals:
Blood pressure
Pulse
Respiration

II. Every 4 to 6 hours:
Central venous pressure
Total serum solids
Hematocrit
Urine specific gravity
Urine output
Fluid intake
Other fluid losses (i.e., chest and nasogastric drainage)

III. Daily:
Body weight
Serum electrolytes (including Ca and Mg in long-term treatment)
Blood urea nitrogen

IV. As necessary:
Blood gases (pH, pCO_2, pO_2)

As emphasized repeatedly, vital signs and clinical response continue to provide the ultimate test of satisfactory homeostasis, but the addition of the supplemental information outlined in Table 2-1 allows a more controlled and intelligent assessment of the infant's requirements.

Abnormal gastrointestinal fluid losses and drainage from body cavities (i.e., chest) should be replaced with a fluid of volume and composition comparable to that lost. Basic replacement of gastric drainage is provided by two-thirds-normal saline containing potassium chloride (3 mEq./100 ml.) (Hyde, 1968). The changing character of gastric secretions during early life, as noted in Chapter 1, may necessitate subsequent alterations in this formula. Losses through intestinal drainage or diarrhea are best replaced with half-strength Ringer's lactate solution containing potassium chloride in a concentration of 4 mEq./100 ml.

The normal output of urine in the adequately hydrated infant should approximate 1 to 2 ml./kg./hour.

Salt-poor albumin, 2 Gm./kg./day, may be administered to maintain satisfactory levels of circulating serum protein. In the absence of hypoproteinemia, the development of periorbital edema, fontanelle swelling, or pulmonary rales may signify fluid overload.

A particular consideration in the determining of parenteral fluid therapy in newborn infants is an increased potential for nursing error. The physician's orders must be explicit! The exact quantity of parenteral fluids, as well as the rate of flow, must clearly be documented in the doctor's orders. An aid to ensuring proper fluid administration is the practice of dividing daily fluid requirements into allotments on the basis of scheduled nursing shifts. This arrangement allows for frequent re-evaluation of therapy (a minimum of every eight hours), and assigns each nurse total responsibility for fluid administration during her shift. The utilization of constant infusion pumps simplifies the problem of administering small aliquots of fluid over protracted periods and is heartily recommended.

Acid-Base Balance

Careful monitoring and regulation of acid-base balance has emerged as an important component of neonatal surgical care. Increased emphasis on treatment of newborn respiratory distress and congenital cyanotic heart disease has stimulated much of this interest. It is now recognized that acidosis increases pulmonary vascular resistance and impairs cardiac output. In this way, a low pH exaggerates the very conditions that the physician is attempting to correct (Filley, 1971).

The Astrup technique provides a convenient method

of determining pCO_2, pO_2, pH, standard bicarbonate concentration, and "base excess" through utilization of the Siggaard-Anderson nomogram. These measurements are now routinely available in most medical centers. The term "standard bicarbonate concentration" (mEq./L.) refers to the amount of bicarbonate in the plasma from whole blood that has been equilibrated at a pCO_2 of 40 mm. Hg at 37°C. Classically the buffer-base of blood (mEq./L.) is determined by titration with strong acid to pH 7.40 at pCO_2 of 40 ml. Hg at 37°C. "Base excess" is obtained by subtracting the normal value for buffer-base from the observed value, providing either a positive or negative result. Negative values of "base excess" actually represent a base deficit. Normal variations in base excess are usually considered to be −2.3 to +2.3 mEq./L. Wider fluctuations in acid-base balance have been noted in healthy newborn infants, however, and it has been suggested that, postoperatively, acid-base disturbances can be definitely identified only when values of standard bicarbonate exceed the range of 19 to 27 mEq./L. or values of base excess exceed the range of −6 to +4 mEq./L. (Borresen and Knutrud, 1967). By the use of measurements of base excess, the total mEq. of base required to correct metabolic acidosis can be obtained by multiplying body weight (kg.) by the Astrup factor of 0.3, and by the negative value for base excess. Initial treatment, however, is usually calculated on a two-thirds replacement. Solutions of sodium bicarbonate and trishydroxymethyl aminomethane (THAM) can be employed for this correction. THAM is particularly useful in those circumstances in which excessive loads of sodium must be avoided (as in congestive heart failure). Both THAM and concentrated bicarbonate are extremely irritating to blood vessels and other body tissues, however, and must be administered with care, preferably into a central venous pool where maximum mixing can be achieved.

Measurements of blood gases provide considerable information on the status of circulatory dynamics, particularly when they are combined with observations of central venous pressure. In the absence of cyanotic heart disease, low blood oxygen tension, in association with low central venous pressure and arterial hypotension, suggests hypovolemia. A low blood oxygen tension, however, in the presence of a high central venous pressure and arterial hypotension, suggests cardiac failure or primary pulmonary disease. Metabolic acidosis, with accumulation of acid metabolites (i.e., lactic acid), results either from hypoxia or from impaired tissue perfusion. Respiratory acidosis, with increased tensions of carbon dioxide, is pathognomonic of impaired ventilatory exchange. Hypercarbic acidosis is best treated by an increase in ventilation to eliminate excess carbon dioxide. Buffer-base administration also may be required in severe cases to raise blood pH, reverse secondary pulmonary hypertension, and improve cardiac output. Care must be exerted to avoid abrupt changes in blood pH, since serum potassium levels are also affected. (Potassium ion rises in acidosis and falls in alkalosis.)

Although respiratory alkalosis with low blood tensions of carbon dioxide has occurred rarely in the past, this finding has become more common with increased reliance on mechanical ventilation. Respiratory alkalosis from hyperventilation may complicate management of a concomitant metabolic acidosis, and blood pCO_2 as well as pO_2 must be monitored for optimal regulation of the ventilator.

Metabolic alkalosis with increased serum bicarbonate levels classically results from persistent vomiting of acidic gastric contents. Since levels of gastric acid production may be relatively high, this problem presents a particular threat to the newborn infant. Potassium replacement is essential for adequate correction of this condition, since metabolic alkalosis results in increased urinary excretion of this cation. In metabolic alkalosis resulting from vomiting, normal saline with added potassium chloride (40 mEq./L.) represents the replacement solution of choice. The ratio of mEq. of sodium to mEq. of chloride is 3 to 2 in serum. Since the ratio of sodium to chloride is 1 to 1 in normal saline, an excess of chloride is available to replace deficits of this ion.

Gastrointestinal Management

Preoperative and postoperative gastrointestinal drainage comprises an essential aspect of newborn surgical care when intestinal stasis or ileus is present. Since the infant is primarily a diaphragmatic breather, any abdominal distention from ingested gas proportionately diminishes his respiratory reserve. Aspiration of vomitus is a potential threat in these cases. Gastrointestinal decompression with small, plastic infant-feeding tubes (all too frequently a 5 or 8 French catheter has been employed for this purpose) is usually worthless. Gastric secretions are thick and viscid and the few small side holes present in the usual plastic tube quickly become plugged. A more reliable and safer approach is achieved if several additional, large side holes are cut near the tip of a 10 or 12 French soft, rubber catheter and this tube inserted through the nasopharynx into the stomach. Any air or fluid that is instilled into the stomach by this route should return readily on aspiration if the tube is correctly positioned.

Nasogastric tubes present a constant threat of airway

obstruction and esophageal and gastric irritation and erosion. Unless the tube is properly functioning, therefore, the patient would be far better without it. Checks on the system must include verification of proper operation of the intermittent low suction apparatus as well as verification of the patency of the tube. It is also essential to maintain an exact account of gastrointestinal fluid losses in these tiny patients. Such checks are achieved by irrigation of the tube every two hours with a calibrated syringe containing 2 ml. normal saline. Retrieval of most of the irrigating solution from the stomach on aspiration confirms proper positioning and patency of the tube itself. The aspirated solution is then placed in a medicine glass and suctioned through the distal end of the connecting tube into the central collecting bottle of the suction apparatus. In this manner, verification of patency and function of the entire system is achieved. An exact tabulation of gastrointestinal losses is easily obtained every four to six hours by subtraction of the total quantity of irrigating solution from the volume of fluid that has been collected in the central suction bottle. If the nurse observes that irrigating solution cannot be aspirated from the stomach, or that the suction apparatus is not functioning, a physician should be notified immediately.

After intra-abdominal operation on the newborn, a gastrostomy provides gastrointestinal decompression while avoiding the potential hazards of prolonged nasogastric intubation. This technique also plays an important role in the preoperative preparation of an infant with a tracheoesophageal fistula. A 16 or 18 French rubber mushroom catheter is preferred for gastrostomy in these tiny patients, since the balloon at the tip of the Foley catheter is frequently excessively large in relation to limited size of the stomach. Suction should not be routinely applied to gastrostomy tubes, since the opposite wall of the stomach may be pulled against the end of the catheter, occluding it and allowing the baby to vomit. A simple expedient is to collect gastrostomy drainage in a small adhesive urine bag, which can remain in the Isolette attached to the end of the tube. These gastrostomy tubes are sufficiently large (16 or 18 French) to be kept patent by intermittent instillation and aspiration of small quantities of air, thus avoiding completely any confusion in the nurses' final tabulation of gastric aspirant.

Various devices have been proposed for administering gastrostomy tube feedings and achieving simultaneous decompression while the feeding is progressing (an automatic "burper"). A simple and reliable procedure in the relatively inactive postoperative newborn infant is to attach a large glass Y-tube to the distal end of the gastrostomy tube. If the system is then elevated, the height of the fluid column within the gastrostomy tube represents the maximum pressure that can be exerted within the stomach itself. Feedings may be administered through one side arm of the Y-tube while simultaneous decompression is achieved through the opposite arm.

Initial feedings may prove troublesome in an infant following gastrointestinal operation or starvation. Sepsis, vitamin deficiency (especially folic acid), electrolyte disturbances (potassium, calcium, and magnesium), and anatomic limitations of intestinal function may contribute to these difficulties. Because of a decreased tendency to form curds, soybean formulas such as Isomil and Nutramigen are preferred when limitations in anatomic function are anticipated, as is often the case at the site of anastomosis of proximal dilated bowel to tiny unused bowel distal to an atretic segment. In these circumstances, curds may produce recurrent obstruction before natural physiologic dilation of the anastomosis and the distal intestine has been achieved. In premature infants, however, feeding of these formulas occasionally produces acidosis; capillary blood gases and pH should be determined intermittently during the early stages of alimentation to exclude this possibility. Initial feedings should be dilute, with gradual progression to full-strength formula as dictated by the infant's response. When gastrostomy feedings are used, small hourly or two-hourly feedings are possible without requiring an inordinate degree of nursing attention or unnecessarily tiring the patient. The quantity of each feeding should be gradually increased, so that the infant eventually receives 150 ml./kg. body weight per day. If the infant still seems hungry, or fails to gain weight, further increases may be required, and a daily intake of 130 to 150 calories is required in some instances. Gastric size may prove to be the limiting factor in these babies, and it may be necessary to increase the frequency or the concentration (up to 1 calorie per ml.) of the feeding. Weight gain in infants over 1500 Gm. body weight is usually adequate on a protein intake of 2 Gm./kg./day.

Medications

The idiosyncrasies of drug metabolism in the newborn infant already have been emphasized, and caution is advised before therapy is instituted (Chap. 1). When in doubt, the physician should seek consultation.

Vitamin K. In order to correct any coagulation deficit related to decreased levels of plasma prothrombin, the newborn infant should receive an intramuscular injection of 1.0 mg. water-soluble vitamin K_1. In the excitement of instituting therapy for a life-threatening neonatal surgical emergency, this injection may be inadvertently omitted. Verification of prior administration of vitamin K_1 is an important component of the preoperative "check-list." In cases of doubt, an additional injection of 1.0 mg. of vitamin K_1 may be given, but further doses should be avoided because of potential hazards described in Chapter 1.

Preoperative Medication. The only premedication required for anesthesia in the newborn is atropine (0.1 mg. total dose). In some instances, depending on the anesthetic agent that is to be employed, the anesthesiologist may prefer to omit this preoperative medication.

Antibiotics. Premature infants are particularly susceptible to infection, and prophylactic antibiotics may be indicated when contamination is either present or anticipated (as in ruptured omphalocele, intestinal obstruction, tracheobronchial aspiration, or pneumonia). Intravenous aqueous penicillin (25,000 u./kg. administered twice daily) and intramuscular kanamycin (7.5 mg./kg. twice daily) are preferred unless resistant organisms are suspected. Cultures of the nasopharynx, bronchial secretions, intestinal contents, and wounds should be obtained at the time of operation to verify the potential effectiveness of this antibiotic regimen or to allow for an early change in therapy if it is indicated. Kanamycin does not appear to be as potentially toxic to the newborn infant as to the adult, but urinary output and serum urea nitrogen levels should be carefully monitored throughout the period of therapy in order to avoid serious nephrotoxicity. Aqueous sodium penicillin may be substituted when hyperkalemia is noted. Infections from Staphylococcus aureus, coliform organisms, enterococci, Klebsiella, Pseudomonas, and Salmonella present a particular threat at this age—a threat that must be appreciated in the selection of an appropriate antibiotic. Pseudomonas is a normal inhabitant of water and may be introduced as a contaminant of inhalation therapy equipment. Gentamicin sulfate, colistin sulfate, or Carbenicillin may be required for treatment of these infections, but the potential toxicity of these drugs must be appreciated when they are used. With the advent of extremely effective broad-spectrum antibiotics, fungal infections (Candida) have become more common, particularly in the presence of protracted intestinal obstruction. Secretions from all body orifices, skin, and blood should be periodically cultured for both bacteria and fungi in babies who require long-term protracted antibiotic therapy so that resistant organisms can be detected before serious complications develop.

Intraoperative Management

Adequate preoperative preparation includes restitution of fluid and colloid losses and maintenance of adequate hydration until the time of operation. An infant who is several days old, if he does not have intestinal obstruction and is not receiving intravenous infusion, should be offered clear liquids until four hours prior to operation, in order to avoid protracted periods of dehydration. When emergency operation is undertaken, however, the stomach should always be aspirated through a 10 or 12 French catheter (as discussed previously) before anesthesia is given.

Provision should be made for monitoring of temperature and pulse rate throughout the operation. Extremities may be wrapped to conserve heat, a thermistor probe should be positioned in the esophagus, or rectum, and the baby should be placed on a circulating-warm-water mattress (temperature not exceeding 100°F). An esophageal or presternal stethoscope should be positioned for audible monitoring of pulse rate, and in many instances, simultaneous electrocardiographic monitoring by way of miniature skin or needle electrodes may be advisable.

All blood and fluid losses should be carefully quantitated and provision should be made for weighing sponges. Fresh blood should be utilized for replacement, to avoid any accentuation of acidosis or hyperkalemia by administration of old, stored blood. Blood or plasma should also be warmed prior to administration (not exceeding 110°F) to avoid dangerous fluctuations in body temperature. Infusion of large quantities of citrated blood may necessitate calcium replacement in newborn infants (1 ml. 10 per cent calcium gluconate per 100 ml. whole blood transfused). This procedure has been followed for many years in adults, but is relatively unimportant in this age group as compared to infants, whose calcium stores are more quickly expended and whose compensatory mechanisms are less able to respond to potential calcium depletion. The administration of large quantities of citrated blood also results in the binding of serum magnesium.

The anesthesiologist must exercise particular caution to avoid overhydration of the newborn through excessive fluid administration for the purpose of infusing medications. Intraoperative monitoring of central venous pressure through a central venous catheter may prevent this complication. If an arterial or central venous catheter is available, periodic sampling of blood gases and pH also may prove helpful in avoiding hypoventilation and acidosis. Such disturbances are most likely to develop during protracted or difficult surgical procedures.

The choice of surgical incision may play an important role in postoperative management. A retropleural approach for repair of congenital tracheoesophageal fistula appears to be associated with a decreased incidence of postoperative pulmonary complications, and with better tolerance of any subsequent anastomotic leak. Abdominal incisions should be positioned so as to preserve the umbilical vein, since postoperative hyperbilirubinemia, particularly in premature infants with intestinal obstruction, may necessitate exchange transfusion. This procedure is best accomplished through umbilical vein cannulation. At the same time, provision must be made for extension of the incision when further exposure is required. Suprapubic retroperitoneal decompression of the bladder by needle aspiration may permit additional exposure. Contamination of the peritoneal cavity must be minimized, since the impaired immunologic response and underdeveloped omentum of these babies restricts their ability to contain intra-abdominal infection.

Bulky wound dressings are to be avoided, since they may restrict diaphragmatic excursion and respiratory exchange. Plastic spray dressings are ideal in these tiny patients.

Finally, a warm Isolette must be available in the operating room at the termination of the procedure for immediate transfer of the baby to an intensive care facility. It may be advisable to keep the endotracheal tube in place until this transfer has been completed and satisfactory respiratory exchange has been assured. The personnel in the intensive care unit must be notified before the baby is removed from the operating room to ensure that all is in readiness for the new arrival.

Cardiopulmonary Resuscitation

Equipment for emergency resuscitation should be readily available in any nursery. Airway obstruction and respiratory arrest present a particular threat to these patients. An infant laryngoscope, small endotracheal tubes, miniature suction catheters, a *reliable* portable suctioning machine, and a self-inflating ventilation bag must be provided. A need for emergency aspiration of an obstructing mucous plug from the trachea is not uncommon in these tiny patients, and a suction catheter of standard 18-gauge intravenous tubing is ideal for this purpose. An electrocardioscope and cardiac defibrillator should be immediately available. Emergency drugs (especially solutions of epinephrine, calcium gluconate, and sodium bicarbonate)

and special infant cut-down trays for venous and arterial catheterization must be provided. Effective cardiac output can be maintained in cases of cardiac arrest by intermittent sternal compression with the tip of the finger or thumb. Excessively wide (as with the palm of the hand) or low thoracic compression in these babies may result in fracture or tearing of the liver. The effectiveness of cardiac massage can be assessed by palpation of a peripheral pulse (usually the femoral artery). Epinephrine (1:10,000 solution) and calcium gluconate (10 per cent solution) may be administered in small quantities for the treatment of persistent cardiac standstill, brachycardia, or poor cardiac output. Intravenous sodium bicarbonate or THAM (5 to 10 mEq. intravenously stat) is almost always required for correction of the severe metabolic acidosis that rapidly ensues in cases of cardiac arrest.

REFERENCES

Anderson, O. S.: The pH-log pCO_2 blood acid-base nomogram revised. Scand. J. Clin. Lab. Invest., *14*:598, 1962.
Astrup, P., et al.: The acid-base metabolism: a new approach. Lancet, *1*:1035, 1960.
Borresen, H. C., and Knutrud, O.: Effects of major surgery on the acid/base homeostasis in the newborn child. J. Pediat. Surg., *2*:493, 1967.
Cooke, R. E., and Levin, S.: The Biologic Basis of Pediatric Practice. New York, McGraw-Hill Book Company, 1968.
Darrow, D. C.: The significance of body size. A.M.A. J. Dis. Child., *98*:416, 1959.
Filley, G. F.: Acid-Base and Blood Gas Regulation. Philadelphia, Lea & Febiger, 1971.
Fink, C. W., and Cheek, D. B.: The corrected bromide space (extracellular volume) in the newborn. Pediatrics, *26*:397, 1960.
Goldberger, E.: A Primer of Water, Electrolyte and Acid-Base Syndromes. Philadelphia, Lea & Febiger, 1965.
Haller, J. A., Jr., and Talbert, J. L.: Trauma and the child. *In* Management of Trauma. Edited by W. F. Ballinger, II. Philadelphia, W. B. Saunders Company, 1968.
Hendren, W. H.: Neonatal surgery. *In* Surgery. Edited by R. Warren. Philadelphia, W. B. Saunders Company, 1963.
Hyde, G. A., Jr.: Gastric secretions following neonatal surgery. J. Pediat. Surg., *3*:691, 1968.
McKay, R. J.: The newborn infant. *In* Textbook of Pediatrics. Edited by W. E. Nelson. Philadelphia, W. B. Saunders Company, 1969.
Peters, M.: The Mechanical Basis of Respiration. Boston, Little, Brown and Company, 1969.
Rickham, P. P.: Preoperative and postoperative care. *In* Pediatric Surgery. Edited by W. T. Mustard. Chicago, Year Book Medical Publishers, Inc., 1969.
Strauss, J.: Fluid and electrolyte compositon of the fetus and the newborn. Pediat. Clin. N. Amer., *13*:1077, 1966.
Swenson, O.: Neonatal Physiology in Pediatric Surgery. New York, Appleton-Century-Crofts, 1969.

3

Monitoring

Treacherous lability is the outstanding characteristic of a newborn infant's response to surgical stress or trauma. Seemingly trivial details, which assume importance only in complicated cases in older children and adults, require routine attention in the pre- and postoperative care of babies. The margin for error at this age is limited, and the physician must maintain constant vigilance to detect those subtle signs that may portend serious alterations in homeostasis.

Valid assessment of the condition of a critically ill infant is feasible only with serial determinations of a variety of clinical measurements. Correlation of these observations not only provides a dynamic evaluation of the state of homeostasis, but also pinpoints the need for specific treatment regimens. Care must be taken not to complicate unnecessarily the care of an infant by blind adherence to any monitoring routine, but in many instances, adoption of a monitoring plan will provide the ultimate determinant of survival.

An important adjunct in assessing these variables in management is the patient's flow chart, which incorporates calculations of fluid intake and output, vital signs, laboratory values, and monitoring results at hourly intervals or more frequently. Important features of this monitoring system include measurements of central venous pressure, total serum solids, hematocrit, blood gases and pH, serum electrolytes, and urine specific gravity. Although the patient's vital signs and clinical response remain the most important criteria of satisfactory return of homeostasis, these signs may be misleading under certain circumstances, and the supplemental information provided in a concise flow sheet allows a more systematic and reasoned approach to management.

An example of the monitoring chart that has been adopted for use in the Pediatric Intensive Care Unit by both the Medical and Surgical Services of the University of Florida is depicted in Figure 3-1. In order to avoid unnecessary duplication of effort, this chart is used by both the nurse and physicians to record hourly observations of the patient's condition. The flow sheet is maintained at the bedside, together with the patient's permanent chart and order sheet, so that all records pertinent to the patient's care are immediately available for meaningful analysis.

Circulatory Monitoring

Alterations in the cardiovascular dynamics of an infant may be evidenced only by changes in skin color, alertness, pulse, and respiratory rate. A small infant's tiny structures may prevent other "routine" signs, such as auscultatory blood pressure, from being easily recognized. In the case of a desperately ill infant, however, this additional information can be critical. A direct indication of the effectiveness of the circulatory system is provided by monitoring of the electrocardiogram and arterial pressure. Methods for observing the pulse rate and electrocardiograms of an infant are similar to those used for adults, except that miniature adhesive or needle electrodes are used.

Arterial Blood Pressure. Monitoring of arterial pressure in these babies requires special adaptations. Customary auscultatory methods are useless at this age and "flush pressures" are unreliable in the presence of impaired cardiac output and poor peripheral perfusion. Under such circumstances, arterial catheterization can be

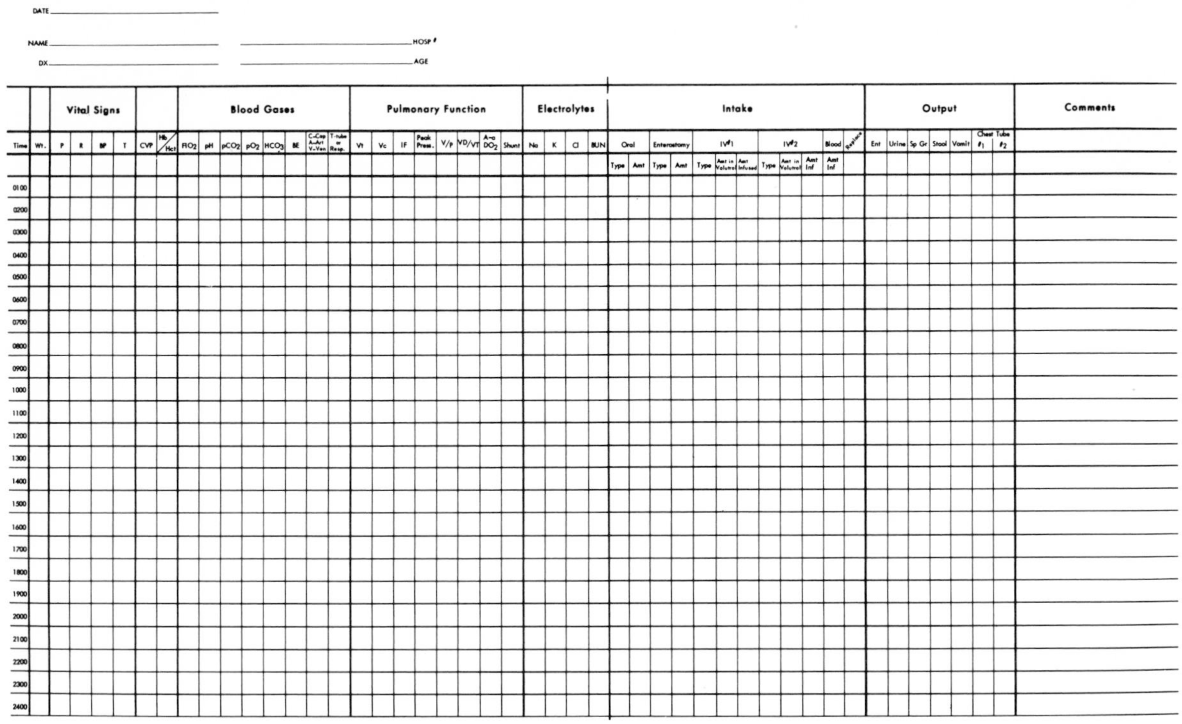

DATE_____

NAME_____ HOSP #_____

DX_____ AGE_____

	Vital Signs					Blood Gases									Pulmonary Function							Electrolytes				Intake														Output						Comments

FIG. 3-1. Pediatric intensive care "flow sheet." (Designed by Dr. Shirley Graves for W. A. Shands Teaching Hospital.)

helpful. The umbilical artery in the newborn is particularly appropriate for this purpose. Special tapered, radiopaque catheters may be inserted through an umbilical artery and positioned in the aorta under fluoroscopic control. Not only can arterial pressures be measured through these catheters, but, of greater importance, arterial blood samples can be withdrawn for analysis of oxygen and carbon dioxide levels, and of electrolyte and acid-base balance. Alternate sites for arterial monitoring in the infant include the temporal artery in the scalp, the femoral artery in the groin, and the radial or brachial arteries in the arm. Serial determinations can be recorded by connection of these catheters to standard pressure transducers to produce visual recordings on an oscilloscope.

When arterial blood gas sampling is not required and only arterial pressure monitoring is desired, the Doppler shifted ultrasound technique for blood pressure measurement provides a convenient and reliable alternative to direct arterial cannulation. As described by Janis and co-workers (1971), a Doppler transducer is placed under a newborn pneumatic blood pressure cuff which is positioned over a superficial artery (Fig. 3-2). The cuff is attached to an aneroid manometer, and blood pressure measurements are obtained in a manner similar to the standard auscultatory technique of Korotkoff, with the exception that signals of arterial wall motion or flow, as distinguished by the Doppler

transducer, are substituted for the usual auscultatory sounds. On deflation of the pneumatic cuff, the first Doppler signal designates the systolic blood pressure, and the point at which the signals either disappear or change markedly is the reading for diastole. The validity of the technique has been verified on numerous occasions by comparisons of blood pressure measurements by the Doppler method with those determined simultaneously through an indwelling arterial cannula.

In interpreting the results of arterial pressure monitoring, it must be remembered that this measurement provides a relatively gross indication of the status of circulatory dynamics. Hypovolemic shock is reflected as an "all or none" condition in peripheral arterial pressure and intervening gradations are obscure. At least 25 per cent of the circulating blood volume must be lost rapidly before a significant fall in arterial pressure is evident. For this reason, other monitoring methods must be employed to supplement observations of arterial pressure in the case of a seriously ill newborn infant.

Central Venous Pressure. Central venous pressure (CVP) often provides a more dependable reflection of functional blood volume than arterial pressure. This is true because the arterial blood pressure may be tenaciously maintained by homeostatic mechanisms, especially arteriolar constriction, in spite of diminished cardiac output and poor perfusion of distal tissues.

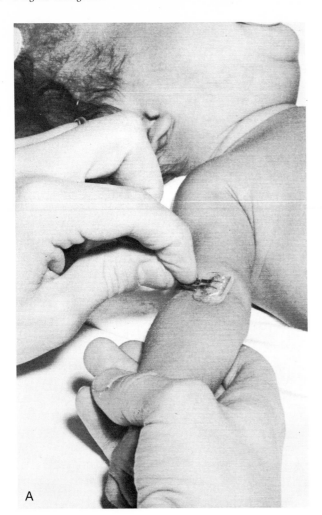

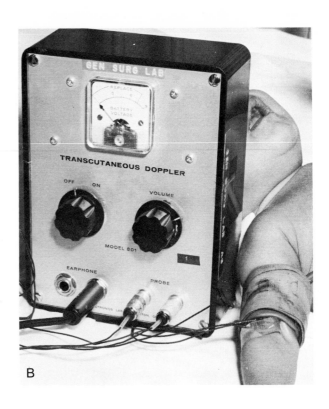

FIG. 3-2.   *A,* Doppler transducer placed over brachial artery. *B,* Cuff over transducer attached to Doppler flow detector (Parks Electronics Doppler Flow Detector, Model 801, Parks Electronics, Beaverton, Oregon). (From Janis, K. M., Kemmerer, W. T., and Hagood, C. O., Jr.: Doppler blood pressure measurement in infants and small children. J. Pediat. Surg., *6:*70, 1971.)

Normal CVP reflects optimal filling pressure of the right ventricle, which in turn ensures normal cardiac output unless the heart muscle is inadequate.

A low CVP or a fall in pressure during observation usually permits safe administration of additional fluids. A normal or moderately elevated venous pressure suggests that cardiac filling pressure is adequate. Under these circumstances some factor other than hypovolemia must be sought to explain poor peripheral perfusion. A high CVP reflects significant hypervolemia or inadequate emptying of the heart and is usually a contraindication to further fluid replacement unless cardiac output can be improved.

Application of CVP monitoring to the management of infants has been delayed by problems in miniaturizing the technique. The importance of placing the monitoring catheter in the central venous pool has been repeatedly emphasized. Both the small size of peripheral

veins in infants and the common association of venous spasm may interpose especially troublesome artifacts between peripheral and central venous pressure. Abdominal distention, particularly following surgical procedures or extensive trauma, has also been shown to give falsely elevated estimations of CVP via the inferior vena cava. Central venous pressure measurements under these conditions reflect the increased intra-abdominal pressure rather than the effective cardiac filling pressure (Fig. 3-3).

Accordingly, the superior vena cava or the right atrium is the preferred site for central venous pressure monitoring. Cannulation may be accomplished through the femoral vein in the groin, the basilic and cephalic veins in the arm and shoulder, or the internal and external jugular veins in the neck (Fig. 3-4). The familiar method of monitoring CVP via a percutaneous catheter in the subclavian vein may be utilized in older

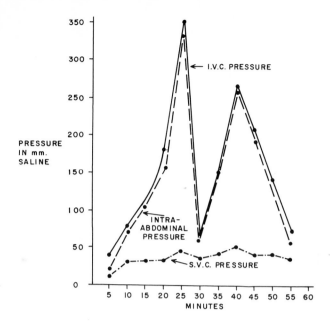

children, but in general the vein is so small in newborn infants and the risk of pneumothorax so great that the technique is rarely justified at this age. The most satisfactory route is the external jugular vein in an infant. Normal values for right atrial and central venous pressures are the same in newborn infants as in older children (5 to 12 cm. water), but fluctuations associated with breathing and crying are much more pronounced. Accordingly, serial determinations are absolutely necessary.

Further indirect evidence of the adequacy of peripheral circulation is provided by observations of blood gases and pH, and of fluid and colloid balance. Although arterial blood pH can be influenced by a variety of factors, persistent metabolic acidosis usually signifies impaired peripheral perfusion with inadequate tissue oxygenation and resultant anaerobic metabolism. Shifts in fluid and colloids also can provide important clues as to the adequacy of peripheral circulation.

Urinary Output and Specific Gravity. Urinary output and specific gravity should be measured in the newborn who requires surgical treatment if the physiologic limitations described previously are to be fully appreciated. Satisfactory recordings of specific gravity are often restricted at this age, however, by the relatively small aliquot of each voided sample. Urinary output may be especially limited in the debilitated or premature infant, and yet it is this patient in whom these

FIG. 3-3. Relationship of inferior vena caval (IVC) and superior vena caval (SVC) pressures to alterations in intra-abdominal pressure produced experimentally in dog by intraperitoneal air injection. Any fluctuation in intra-abdominal pressure consistently induces similar change in IVC pressure, while SVC pressure remains unaltered. (From Talbert, J. L., and Haller, J. A., Jr.: The optimal site for central venous measurement in newborn infants. J. Surg. Res., 6:168, 1966.)

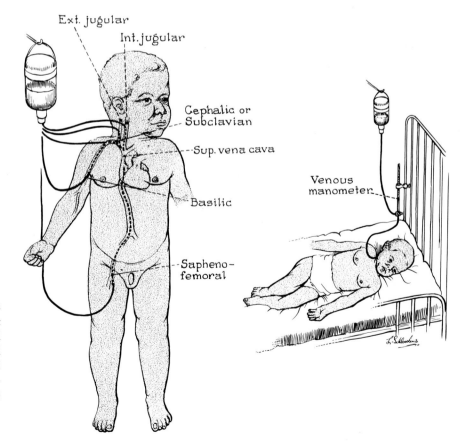

FIG. 3-4. Sites for central venous (superior vena cava and right atrium) cannulation in infant and child. (From Talbert, J. L., and Haller, J. A., Jr.: Technic of central venous pressure monitoring in infants. Amer. Surg., *32:*767, 1966.)

measurements might prove most useful. In such circumstances, hand refractometers provide accurate readings of specific gravity on only a few drops of urine (Fig. 3-5).

Total Serum Solids and Hematocrit. A small, accurate hand refractometer also is available for estimating levels of total serum solids. The overwhelming proportion of total serum solids are composed of the protein fraction. Any assessment of circulating serum solids, therefore, concomitantly provides a reliable means for estimating total serum proteins. With the hand refractometer, an accurate index of total serum solids can be determined (within 0.1 per cent) from the serum contained in two small microhematocrit tubes. Observations in our laboratories have confirmed the reliability of this method for determining total serum proteins on both venous and capillary blood samples (Fig. 3-6). With a simple bedside determination, the clinician is presented with a quick, easy method for simultaneously obtaining two important measurements, those of total serum solids and hematocrit.

Serial recordings of urinary output and arterial and central venous pressure provide the observer with insight regarding the functional adequacy of circulating blood volume. When observations of body weight, total serum protein, hematocrit, electrolytes, and blood gases and pH are added to this information, an informed estimate of the need for water, electrolyte, plasma, and blood replacement is continuously available.

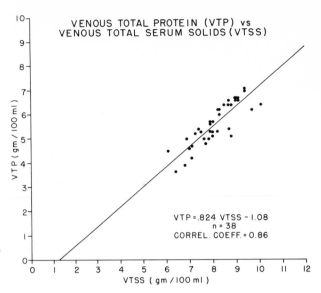

FIG. 3-6. Consistent correlation is seen between total serum solids of venous blood, as determined by hand refractometer using serum contained in two microhematocrit tubes, and total serum proteins, as determined by standard laboratory methods. Similar relationship exists between total serum solids of capillary blood and total serum protein of venous blood. (From Thoene, J. G., Talbert, J. L., Subramanian, S., and Odell, G. B.: Use of the hand refractometer in determining total serum proteins of infants and children. J. Pediat., *71*:413, 1967.)

Data on hydration and intravascular volume are particularly valuable in situations in which one is uncertain whether the oliguria (or anuria) that so often follows severe trauma or major operations is due to physiologic stress responses, primary renal insult, or inadequate fluid replacement. A flow chart of the type outlined provides a valuable indicator of unusual trends in therapy, and may warn the physician of impending complications prior to their overt development. The dangers of overhydration and excessive transfusion in a newborn infant, for example, can be minimized by this approach.

Respiratory Monitoring

Respiratory function is immediately evaluated at birth by use of the Apgar index. Babies with low scores should be suspected of having a pathologic condition that causes respiratory distress (see Chapter 5).

Whatever the etiology, whether the treatment indicated is medical or surgical, a need for respiratory assistance and/or aspiration of tracheobronchial secretions is signaled by a variety of signs and symptoms. Noisy respirations, croupy cough, stridor, and aphonia are self-evident. Signs of restlessness, apprehensive-

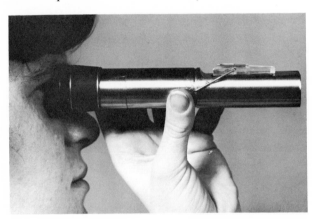

FIG. 3-5. Hand refractometer (TS Meter, The American Optical Company, Instrument Division, Buffalo, N.Y.) provides a quick, simple, and reliable method for determining urine specific gravity as well as serum total solid and protein content. Drop of urine or serum is placed under cover glass on top, and if instrument is held horizontal with light source above, direct reading of specific gravity or total solid or total protein content may be obtained through viewer. (From Haller, J. A., Jr., and Talbert, J. L.: Trauma and the child. *In* The Management of Trauma. Edited by W. F. Ballinger, II. Philadelphia, W. B. Saunders Company, 1968.)

ness, or fatigability are more subtle, but may be equally significant. Physical evidence of distress includes tachypnea; tachycardia; flaring of the nares; suprasternal, epigastric, and intercostal retraction; use of accessory muscles of respiration; and forced or exaggerated respiratory excursions. In the late stages of respiratory decompensation, the patient may become somnolent, pale, and cyanotic.

Blood Gas Determination. The technique of blood gas analysis has received increasing recognition as a diagnostic test and therapeutic guide in these patients. Accurate assessment of the significance of an infant's clinical signs, as well as a measure of his compensatory efforts, is provided by this approach. The development of quick, accurate micro methods for blood gas determinations, coupled with an increasing awareness of their potential importance in intensive care, has contributed to the rapid adoption of these tests as "routine" procedures in many hospitals. Under most circumstances, arterialized capillary samples provide adequate blood gas determinations. In the presence of impaired tissue perfusion, however, as may occur with hypovolemic or hypoxic shock, analysis of peripheral blood samples may prove misleading. Arterial, or even central venous, blood with serial determinations provides a more accurate index of respiratory efficiency and serves as a dependable guide for specific therapy.

Apnea Monitor. Additional help in the management of a premature or debilitated infant who has a relatively immature respiratory mechanism and is susceptible to apneic spells is provided by electronic breathing sensors (i.e., apnea monitors). They provide a convenient and simple method for monitoring the respiratory rhythm of a tiny patient enclosed in an Isolette (Fig. 3-7). Immediate recognition of an "apneic spell' and stimulation of the infant often can prevent the irreversible *sequelae* of prolonged respiratory arrest.

Since hypoxemia is rapidly manifested by bradycardia in the newborn infant, monitoring of the heart rate provides a reliable alternate method for detecting hypoventilation and/or apnea. In some neonatal units, heart rate monitors are preferred for this purpose.

Temperature Monitoring

As noted previously, control of body temperature in a newborn requires particular attention. The thermal regulatory mechanism of the debilitated or premature infant is extremely labile, and insulating stores of subcutaneous body fat may be rapidly depleted. Tissue hypoxia and acidosis may inhibit the maintenance of an adequate temperature at this age. These natural limitations are compounded when an infant is exposed

in a cool environment, since the ratio of body surface area to body weight is relatively greater at this age and body heat is rapidly dissipated.

It is essential that an infant be placed on a circulating-warm-water blanket in the operating room and that an esophageal or rectal thermistor probe be utilized to monitor temperature during any surgical procedure. It is imperative that infusions of large quantities of cold blood or plasma be warmed prior to administration, if by no other means than the coiling of a plastic intravenous tubing in a container of warm water. The temperature of this warming solution should not exceed 110°F.

An important recent advance in the intraoperative management of infants has been the addition of a heated humidifying system to the anesthesia ventilating circuits. In these systems, heated, fully humidified anesthesia gases not only decrease the incidence of pulmonary complications, but also provide valuable assistance in the maintaining of normal body temperature during the surgical procedure.

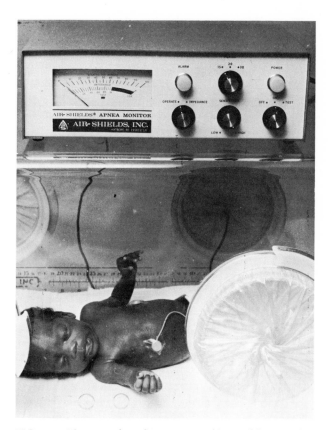

FIG. 3-7. Electronic breathing monitor (Apnea Monitor, Air Shields, Inc., Hatboro, Pa. 19040) is activated by chest wall sensor and provides immediate warning of respiratory arrest in premature or debilitated infant. (From Talbert, J. L.: Intraoperative and postoperative monitoring of infants. Surg. Clin. N. Amer., *50*:787, 1970.)

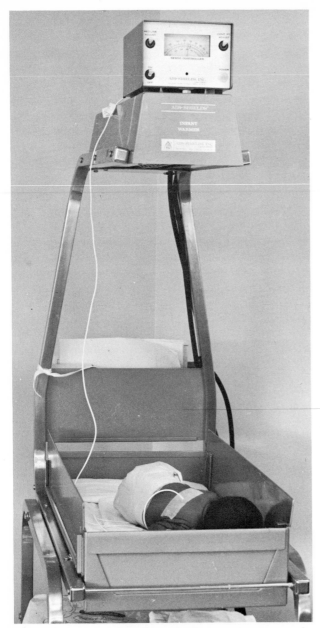

FIG. 3-8. Several models of special bassinets are equipped with radiant heat shields that are autoregulated by skin thermal sensors. (Infant Warmer, Air Shields, Inc., Hatboro, Pa. 19040). These bassinets are particularly helpful in the management of infants who require ventilatory support or in facilitating performance of minor operative procedures, such as venous cutdown or tracheostomy, in pediatric intensive care unit. (From Talbert, J. L.: Intraoperative and postoperative monitoring of infants. Surg. Clin. N. Amer., *50*:787, 1970.)

For pre- and postoperative support of newborn infants, a standard Isolette provides a satisfactory means of maintaining warmth and humidity. Newer models provide for automatic regulation of environmental temperature by skin thermal sensors. Infants who require connections to respirators, intravenous tubing, drainage tubes, and ancillary equipment may be placed in special bassinets with radiant heat shields, which are also regulated by skin thermal sensors. This latter arrangement provides constant access to the critically ill baby by eliminating the confining wall of an Isolette. Current models of the radiant heat bassinet facilitate performance of minor operative procedures, such as venous cutdowns, in the intensive care unit (Fig. 3-8).

Monitoring of Monitors

The complexity of modern monitoring routines demands constant checks on the adequacy of each individual system. Such checks must include verification of the presence as well as the position of each sensing electrode. A composite roentgenogram, which includes the head, neck, chest, abdomen, and extremities, often can provide valuable information relating to this question. Adoption of radiopaque catheters and tubes has facilitated this aspect of monitoring. The necessity for a routine check on the monitors emphasizes the continuing need for experienced human judgment behind all electronic devices.

In summary, the application of monitoring techniques to pediatric surgery has permitted important advances in the care of the newborn patient. This approach has proved particularly valuable in the areas of cardiovascular function, fluid and colloid balance, serum electrolyte and acid-base levels, temperature regulation, and respiratory support. Correlation of serial observation of each of these functions provides the pediatrician and surgeon with precise guidelines for management. The smaller the patient, the greater the potential contribution of these monitors in intensive treatment.

REFERENCES

Janis, K. M., Kemmerer, W. T., and Hagood, C. O.: Doppler blood pressure measurement in infants and small children. J. Pediat. Surg., *6*:70, 1971.

Talbert, J. L.: Intraoperative and postoperative monitoring of infants. Surg. Clin. N. Amer., *50*:787, 1970.

4

Special Techniques

Support techniques required for the management of neonatal surgical emergencies are similar to those developed previously for use in adult intensive care. The successful application of these methods to the care of newborn infants, however, requires special adaptations, owing primarily to the anatomic restrictions imposed by the patient's tiny structures.

Respiratory Support

The two major indications for respiratory assistance in newborn infants are a need for improved ventilatory exchange and a need for better removal of tracheobronchial secretions. In many instances, these two requirements occur simultaneously, and the techniques of nasotracheal intubation and tracheostomy are widely utilized for their management.

Nasotracheal Intubation. Relief of acute respiratory obstruction and/or insufficiency is best achieved with an endotracheal tube and artificial ventilation. The use of nasotracheal tubes for this purpose has provided an important adjunct to therapy, particularly in those infants in whom the period of ventilatory insufficiency is expected to be brief. In some pediatric centers, nasotracheal intubation has also been utilized for long-term support, whereas in other centers it is believed that extended treatment is best achieved with tracheostomy. In general, a nasotracheal tube must be longer and narrower in caliber than a tracheostomy tube for use in the same patient. The longer, narrower tube adds the penalties of increased dead space and airway resistance. From the standpoint of nursing care, a tracheostomy provides a more direct access to the

tracheobronchial tree, an important aid in aspirating secretions. The tracheostomy leaves the face and mouth of the infant unencumbered and allows normal care and feeding, even under circumstances requiring prolonged ventilatory support. Specific hazards of prolonged nasotracheal intubation, which have been documented in some reports, are the production of nasal and laryngotracheal scarring, ulceration, and stenosis. Management of tracheostomy in infants, however, has also been associated with a number of complications in the past, and the experience of the individual clinic and physician must dictate the method of choice for the individual patient.

The successful management of an infant with prolonged nasotracheal intubation requires meticulous nursing care and attention to tracheobronchial toilet as described subsequently. Of particular importance are secure attachment of the nasotracheal tube (to avoid the hazards of accidental dislodgment or excessive motion), use of the smallest tube practical (to reduce trauma and erosion of adjacent tissues), avoidance of too frequent or too vigorous suctioning, and use of nontoxic polyvinyl endotracheal tubes (tubes containing tin have produced increased tissue reaction).

Tracheostomy. In the past, physicians often have been discouraged from utilizing tracheostomy in newborn infants because of a high incidence of complications. The efforts of Holinger and of Aberdeen (1965) have recently demonstrated the usefulness of this technique for neonatal ventilatory support, and have defined methods by which previous difficulties can be avoided. In general, sources of error in the management of tracheostomy in infants can be attributed to (1) improper surgical techniques, (2) lack of a suitable tracheostomy tube for long-term attachment to a mechanical ventilator, and (3) errors in nursing care. With specific adaptations for neonatal tracheostomy care, experience with tracheostomy in numerous pediatric surgical clinics throughout the world has confirmed the value of this technique in salvaging infants with serious respiratory disturbances (Haller and Talbert, 1970).

Surgical Technique. Three salient features of the operative technique of tracheostomy in an infant require emphasis:

1. A tracheostomy in a baby should never be attempted without prior intubation to ensure an adequate temporary airway; circumstances preventing this measure are exceedingly rare.

2. **No tracheal tissue should be excised for any reason.** A vertical incision through two, three, or more cartilages will ensure an adequate opening (Fig. 4-1). The elastic tracheal rings subsequently reconstitute the airway cylinder on removal of the tube. Otherwise, if the adult technique of window excision is utilized, the infant's poorly supported trachea will collapse and the soft tissues will fall inward and plug the lumen. This technical error of excising the anterior tracheal wall is the single most important factor contributing to difficult extubation, airway obstruction, and secondary tracheal stenosis in babies.

3. The infant's tracheostomy tube must be securely and snugly tied in position. Accidental tube dislodgment occurs more easily in the unsupported neck of the baby, and re-insertion of the tube under these circumstances may prove exceedingly hazardous.

Infant Tracheostomy Tubes. Failure to recognize signifi-

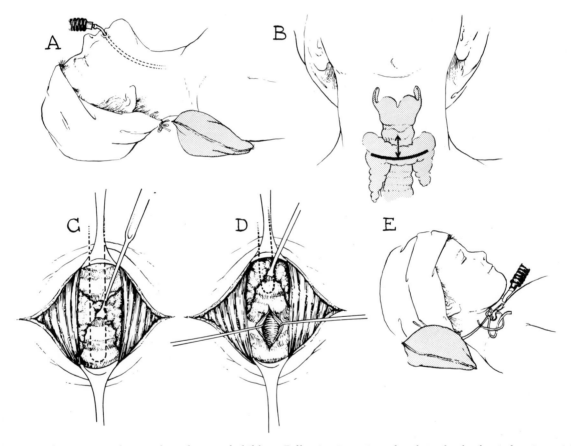

FIG. 4-1. Tracheostomy technique for infants and children. Following insertion of endotracheal tube, infant is positioned with neck extended, *A. B*, Transverse skin incision at level of thyroid isthmus has proved preferable for use with Silastic tube, which is equipped with inferior "tracheostomy incision shield" to prevent angulation and erosion of edge of tube into lower margin of skin wound. *C*, Strap muscles are separated vertically by blunt dissection and thyroid isthmus is reflected cephalad after division of pretracheal fascia. Anterior tracheal wall is then incised vertically, dividing second, third, fourth, and, if needed, fifth tracheal cartilages in midline. *No transverse counter-incision is employed and no tracheal flap or window is ever removed in infants. D*, Endotracheal tube is then withdrawn into proximal trachea, tracheostomy margins are reflected laterally by small hooks, and appropriate Silastic tube is inserted. *E*, Tube is tied securely in place with neck flexed, in order to ensure snugness and guard against subsequent accidental dislodgment. (*C* and *D* from Haller, J. A., Jr., and Talbert, J. L.: Clinical evaluation of a new Silastic tracheostomy tube for respiratory support of infants and young children. Ann. Surg., *171:*915, 1970.)

cant differences between infants and adults has led to a major problem in tracheostomy management, namely, use of inappropriate, miniaturized adult metal tracheostomy tubes. Aberdeen and Holinger have emphasized anatomic differences between the trachea of an infant and that of an adult. Miniature adult metal tubes are unsatisfactory in size, length, and configuration. The narrow lumen of an infant's trachea, the extreme flexibility of the cartilages, and the increased activity and movement of the body, head, and neck are all factors requiring particular attention. In order to achieve satisfactory air exchange and avoid additional airway resistance, a relatively larger tube is required for an infant than for an adult.

A rigid tube that does not conform to the length and shape of the infant's trachea could cause mucosal trauma and the resultant complications of ulceration, granulation, bleeding, obstruction, and/or perforation. The infant requires a tracheostomy tube of special design. Various materials have been employed in the construction of such tubes, but experience in a number of pediatric surgical clinics has confirmed the advantages of a plastic or Silastic* pediatric-size tracheostomy tube for this purpose (Fig. 4-2). The smallest of these tubes (No. 1) is designed for use in newborn infants and has been inserted in babies weighing as little as 1300 Gm. In addition to their fabrication from an inert material that is well tolerated by body tissues, silicone rubber tubes also provide the following advantages:

1. They conform to the unique anatomic configuration of the infant's trachea with regard to length, diameter, and shape.

2. The tubes are quite flexible and present a relatively slick surface, which discourages the adherence of mucous plugs.

3. The tubes can be readily cleaned; Silastic is relatively nonadherent and can be autoclaved without resultant alteration in its shape or consistency, facilitating immediate re-use.

4. The silicone rubber contains barium, rendering the tubes radiopaque and permitting confirmation of their position in the trachea by x-ray study (Fig. 4-3).

5. Tube length can be quickly modified with a pair of scissors or knife; sharp edges may be removed by abrasion with a rough towel or fine sandpaper; in newborn and premature infants the bevel may be cut off so that the opening of the tube does not become occluded by the posterior tracheal wall.

6. The tubes are specifically designed for attachment to mechanical ventilators. The "tripod incision shield"

*Silastic—Medical Products Division, Dow Corning Corporation, Midland, Michigan 48640.

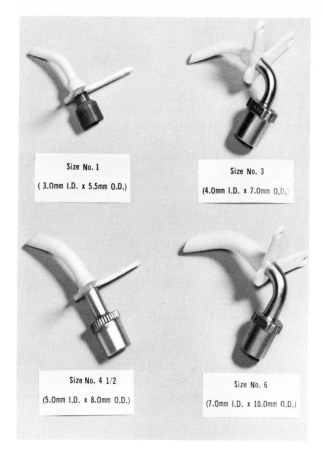

FIG. 4-2. Four sizes of Silastic tracheostomy tube (Aberdeen design) are demonstrated with representative types of ventilator connectors, which fit into special well at tube orifice. (From Talbert, J. L., and Haller, J. A., Jr.: Improved silastic tracheostomy tubes for infants and young children. J. Pediat. Surg., *3*:408, 1968.)

on the outer surface provides additional support and prevents angulation of the tube when ventilator tubing is attached. The outer orifice includes a well that accepts an adaptor from the ventilator connector without limiting the effective lumen of the tube. The lateral flanges of the surface shield are curved obliquely to conform to the natural shape of the infant's neck, facilitating a snug fit and minimizing the chance of accidental dislodgment. Finally, the flexible tube buffers any sudden shock or movement of the ventilator or its connecting tubing (Fig. 4-4).

Nursing Care of Infants With Nasotracheal Tubes and Tracheostomies. Nursing care is the single most important consideration in the successful management of any infant with a nasotracheal or tracheostomy tube in place. A nursing attendant must be present at all times.

The clinical challenge of an infant with airway intubation compares to that of a comatose patient who is unable either to care for himself or to communicate his needs. An effective nurse must be trained to recog-

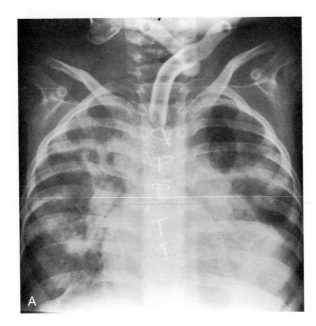 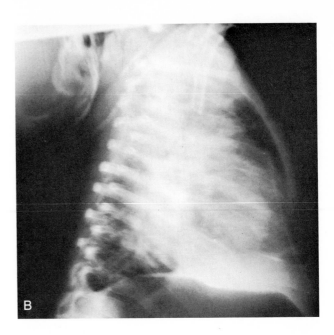

FIG. 4-3. Because of its barium content, position of Silastic tracheostomy tube is readily monitored radiographically. In above chest roentgenogram, *A,* distal tip of tube is apparent just proximal to tracheal bifurcation, thereby assuring free access to both main stem bronchi for suctioning and air exchange. In lateral view, *B,* position of tracheostomy tube is in center of trachea, even with hyperextension of baby's head. (From Haller, J. A., Jr., and Talbert, J. L.: Clinical evaluation of a new Silastic tracheostomy tube for respiratory support of infants and young children. Ann. Surg., *171*:915, 1970.)

nize the danger signs of impending airway obstruction. In general, these signs are identical with those that initially indicated the need for intubation: restlessness, agitation, tachypnea, tachycardia, paleness, cyanosis, and suprasternal, epigastric, and intercostal retraction. Sudden phonation in an infant with a tracheostomy suggests obstruction of the lumen, with bypass of air around the tube and through the larynx. Even in the absence of distress, phonation provides a warning of impending disaster. Bubbling secretions in the trachea or the tube are obvious evidence of partial obstruction. Significant protrusion of the tracheostomy tube above the skin surface, or of the nasotracheal tube from the nares, may indicate dislodgment.

Adequacy of the airway can usually be verified by a series of simple maneuvers. An aspirating catheter passed into the trachea, effecting removal of secretions and stimulation of coughing, confirms patency of the tube. A mucous plug at the tip of the tube can produce a ball-valve effect, however, allowing inspiration while blocking expiration. In this circumstance, the suction catheter may pass beyond the plug or temporarily dislodge it distally, only to have the obstruction recur on withdrawal of the catheter. To verify normal air exchange, the attendant should listen over the tube orifice. Not only can the passage of air into and out of the tube be heard, but the air stream can also be felt against the side of the observer's ear and face. Finally, periodic auscultation of the lungs can provide important information. Not infrequently an obstruction may be peripheral in location and involve only one main stem bronchus (usually the left). This complication is signaled by differential changes in breath sounds. Nurses and physicians responsible for such patients must routinely auscultate both lungs, prior to and following suctioning, in order to confirm the adequacy of tracheobronchial toilet.

Proper management of the intubated patient requires preparation for any emergency. A duplicate tube must be available at all times with a laryngoscope and resuscitation equipment (including a self-inflating ventilation bag). With trained personnel and correct equipment, no child with a nasotracheal or tracheostomy tube should ever succumb to airway obstruction.

Inhalation of dry gases predisposes to mucous plug formation. Prevention hinges on adequate humidification and aspiration. Optimal humidification requires a combined program of adequate patient hydration and periodic instillation of small amounts of normal saline directly into the tube orifice. In general, simple bubble humidifiers are inadequate for support. Heated humidifiers or ultrasonic nebulizers are preferable, although caution must be exerted to avoid overhydration with the latter. The general state of hydration of the patient bears an important relationship to the viscidity of his bronchial secretions. In recent years, there has been a tendency to underhydrate pediatric patients postoperatively, a natural reaction to earlier difficulties with excessive fluid administration. Overcompensation by fluid restriction, however, may lead to increased respiratory complications resulting from tenacious bronchial secretions.

Adherence to sterile technique in suctioning the trachea minimizes contamination and infection. Bronchopulmonary inflammation, in itself, favors increased production of viscid secretions. A fresh sterile suction catheter should be employed for each aspiration. A sterile clamp or gloved hand should be employed to grasp the suction catheter. The frequency of tracheal aspiration must be individualized on the basis of each infant's condition and the length of time he has had the tracheostomy, but failure to institute a program of periodic tracheal aspiration will favor the inadvertent accumulation of secretions. Since the airway is completely obstructed during the process of suctioning, deliberate haste must be employed (not exceeding 10 seconds) and the infant must be allowed to recover

from his temporary anoxia before the aspiration is repeated. It is also essential that secretions be aspirated from both bronchial trees, with the effectiveness of suctioning confirmed by auscultation of both lungs.

Mechanical Ventilation. An infant with respiratory distress presents the ultimate test for any mechanical ventilator. Adults, in whom the margin for error is greater, can usually compensate for the inaccuracies of a particular machine, but similar deficiencies may prove overwhelming for newborn infants.

One essential feature of any ventilator is an adequate humidification system. Heated humidifiers are preferable for this purpose, not only because they provide moisture, but also because they assist in maintaining body temperature. Ultrasonic nebulizers are valuable, but excessive hydration must be avoided.

The argument of pressure- versus volume-regulated ventilators is an additional consideration. In many instances, particularly in the absence of primary pulmonary disease, differences in the two systems are unimportant. In cases of impaired or fluctuating pulmonary compliance, however, as associated with some forms of congenital heart disease, hyaline membrane disease, or bronchospastic disease of the lung, volume-regulated ventilators may prove preferable. With this system, adequate ventilatory exchange is assured in spite of changes in airway resistance.

A piston ventilator that is specifically modified for use in infants may be employed for this purpose. These machines offer simplicity of operation in addition to the advantages listed above. This last point is especially important when skilled nursing personnel are at a premium. In most instances, infants adjust to pre-set respiratory rates and do not require a self-triggering system. In any case, blood gas monitoring is essential for accurate assessment of the adequacy of ventilation. Adjustment of inspired oxygen concentrations on the basis of blood pO_2 aids in determining the needs of the patient and diminishes the danger of chronic oxygen toxicity. Symptoms of oxygen toxicity have been noted with concentrations as low as 40 per cent, and whenever feasible, room air is preferred.

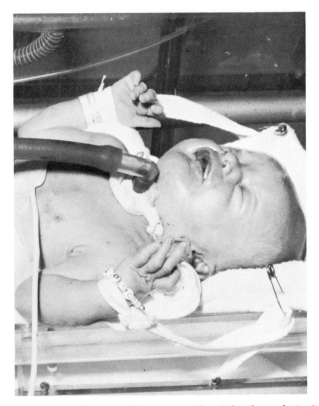

FIG. 4-4 Silastic tracheostomy tube (Aberdeen design) should be attached to ventilator by passage of connecting tubing from below upward over chest wall. This approach minimizes traction on trachea with movement of body and neck, and frees face and neck for suctioning and feeding.

Cardiovascular Support

The successful application of sophisticated monitoring techniques to the management of newborn infants requires specific adaptations in the usual methods of venous and arterial catheterization. A special cutdown tray, equipped with small instruments and retractors, should be available in the newborn intensive care unit. Absorbable fine gut ligatures are preferred, to lessen the risk of contamination and infection. For this same reason, whenever feasible, the catheter is brought out through a small stab wound separate from the original cutdown incision, and a regimen of meticulous daily wound care is adopted, including cleansing of the catheterization site, application of broad-spectrum antibiotic ointment, and frequent changes of the sterile dressing. Close observation must be maintained for any evidence of wound sepsis or phlebitis. In instances of long-term venous cannulation, blood cultures should be obtained weekly and urine cultures twice weekly for both bacteria and fungi. With these measures, septic complications may be detected prior to the appearance of clinical signs and symptoms.

Central Venous Catheterization. In infants requiring close surveillance of fluid and colloid balance or long-term parenteral alimentation, the techniques of central venous cannulation are invaluable (Talbert and Haller, 1966). For reasons noted previously, these catheters are optimally positioned in the superior vena cava or right atrium. Although the antecubital veins and the saphenous vein in the groin provide alternative sites for peripheral cannulation, the internal and external jugular veins or the common facial vein in the neck are preferred for this purpose. Percutaneous puncture of the subclavian vein in the shoulder, a technique that is frequently utilized in the adult, is considered excessively hazardous in infants. The umbilical vein also is avoided for this procedure because of the risk of thrombosis and phlebitis, and the subsequent sequela of portal hypertension. Umbilical vein catheterization,

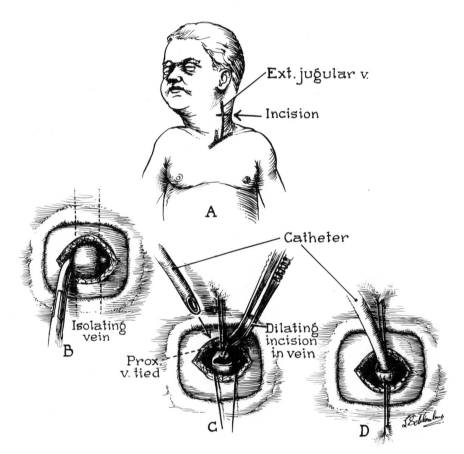

FIG. 4-5. Catheterization of external jugular vein in infant. *A,* Incision. *B,* Vein is isolated with small curved clamp through short, transverse skin incision. *C,* Fine absorbable ligature is tied about cephalic end of vein. Second ligature is placed distally with traction exerted in opposite directions by ties clamped to adjacent drapes. Transverse incision is made in anterior wall of vein. This opening is then enlarged by insertion and spreading of tips of small curved forceps. While vein lumen is thus exposed, beveled cannula may be introduced with relative ease. *D,* When catheter has been positioned at level of innominate vein or superior vena cava, second ligature is secured. Internal jugular vein can be exposed and cannulated in similar manner by mobilization and lateral retraction of overlying sternocleidomastoid muscle. After venous cannulation is completed, catheter is preferably exteriorized through separate stab wound high in skin of neck or in postauricular area of scalp, by subcutaneous tunneling with large-bore, thin-wall needle. Skin incision is closed with fine interrupted subcuticular absorbable sutures, antibiotic ointment is applied to wound, and catheter is secured with sterile dressing. (From Talbert, J. L., and Haller, J. A., Jr.: Technic of central venous pressure monitoring in infants. *Amer. Surg., 32:*767, 1966).

however, continues to be the method of choice for exchange transfusion.

The jugular veins in the neck are exposed through a short transverse skin incision over the sternocleidomastoid muscle (Fig. 4-5). If the external jugular vein proves excessively small, as is often the case in premature infants, the internal jugular vein may be cannulated, either directly or via the common facial vein (Fig. 4-6). The same skin incision used for external jugular vein cutdown also provides exposure of the internal jugular vein with lateral retraction of the sternocleidomastoid muscle and blunt dissection of the adjacent structures of the carotid sheath (carotid artery; vagus and hypoglossal nerves) (Fig. 4-7). Since all other major routes of venous drainage from the neck and head are preserved intact, no serious sequelae are anticipated in these infants from sacrifice of a single internal jugular vein. Following isolation, the vein is secured cephalad with a fine absorbable ligature. A second ligature is placed distally, with traction exerted in opposite directions by the two ties clamped to the adjacent drapes. A transverse incision is then made in the anterior wall of the vein by insertion of the point of a No. 11 scalpel blade through the midportion of the vein, and cutting upward with the blade edge. The vein opening is then enlarged by the insertion and spreading of the tips of a small, curved iris forceps. Although the vein lumen is exposed in this manner, a beveled, radiopaque cannula may be introduced with relative ease. Silastic tubing is preferred for this purpose, because of the decreased risk of tissue reaction and intravascular thrombosis, factors favoring prolonged use. Special radiopaque Silastic tubing has been recently introduced for this purpose. The catheter should be positioned in the superior vena cava or right atrium, and measurement of the tubing prior to insertion will assist in optimal placement. *A roentgenogram always should be obtained at completion of the procedure to confirm location* (Fig. 4-8). Since these fine, soft cannulas are easily occluded by tight ligatures, a free flow of solution should be ascertained before the distal connection is passed off the sterile operative field. After venous cannulation has been completed, the catheter is preferably exteriorized through a separate stab wound high in the skin of the neck or the postauricular area of the scalp, by subcutaneous tunneling with a large-bore, thin-wall needle. The skin incision is then closed with fine, interrupted, subcuticular absorbable sutures; antibiotic ointment is applied to the wound; and the catheter is secured by a sterile dressing.

Arterial Catheterization. Although investigators of hemodynamic alterations associated with shock have long since discarded determinations of arterial blood pressures as the sole indicator of effective cardiac out-

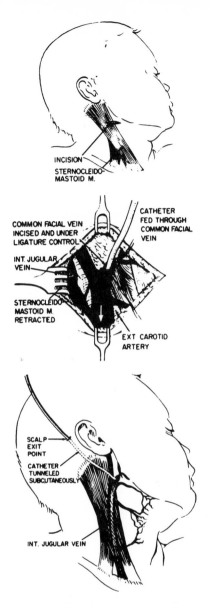

FIG. 4-6. Technique for central venous catheterization via common facial vein. *Top,* Under local anesthesia, short transverse incision is made over anterior border of sternocleidomastoid muscle at junction of upper and middle thirds of muscle. *Center,* Incision is deepened beneath muscle border and common facial vein is easily located just beyond its formation from anterior and posterior facial veins. Common facial vein is partially incised transversely, under ligature control, approximately 1 cm. from its entrance into internal jugular vein. Catheter is inserted into common facial vein and advanced into internal jugular vein for distance of approximately 5 cm., placing catheter tip within superior vena cava near right atrium. Final position of catheter tip is confirmed roentgenographically. *Bottom,* Catheter is fixed into position by silk ligature around common facial vein, then tunneled subcutaneously to exit point behind ear. (From Zumbro, G. L., Jr., et al.: Catheter placement in infants needing total parenteral nutrition utilizing common facial vein. Arch. Surg., *102:*71, 1971).

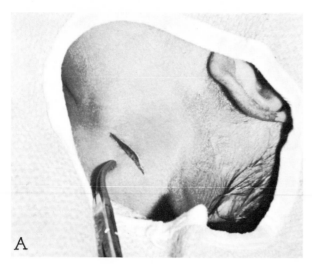
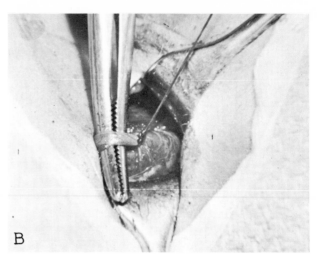

FIG. 4-7. Catheterization of internal jugular vein in infants. *A,* Short transverse skin incision is made over medial border of sternocleidomastoid muscle. *B,* This muscle is retracted laterally, and internal jugular vein is exposed by blunt dissection. Adjacent nerves and vessels are carefully identified and preserved. Vein is ligated cephalad with plain catgut ligature while second untied ligature is placed caudally. (From Talbert, J. L., and Haller, J. A., Jr.: Technic of central venous pressure monitoring in infants. Amer. Surg., *32:*767, 1966).

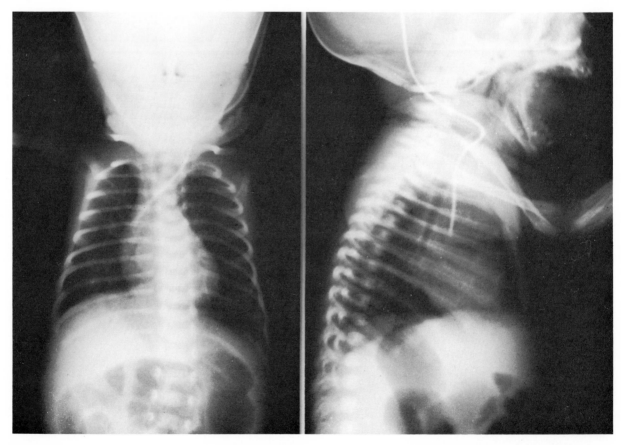

FIG. 4-8. Radiographic monitoring of central venous catheter position. Distal tip of CVP catheter, inserted via jugular vein in neck, is localized at junction of right atrium and superior vena cava by AP and lateral chest roentgenograms, which also include lower neck and upper abdomen. Central venous pressure measurements are valid only when catheter tip is positioned in superior vena cava or right atrium. Catheterization of atrial appendage or right ventricle poses a significant threat of myocardial perforation and pericardial tamponade.

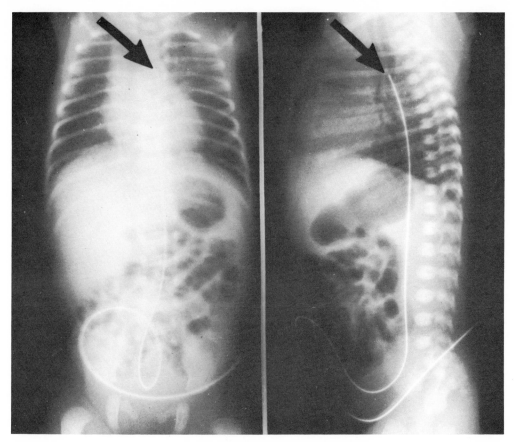

FIG. 4-9. Radiographic monitoring of umbilical artery catheter by AP and lateral chest roentgenograms, which demonstrate position of tip of catheter in thoracic aorta.

put and peripheral perfusion, serial measurements continue to provide important assistance when correlated with other observations. Of greater importance than the measurement of arterial pressure is the use of arterial monitoring catheters for serial sampling and determinations of arterial pH, pCO_2 and pO_2. These measurements have been accepted as routine guidelines for respiratory support and artificial ventilation in the care of small infants (Lucey, 1969).

The technique of umbilical artery catheterization has been popularized for determination of arterial blood gases and pressures in the newborn infant (Vidyasagar, 1970). This approach provides a unique means for obtaining arterial blood samples and monitoring pressure while providing a simultaneous route for the administration of fluid and colloids through a constant infusion pump. A radiopaque catheter is inserted through the umbilical artery, and with x-ray monitoring, is positioned in the aorta at the level of the diaphragm or above. (A smooth-tipped, end-hole catheter should be used, and blood flow should be easily obtained on aspiration.) Since the ductus arteriosus is frequently patent at this age, it is essential that the exact location of the cannula be confirmed (Fig. 4-9).

The position of the catheter tip relative to the ductus arteriosus obviously influences the anticipated blood gas results. Major complications of umbilical artery catheterization have been arterial thrombosis or perforation when inappropriate catheters have been employed, and partial or complete obstruction of the femoral artery on the side of the umbilical artery catheterization. This latter complication is usually signaled by ischemic changes in the affected lower extremity. Signs of ischemia usually disappear when the catheter is removed, although in a few instances, arterial thrombosis has been documented. Reflex vasodilatation of the affected leg is encouraged by warming of the opposite extremity. To minimize the danger of hemorrhage, catheter removal is ideally delayed for six hours after the last administration of flushing solutions containing heparinized saline.

Another technique that has been developed for arterial blood sampling in infants is that of temporal artery catheterization (Fig. 4-10). This method is particularly useful after the fourth or fifth day of life, when the umbilical artery has usually thrombosed and cannulation is impossible. Repeated percutaneous needle punctures of the femoral artery in these circumstances

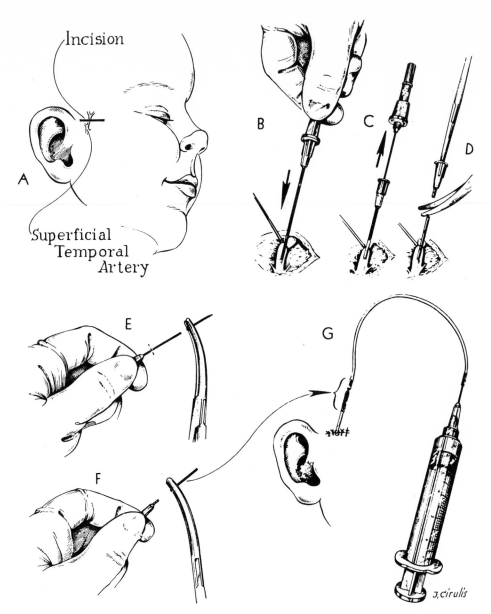

FIG. 4-10. Temporal artery catheterization. *A,* Location of incision on line between outer canthus of eye and helix of ear. *B,* Insertion of Angiocath needle into temporal artery. *C,* Removal of needle stylet. *D,* Amputation of needle hub. *E* and *F,* Fashioning of metal connector from No. 20 disposable needle. *G,* Polyethylene cutdown catheter used as extension line between Angiocath needle and syringe. (From McGovern, B., and Baker, A. R.: Temporal artery catheterization for monitoring of blood gases in infants. Surg. Gynec. Obstet., *127:*601, 1968).

is difficult, and presents potential hazards of sepsis and arterial injury. In the technique of temporal artery catheterization, the vessel is exposed through a short transverse skin incision just anterior to the cephalad attachment of the helix of the ear. The artery is isolated from the accompanying vein and is cannulated proximally with an 18.5-gauge Angiocath needle. The catheter is connected to a syringe filled with heparinized saline and the system is periodically flushed with small amounts of solution to ensure patency over the next three to four days. Clinical improvement in the infant's condition usually allows removal of the catheter by this time.

A final method for monitoring arterial pressures and gases in larger infants is cannulation of the radial artery of the wrist (Fig. 4-11). The catheter is connected to an appropriate transducer for pressure monitoring and a stopcock for arterial blood sampling. A mattress suture is placed through the skin, beneath the proximal artery, and left untied. Following the removal of the catheter, this suture is tied and kept in position for 48 to 72 hours. No instance of bleeding has been encountered following subsequent removal of the ligature.

Nutritional Support

A variety of special operative procedures, including gastrostomy and enterostomy, are particularly valuable in initiating gastrointestinal alimentation in the postoperative newborn (see Chapter 7). Not infrequently, however, the neonatal patient who has had corrective surgery for a gastrointestinal anomaly requires a protracted period before normal function can be achieved. In the past, the surgeon and pediatrician faced a potential race for survival in such circumstances, with the constant threat of exhausting the baby's limited metabolic reserves before a satisfactory mechanism for restoring them could be established. Utilizing new techniques of parenteral feeding, this critical time period has been significantly extended, and in some instances, progression of normal growth has continued uninter-

rupted. Developments that have contributed to this progress include (1) new methods for central venous cannulation of the newborn infant, (2) new equipment (such as inert silicone rubber tubing, which incurs less intravascular reaction and clotting, and special infusion pumps, which facilitate administration of small amounts of fluid and colloids over protracted periods), and (3) new preparations of parenteral solutions, which provide most essential metabolic needs. Not only do these new techniques provide total parenteral nutrition when required, but they also allow supplementary support during that critical phase of transition from parenteral to alimentary feeding. The use of constant infusion pumps, for both parenteral and alimentary feedings, provides a method by which a critical fluid balance may be maintained in these situations, allowing limited, exact quantities of fluid to be administered simultaneously by both routes.

The exact composite of the infusate has been documented in articles by Wilmore and Dudrick (1969) and by Filler and associates (1970). This is a fat-free solution that is prepared by admixture of 5 per cent fibrin hydrolysate (Aminosol) with 50 per cent glucose, so that the final solution contains 20 per cent glucose and

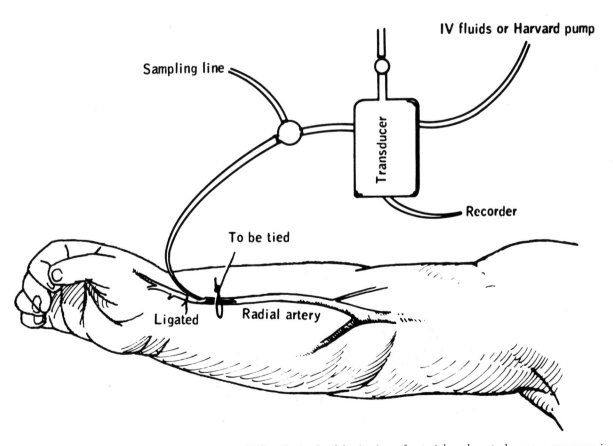

FIG. 4-11. Radial artery catheterization. (From Haller, J. A., Jr.: Monitoring of arterial and central venous pressure in infants. Pediat. Clin. N. Amer., *16*:640, 1969).

TABLE 4-1.   Infusate for Parenteral Feeding (Content Per Liter)

Protein (amino acids)	33 Gm.
Glucose	200 Gm.
Sodium*	5 mEq.
Potassium*	16 mEq.
Chloride*	11.7 mEq.
Calcium*	183 mg.
Phosphorus*	67 mg.
Multivitamin infusion†	5.0 ml.
Vitamin B$_{12}$	6 mg.
Vitamin K$_1$ (AquaMEPHYTON)	0.2 mg.
Folic acid	0.45 mg.

*The concentration of electrolytes should be adjusted daily on the basis of the requirements of the individual patient. In general, 30 mEq. of sodium chloride and 20 mEq. of potassium chloride should be added to each liter of infusate. The exact needs, however, will be dictated by the infant's serum electrolyte levels, renal function, and external fluid and electrolyte losses.

†U.S. Vitamin and Pharmaceutical Corporation, New York, New York. Adapted from Filler, R. M., et al.: Long-term total parenteral nutrition in infants. New Eng. J. Med., *281*:589, 1969.

0.94 calories per ml. (Table 4-1). Concentrations of sodium, chloride, potassium, calcium, magnesium, and phosphorus are adjusted daily as dictated by the patient's requirements. Increased daily increments of sodium, potassium, and chloride are required almost routinely. Additional magnesium may also be needed if the infant is sustaining excessive, prolonged losses of intestinal fluids. Trace metals (zinc, cobalt, manganese, and copper) and essential fatty acids are provided by plasma transfusions (10 ml. per kg.) twice weekly, and iron requirements are satisfied either by weekly intramuscular injections of iron dextran or by blood transfusions. Daily vitamin requirements are provided by the standard infusate solution.

These solutions should be administered by constant infusion pump through a catheter inserted in the superior vena cava (utilizing the techniques described previously) (Fig. 4-12). An infusion of 135 ml./kg./day of the infusate will provide 122 calories/kg./day, a quantity sufficient to satisfy the normal metabolic re-

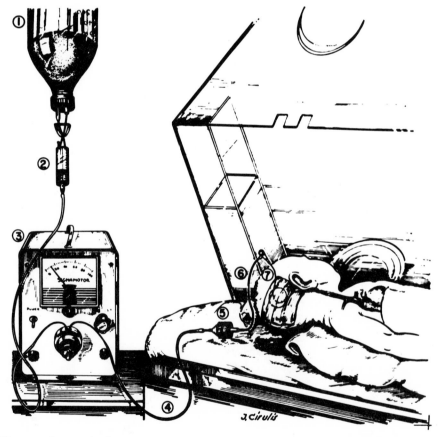

FIG. 4-12.   System for long-term intravenous alimentation (Lifeline). *1,* Amino acid-glucose infusate. *2,* Calibrated burette. *3,* Constant infusion pump. *4,* Disposable tubing with compressible section which adapts to pump head. *5,* Millipore filter. *6,* "T" connector. *7,* Silicone rubber intravenous catheter. (From Filler, R. M., and Eraklis, A. J.: Care of the critically ill child: intravenous alimentation. Pediatrics, *46:*456, 1970.)

quirements for tissue repair and growth in an infant. Administration at a slow, uniform rate is essential to achieve maximal dilution in the central venous pool, to avoid the complications of venous irritation and thrombosis, and to ensure optimal utilization of the nutrients.

A 0.22-micron filter must be interposed in the circuit to remove any particulate matter or microorganisms that might otherwise contaminate the solution. Meticulous wound care at the skin catheterization site, as described, is also essential for avoiding sepsis. Routine periodic blood cultures for bacteria and fungi may permit the early detection of any septic complication. Metabolic acidosis also must be guarded against, particularly in premature or seriously ill infants, by routine monitoring of blood gases and pH. An osmotic diuresis and dehydration of the patient may result from administration of these hypertonic solutions, and serial determinations of body weight, urine output, serum osmolality and electrolytes, and urinary glucose are required for successful management. Although the technique for long-term parenteral alimentation has proved to be an invaluable addition to the armamentarium of the pediatrician and surgeon, the physician should refer to excellent detailed descriptions by Dudrick and Filler before undertaking this method for the first time.

REFERENCES

Aberdeen, E.: Mechanical pulmonary ventilation in infants. Tracheostomy and tracheostomy care in infants. Proc. Roy. Soc. Med., *58*:900, 1965.

Filler, R. M., and Eraklis, A. J.: Care of the critically ill child: intravenous alimentation. Pediatrics, *46*:456, 1970.

Haller, J. A., Jr., and Talbert, J. L.: Clinical evaluation of a new Silastic tracheostomy tube for respiratory support of infants and young children. Ann. Surg., *171*:915, 1970.

Holinger, P. H., Brown, W. T., and Maurizi, D. G.: Tracheostomy in the newborn. Amer. J. Surg., *108*:771, 1965.

Lucey, J. F.: Problems of Neonatal Intensive Care Units, Report of the Fifty-Ninth Ross Conference on Pediatric Research. Columbus, Ross Laboratories, 1969.

McGovern, B., and Baker, A. R.: Temporal artery catheterization for monitoring of blood gases in infants. Surg. Gynec. Obstet., *127*:601, 1968.

Talbert, J. L., and Haller, J. A., Jr.: Technic of central venous pressure monitoring in infants. Amer. Surg., *32*:767, 1966.

Vidyasagar, D., Downes, J. J., and Boggs, T. R., Jr.: Respiratory distress syndrome of newborn infants: II. Technic of catheterization of umbilical artery and clinical results of treatment of 124 patients. Clin. Pediat., *9*:332, 1970.

Wilmore, D. W., Groff, D. B., Bishop, H. C., and Dudrick, S. J.: Total parenteral nutrition in infants with catastrophic gastrointestinal anomalies. J. Pediat. Surg., *4*:181, 1969.

5

Respiratory Emergencies

Respiratory distress is largely responsible for morbidity and mortality in the neonatal period. The critical transition from intrauterine to extrauterine life requires many complex adjustments. Inadequacies in any one may prove fatal.

During fetal life the respiratory system undergoes a remarkable series of morphologic changes in preparation for extrauterine function (Reid, 1967). The lung originates as a ventral evagination of the primitive foregut, the upper end retaining its communication with the alimentary tract as the larynx. The caudal end of the primordial pulmonary tree differentiates into lung buds, each of which subsequently redivides to form two major branches on the left and three on the right. This process of branching is then repeated until the major components of the tracheobronchial system are completed by the fourth month of gestation. At this time the peripheral portions of the bronchial tree begin to differentiate into complex canalicular spaces. By the seventh month of gestation (at an approximate fetal weight of 1000 Gm.), bronchopulmonary development usually has sufficiently matured to sustain extrauterine survival, and each week of subsequent gestation enhances this potential. Alveolar differentiation continues postnatally, with an increase in number until the age of eight years and an increase in size until growth of the chest wall is completed.

Inadequacies in bronchopulmonary differentiation can result in a variety of anomalies that are capable of producing neonatal respiratory distress (Burford and Ferguson, 1969). Esophageal atresia, tracheoesophageal fistula, and bronchogenic cyst probably represent examples of abnormalities of the initial phases of esophageal and tracheobronchial budding. An arrest in a subsequent stage of bronchopulmonary differentiation can produce pulmonary agenesis, aplasia, or hypoplasia. Bilateral pulmonary agenesis represents a complete failure in tracheobronchial budding. Unilateral pulmonary agenesis occurs more frequently on the left side and must be differentiated from other conditions producing mediastinal shift. Unilateral agenesis may be associated with anomalies of the spine, heart, and gastrointestinal tract. Pulmonary aplasia is characterized by a rudimentary tracheobronchial tree with no evidence of pulmonary parenchymal formation. Hypoplasia of the lung represents an interruption in alveolar development during the final months of gestation and may be associated with anomalies of the heart or skeleton. Compression of the fetal lung by coexistent intrapleural space-occupying lesions, such as abdominal viscera herniated through a foramen of Bochdalek defect in the diaphragm, can also result in pulmonary hypoplasia.

During delivery the normal compression of the baby's thorax in the vaginal canal helps in the expression of amniotic fluid and secretions from the tracheobronchial tree when the baby's head is finally outside. At birth, initiation of ventilation may require transient intrapulmonary pressures as high as 40 to 80 cm. of water to overcome the viscosity of fluid in the airway and the forces of surface tension, and to stretch the lung parenchyma. The process of inflation is usually uneven, and if excessively high pressures are maintained in the aerated alveoli because of persistent obstruction and/or atelectasis elsewhere in the lung, spontaneous rupture may ensue. In most instances, however, the process of expansion is rapid and smooth, and complete functioning residual capacity is attained within the first 18 minutes of life (Chernick and Avery, 1963).

Concomitant with inflation of the lung, the pulmonary blood flow increases rapidly as a result of marked decrease in pulmonary vascular resistance. The right-to-left shunt through the ductus arteriosus reverses, and left atrial filling increases. With diversion of blood via the lungs into the left heart, functional closure of fetal shunts through the ductus arteriosus and foramen ovale is normally achieved. Anatomic closure of these fetal remnants, however, may require weeks, and interim alterations in intrathoracic or pulmonary artery pressure can reactivate the potential right-to-left shunts (Dawes, 1968).

A major determinant of successful extrauterine adaption is the degree to which adequate tissue oxygenation is achieved. Although the brain of the newborn appears relatively resistant to the effects of hypoxia, other systems are exquisitely sensitive. Tissue anoxia, as a result of hypoxia or circulatory failure, produces a significant metabolic acidosis. This combination (hypoxia and acidosis) may then initiate a vicious cycle of pulmonary vasoconstriction, recurrent pulmonary hypertension, reactivation of fetal right-to-left shunts, and exaggeration of arterial oxygen desaturation. If uncorrected, the process may result in cardiac arrhythmias, depressed cardiac or renal function, hyperkalemia, impaired end-organ response to catecholamines, impaired metabolic response to cold, spontaneous tissue hemorrhage, and hyperbilirubinemia (Scarpelli, 1968).

It is essential, therefore, that neonatal respiratory distress be promptly corrected (Behrman et al., 1969). An immediate assessment of the baby's condition is obtained by the method of Apgar (Table 5-1). Most infants should score over 6 by one minute and 8 by three minutes of life. The lower the score, the greater the urgency for instituting corrective measures. Of the five functions assessed by the Apgar score, heart rate provides the most reliable index to the severity of hypoxia (Apgar, 1953 and 1966).

Differential Diagnosis

The cause of most cases of neonatal respiratory distress can be determined by history, physical examination, and x-ray examination of the chest.

History. Damage to the central nervous system or respiratory depression can result from injury during labor. Massive bronchopulmonary aspiration may occur in infants with low birth weight, in breach presentation, or with placental hemorrhage or prolapse of the umbilical cord. Bacterial pneumonitis and sepsis

TABLE 5-1

Sign	0	1	2
Heart rate	Absent	Slow (below 100)	Over 100
Respiratory effort	Absent	Slow, irregular	Good crying
Muscle tone	Limp	Some flexion of extremities	Active motion
Reflex irritability	No response	Grimace	Cough, sneeze
Color	Blue Pale	Body pink, extremities blue	Completely pink

Technique of APGAR scoring: Values of 0, 1, or 2 points are assigned to these five observations of activity and physiologic function. Summation of the results provides a helpful assessment of the state of homeostasis in the newborn infant. (Modified from Apgar, V.: The newborn (Apgar) scoring system. Reflections and advice. Pediat. Clin. N. Amer., *13*:645, 1966.)

may result from intrauterine infections. Prematurity or maternal diabetes predisposes to hyaline membrane disease.

Physical Examination. When dyspnea is present, the time of onset may suggest its cause. Immediate distress results from major malformations of the airway or tension pneumothorax. Progressively increasing dyspnea is seen with the respiratory distress syndrome (hyaline membrane disease) and diaphragmatic hernia. Sudden onset of dyspnea in a previously stable infant is characteristic of acute pneumothorax.

When noisy respirations are present, their character may suggest the level of airway obstruction or the source of distress. Moist, rattling inspiratory and expiratory noises suggest nasopharyngeal blockage, either from micrognathia and macroglossia or from the excessive mucus that overflows from the blind proximal pouch of an esophageal atresia. Inspiratory stridor, hoarseness, or aphonia suggests a laryngeal abnormality. Expiratory grunting is characteristic of hyaline membrane disease, pneumonia, or aspiration; expiratory wheezing accompanies partial obstruction of a major bronchus.

Physical examination assists in the localization of these processes. By the passage of a catheter through the nares, pharynx, and esophagus into the stomach, either choanal or esophageal atresia can be detected. The presence of micrognathia or macroglossia is readily apparent. Visual inspection and digital palpation of the posterior pharynx exclude any obstructing lesion at this level. Examination of the neck usually defines any extrinsic mass that compresses the larynx or trachea.

The configuration of the chest wall or the character of respiratory movements can suggest the source of distress. Asymmetry of thoracic expansion accompanies unilateral lesions, such as diaphragmatic hernia, pneumothorax, chylothorax, or lobar emphysema. Inspiratory retraction of the suprasternal, subxiphoid, or intercostal spaces accompanies upper airway and/or laryngeal obstruction. Percussion of the chest wall may demonstrate unilateral hyperresonance in tension pneumothorax or lobar emphysema, whereas dullness may accompany diaphragmatic hernia or pleural effusion. Auscultation may reveal diffusion rales in pneumonia or cardiac failure. Unilateral absence of breath sounds is noted in pneumothorax, lobar emphysema, and diaphragmatic hernia. Generally diminished breath sounds accompany aspiration pneumonia and hyaline membrane disease.

Cyanosis of the hands and feet can occur normally in the newborn infant. Generalized cyanosis with improvement on stimulation characterizes those conditions producing lethargy or respiratory depression, such as sepsis or central nervous system damage. The cyanosis of congenital heart disease usually persists, and may even intensify, with stimulation of respiration. Cyanosis resulting from a right-to-left intracardiac shunt is not corrected by administration of 100 per cent oxygen. The combination of cyanosis and dyspnea usually indicates a primary airway or bronchopulmonary problem.

Chest Roentgenogram. Posteroanterior (PA) and lateral views of the chest should be obtained immediately in any newborn infant with respiratory distress or persistent cyanosis. Since the condition responsible may exist above the thoracic inlet as well as below the diaphragm, the initial examination must always encompass the neck (including the mandible) as well as the abdomen (Capitanio and Kirkpatrick, 1969). Abnormalities of the thorax and spine may indicate asphyxiating thoracic dystrophy, osteogenesis imperfecta, duplication cysts, pulmonary agenesis, or tracheoesophageal fistula. A lateral roentgenogram of the chest and neck is particularly helpful in excluding tracheal narrowing, retropharyngeal masses, or obstructing lesions. The trachea normally buckles slightly to the right at the thoracic inlet, and deviation to the left suggests a right-sided aortic arch. A normal thymic density is evident on both PA and lateral films, and retrosternal lucency in the first few days of life suggests the syndrome of congenital absence of this gland. The heart normally appears large for the first three days of life. Intrathoracic tumors in the newborn are usually included in the mediastinal shadow. The configuration and position of the diaphragm may indicate hernia or eventration. Integrity of the esophagus is confirmed by

passage of a radiopaque catheter into the stomach. Instillation of barium assists in demonstrating a tracheoesophageal fistula, mediastinal tumor, or constricting vascular ring. (*Barium should never be administered to a newborn infant by bottle* because of the danger of aspiration and flooding of the lungs.) Abnormal abdominal gas patterns are present in diaphragmatic hernia, tracheoesophageal fistula, and intestinal obstruction. Unilateral opacification of the pleural cavity with shifting of the mediastinum to the opposite side suggests effusion, diaphragmatic eventration, or hernia. Tension pneumothorax is characterized by unilateral absence of pulmonary markings and contralateral shifting of the mediastinum. Small degrees of pneumomediastinum are commonly present in the newborn infant and usually prove inconsequential. Localized or unilateral overaeration of the lung is seen with lobar emphysema, adenomatoid malformation of the lung, and ball-valve obstruction of the bronchus. Chest fluoroscopy may be required to differentiate primary pulmonary atelectasis from a contralateral process that has produced mediastinal shifting and secondary compression. Agenesis or hypoplasia of the lung may also be associated with mediastinal shift and contralateral hyperaeration. Bronchography and pulmonary angiography may be required to confirm this diagnosis (Booth and Berry, 1967). Diffuse overaeration of the lungs results from proximal airway obstruction or meconium aspiration. Diffuse underaeration, with a "granular" appearance of the lung parenchyma, characterizes hyaline membrane disease or may occur less commonly in pulmonary hemorrhage or neonatal atelectasis. "Kerby lines" and pleural effusion may accompany abnormalities of pulmonary venous drainage and cardiac failure.

Special Diagnostic Procedures. The usefulness of esophagography and chest fluoroscopy in differential diagnosis of neonatal respiratory distress has been noted. Other special procedures, which may be required less frequently, are bronchoscopy, bronchography, arteriography, and radioactive pulmonary scan.

Bronchoscopy occasionally serves to remove a persistent mucous plug that partially or totally occludes a major bronchus. In general, this technique is less useful in newborn infants than in older children, and during laryngoscopy, suctioning of the trachea directly through a laryngoscope or through an endotracheal tube usually suffices. In rare cases, however, particularly if the mucous plug produces a ball-valve obstruction that simulates lobar emphysema, bronchoscopy may prove curative (Fig. 5-1). In these circumstances, bronchoscopy must be performed *in the operating room* with a "double surgical set-up," providing for an immediate thoracotomy if progressive emphysema results

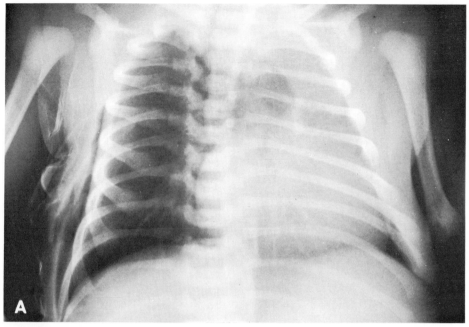

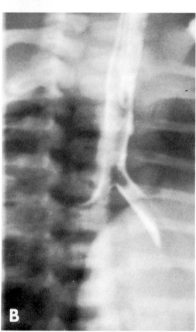

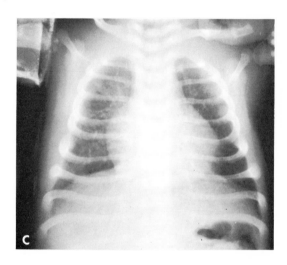

FIG. 5-1. Obstructive lobar emphysema of newborn infant. *A,* Hyperinflation of right lung with mediastinal shift and compression of left lung. *B,* Bronchogram confirming patency of left main-stem bronchus and ball-valve obstruction of right. *C,* Postoperative chest roentgenogram one week following extraction of obstructing mucous plug from right main-stem bronchus. (From Murray, G. F., Talbert, J. L., and Haller, J. A., Jr.: Obstructive lobar emphysema of the newborn infant. J. Thorac. Cardiov. Surg., *53*:886, 1967.)

or the respiratory distress increases. Bronchography is also rarely required for differential diagnosis at this age, but may prove helpful in the defining of pulmonary atresia or obstructive processes. Angiography is particularly useful in the diagnosing of congenital cardiac disease or vascular abnormalities, and of pulmonary sequestration, hypoplasia, or agenesis. Finally, the use of radioactive pulmonary scans has been reported recently for the diagnosis of congenital lobar emphysema (Mauney and Sabiston, 1970).

Extrathoracic Causes of Respiratory Distress

Extrathoracic airway obstruction may occur at any level from the nose to the larynx and is usually characterized by difficulty with inspiration (i.e., retraction) (Ferguson, 1967).

NOSE AND NASOPHARYNX

Obstructing lesions include nasal atresia or agenesis, cystic masses (especially nasal encephaloceles), tumors (usually dermoids or teratomas), and congenital choanal atresia.

Congenital Choanal Atresia. This is the most common anomaly of the nasopharynx and must be excluded in any case of neonatal respiratory distress by immediate passage of a 10 Fr. catheter through each nares into the posterior pharynx. The newborn infant is of necessity a nasal breather. Accordingly, bilateral nasal obstruction results in rapid asphyxiation (Polgar, 1965). In 90 per cent of cases of bilateral choanal atresia, the obstruction is bony and requires definitive operation for correction. During the first two to three weeks of life, a mouth gag, airway, or McGovern's nipple, in conjunction with constant careful nursing supervision, serves to support these patients until a pattern of mouth breathing is established. (Key and Mendel, 1968). A definitive, transpalatal surgical attack on the atretic lesion can be performed later.

ORAL CAVITY

Obstructions at this level can result from micrognathia, macroglossia, or various cysts or tumors involving the posterior tongue or pharyngeal wall.

Micrognathia. Mandibular hypoplasia represents an anomaly of the first branchial arch and may be associated with the Treacher-Collins syndrome (mandibulofacial dysostosis) or Pierre Robin syndrome. The first condition can be distinguished by the presence of a characteristic antimongoloid slant to the eyelids and large low-set ears. In the Pierre Robin syndrome, there is usually an incomplete cleft of the palate and a relative macroglossia in addition to the typical "bird-like" facies (Fig. 5-2). Airway obstruction in both conditions results from glossoptosis, and is relieved if the infant is placed in the prone position, which allows the tongue to fall forward. In severe cases that do not respond to positional management, the Douglas procedure of temporary glossopexy may alleviate the obstruction until normal mandibular growth provides permanent relief (Fig. 5-3) (Douglas, 1950; Randall, 1964). Tracheostomy is useful in babies who require mechanical

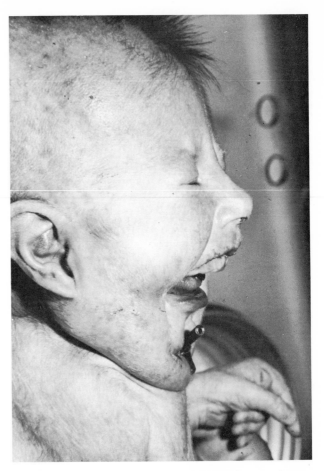

FIG. 5-2. Newborn infant with Pierre Robin syndrome. Note characteristic "bird-like" facies secondary to mandibular hypoplasia. Airway obstruction, as result of glossoptosis, was relieved by Douglas procedure of temporary glossopexy.

ventilatory support (McEvitt, 1968). Feedings can be administered to these patients by a variety of methods, including the use of small plastic feeding tubes, cleft palate feeders, the McGovern nipple technique, or gastrostomy. With gastrostomy, performed under local anesthesia, the most dependable method of feeding is provided and additional narrowing of the airway is avoided.

Macroglossia. A relative macroglossia may be present in micrognathia. True macroglossia results from neoplasms involving the tongue or from excessive muscular hypertrophy and hyperplasia. The most frequent tumors are plexiform neurofibroma and lymphangioma (Ayres et al., 1952; Koop and Moschakis, 1961). These lesions may require excisional therapy and can be differentiated by biopsy of the tongue.

Oropharyngeal Tumors. A large polypoid dermoid or teratoma (epignathus) or a congenital epulis may arise from the mandible or maxilla and may be associated with respiratory obstruction (Chamberlain, 1967). Teratomatous lesions also can involve the palate or pharyngeal wall (Boeckman, 1968). Extensive lymphangiomas can infiltrate both the larynx and pharynx and can require immediate treatment (Fig. 5-4). The thyroid gland arises from the foramen cecum at the base of the tongue, and this may be the site of an aberrant thyroid or thyroglossal duct cyst. Since this tissue may represent all the thyroid gland present in the infant, whenever feasible, a preoperative radioactive scan is advised. Cystic duplications also can occur in the tongue (Lister and Zachary, 1968). Simple marsupialization by surgical unroofing may provide immediate relief of cystic lesions. Solid masses must be excised.

LARYNGEAL LESIONS

Laryngeal obstruction can result from congenital atresia, subglottic stenosis, webs, laryngomalacia, bi-lateral vocal cord paralysis, laryngoceles, hemangiomas, or lymphangiomas (Ferguson, 1967). Papillomatosis, a common condition in older children, rarely appears before a child is one year of age. Laryngoscopy is usually required for differentiation of these lesions. In some cases, such as atresia or web, survival can be assured only by immediate tracheostomy. Bilateral paralysis of the vocal cords usually accompanies central nervous system damage and may subsequently improve as the central lesion responds. Unilateral paralysis occurs most frequently on the left and suggests cervical trauma or compression of the nerve within the thorax, where it loops around the ductus arteriosus. A laryngeal web may be alleviated immediately by puncture with a bronchoscope or endotracheal tube, but thicker webs may require direct incision and subsequent dilatation for complete correction. Hemangiomas are the most common tumors involving the larynx and have been treated in the past by irradiation. Recent results suggest that steroid therapy may prove helpful

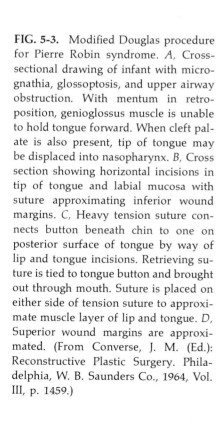

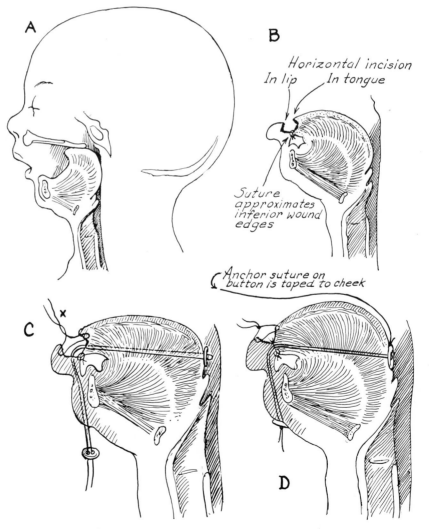

FIG. 5-3. Modified Douglas procedure for Pierre Robin syndrome. *A,* Cross-sectional drawing of infant with micrognathia, glossoptosis, and upper airway obstruction. With mentum in retroposition, genioglossus muscle is unable to hold tongue forward. When cleft palate is also present, tip of tongue may be displaced into nasopharynx. *B,* Cross section showing horizontal incisions in tip of tongue and labial mucosa with suture approximating inferior wound margins. *C,* Heavy tension suture connects button beneath chin to one on posterior surface of tongue by way of lip and tongue incisions. Retrieving suture is tied to tongue button and brought out through mouth. Suture is placed on either side of tension suture to approximate muscle layer of lip and tongue. *D,* Superior wound margins are approximated. (From Converse, J. M. (Ed.): Reconstructive Plastic Surgery. Philadelphia, W. B. Saunders Co., 1964, Vol. III, p. 1459.)

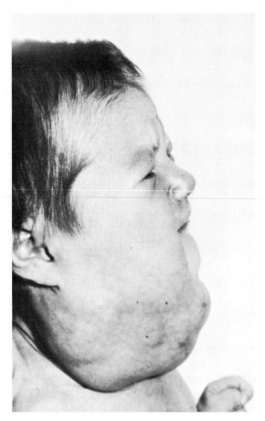

FIG. 5-4. Cystic hygroma in newborn infant. Huge, beard-like lymphangioma infiltrated larynx and pharynx, tongue, parotid gland, and muscles and soft tissues of face and neck. Staged resection with temporary tracheostomy and gastrostomy eventually restored normal breathing and swallowing.

in inducing spontaneous regressions of these lesions (Fost and Esterly, 1968). Lymphangiomatous cysts may cause laryngeal obstruction and have been successfully managed with cryosurgery. Congenital subglottic stenosis may respond to dilatation.

Laryngomalacia is the most common cause of laryngeal obstruction, but rarely produces symptoms at birth. This entity is usually characterized by progressive respiratory distress appearing during the second to third week of life. The aryepiglottic folds are floppy in appearance and respiratory obstruction is alleviated by retraction of the epiglottis and larynx with the laryngoscope. The obstruction occurs on inspiration and the condition is differentiated from a web by the presence of a strong cry. In most instances, the associated stridor resolves spontaneously within six to twelve months through progressive laryngeal growth and development. Laryngoceles are rare at birth, but present signs and symptoms similar to those encountered in older patients.

LESIONS OF THE NECK

A variety of cervical tumors may produce extrinsic compression of the larynx and trachea or may directly infiltrate these structures. Goiter, teratoma, and cystic hygroma are the most common of these growths.

Goiter. Congenital goiter may be diagnosed by a PBI, and usually occurs in infants whose mothers have taken iodides or antithyroid preparations during pregnancy. The condition responds to thyroid administration within a few days, but emergency excision of the isthmus of the gland occasionally may be necessary when respiratory obstruction is marked (Packard et al., 1960). The isolated midline ectopic thyroid is a rare condition and requires careful identification, since excision usually results in total extirpation of functioning glandular tissue with the inevitable development of myxedema (Parodi-Hueck and Koop, 1968). This lesion can be identified preoperatively by a radioactive iodine scan.

Tumors. *Teratoma* of the neck is rare and often arises in association with the thyroid gland. The presence of calcium in the lesion aids identification. Immediate excision is advised and usually produces complete alleviation of symptoms as well as long-term cure (Hajdu et al., 1966; Hurlbut et al., 1967).

Of all congenital tumors of the neck, *cystic hygroma* is the most striking (see Fig. 5-4). The lesion represents a congenital malformation of the lymphatic system, and it is noted at birth in 50 to 65 per cent of cases. The lymphatic vessels develop from endothelial buds derived from the lining of the jugular sacs. The vessels, which penetrate the surrounding tissue and radiate outward over the body, have some secretory action. Some of the lymphatics may fail to establish communication with the venous system, and this failure can result in sequestration of the lymphatic tissue, which gives rise to the cystic malformation characterized by cystic hygroma. Grossly, these lesions consist of multilocular cysts that contain serous fluid. Although they are usually located in the neck, they may occur in the thorax, axilla, groin, or abdomen. Cystic hygromas may appear quite different clinically from cavernous lymphangiomas, but there is little other basis for differentiation (Bill and Sumner, 1965). Malignant degeneration has not been reported. Most patients are seen because of the presence of a mass in the neck, and usually the history is that of a tumor, which developed after birth and has been growing persistently, sometimes with rapid enlargement after infection of the upper respiratory tract. Characteristically the mass is soft, fluctuant, and nontender and can be transilluminated. The tumor is rarely painful and usually does not produce functional disturbances. However, lesions located in the tongue and foremouth or in the mediastinum may result in difficulty in swallowing or in respiratory distress caused by tracheal compression.

Nonoperative forms of treatment directed at these lesions have included aspiration, injection of sclerosing solutions, an irradiation. Aspiration may be employed as an emergency measure in cases of severe respiratory embarrassment, but it is not definitive therapy and may result in infection. The presence of septa between loculated areas of the lymphangiomatous mass prevents dispersion of sclerosing agents. These agents are used infrequently, because the marked inflammatory reaction that they cause may result in significant scar tissue. Cystic hygromas are relatively radioresistant; irradiation or radium implantation is used mainly for recurrence or when radical operation is not feasible. Radiation to the neck should be studiously avoided because of the increased incidence of postirradiation carcinoma of the thyroid.

Surgical procedures offer the most reliable mode of management; the results have been excellent and the complications few (Galofre, 1962). The tumor should be removed as completely as possible without sacrificing functional result or cosmesis. Recurrence does not always follow incomplete removal. In general, the surgical wound should be drained, since there is a tendency for lymph to reaccumulate in the subcutaneous tissues from the remaining open lymphatic radicals. Concomitant thoracotomy may be required for excision of mediastinal extensions of the tumor, and if there has been evidence of prolonged tracheal compression, a tracheostomy may be indicated. After sur-

gical excision, less than 20 per cent of patients require additional therapy. Nearly all recurrences take place in the first year after surgical treatment.

Intrathoracic Causes of Respiratory Distress

Respiratory distress of intrathoracic etiology may result from aspiration of secretions (e.g., tracheoesophageal fistula), intrinsic and extrinsic obstruction of the tracheobronchial tree, and intrapleural space-occupying lesions which compress pulmonary tissue.

TRACHEOESOPHAGEAL FISTULA

Newborn respiratory distress resulting from a communication between the trachea and esophagus is a common indication for emergency surgery. The respiratory difficulty is associated with an unusually large amount of oral secretions, which require repeated aspiration. Often the problem is first called to a physician's attention by a nurse in the newborn nursery who notices that the baby is constantly bubbling from the secretions.

The most common anatomic arrangement (about 85 per cent of all cases) is a blind proximal esophageal pouch (esophageal atresia), with the distal esophagus arising from the tracheal bifurcation (fistula) (Fig. 5-5). The pathologic physiology of this abnormality consists of (1) obstruction of the esophagus and overflow of oral secretions into the trachea, and (2) reflux of gastric juice up the distal esophageal segment into the pulmonary parenchyma. Both processes result in aspiration

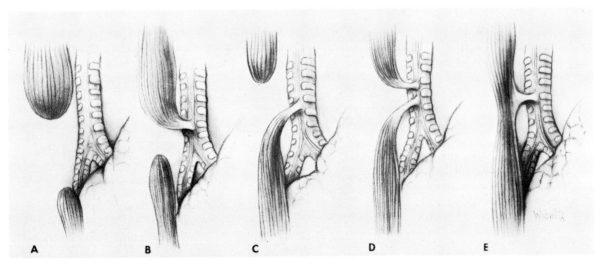

FIG. 5-5. Five major varieties of esophageal atresia and tracheoesophageal fistula. *A,* Esophageal atresia without associated fistula. *B,* Esophageal atresia with tracheoesophageal fistula between proximal segment of esophagus and trachea. *C,* Esophageal atresia with tracheoesophageal fistula between distal esophagus and trachea. *D,* Esophageal atresia with fistula between both proximal and distal ends of esophagus and trachea. *E,* Tracheoesophageal fistula without esophageal atresia (H-type fistula). (From Schwartz, S. I.: Principles of Surgery. New York, McGraw-Hill, 1969.)

4

pneumonitis, but by far the most significant is the reflux of gastric juice. Actually the secretions of the mouth and pharynx of a newborn infant are relatively free of bacteria and, therefore, do not constitute a significant insult to the lungs. Gastric juice, on the other hand, is a powerfully activated solution of enzymes and rapidly digests the pulmonary parenchyma, causing a necrotizing, destructive pneumonia which is rapidly followed by secondary bacterial invasion and lethal sepsis.

The most common cause of death in infants with tracheoesophageal fistula is not pneumonia and secondary septicemia, as might be expected from the foregoing comments, but rather lethal complications from associated congenital anomalies. Serious associated congenital anomalies are found much more commonly in the premature infant with tracheoesophageal fistula. The most significant anomalies are cardiovascular, of which patent ductus arteriosus, ventricular septal defect, and atrial septal defect are the most common (Mehrizi et al., 1966). Many of these infants are already in trouble with congestive failure; the secondary insult of aspiration pneumonia is enough to tip the scales. The most common associated gastrointestinal anomalies are imperforate anus and duodenal atresia. These can be handled very successfully in the newborn, but their diagnosis often is not suspected. One of the indications for a staged operative repair of the tracheoesophageal fistula is the presence of multiple congenital anomalies.

Even when there are no other lethal anomalies, infants with tracheoesophageal fistulas can die of overwhelming pulmonary sepsis unless the abnormality is corrected. Since pulmonary contamination is obviously related to the period of exposure to aspiration, the earlier the condition is diagnosed and surgically corrected the better the survival and overall salvage rate.

Diagnosis. The diagnosis of tracheoesophageal fistula is easily made once it is suspected. As noted above, the diagnosis should be considered in any newborn with respiratory distress combined with hypersecretion, and confirmed by unsuccessful attempts to pass a small rubber catheter into the stomach, and by percussion over the stomach area that reveals hyperresonance caused by air in the gastrointestinal tract. These findings also indicate that the anatomic type is a blind proximal pouch with the distal esophagus coming off the trachea. In the 5 to 10 per cent of infants with other types of tracheoesophageal communication, there may be no air in the gastrointestinal tract because the distal esophagus is not in communication with the bronchial tree. These more complicated anatomic arrangements require different management and will be discussed separately.

X-ray examination of the chest is the next step. A small amount of contrast medium, preferably water-soluble, will fill the blind proximal pouch, and the presence of air in the stomach and upper gastrointestinal tract will confirm the presence of the communication at the distal esophagus. The x-ray study constitutes an important part of the child's hospital record and confirms the nature of the tracheoesophageal fistula. Of more significance is the roentgenographic evaluation of the pulmonary parenchyma, since the extent of pneumonitis and the degree of aspiration in the tiny infant are difficult to evaluate by auscultation alone.

Treatment. The first step in the management of the infant with a tracheoesophageal fistula is prevention of further aspiration of gastric contents. Total correction of the intrathoracic anomaly is not an emergency procedure, but a gastrostomy is imperative and should be performed immediately after the child reaches an appropriate medical center. This is the only dependable way of draining gastric contents and preventing further reflux and aspiration into the tracheobronchial tree.

The gastrostomy is carried out at any hour and is usually performed under local anesthesia. A Stamm gastrostomy is satisfactory. We prefer two chromic catgut purse-string sutures on the stomach and four nonabsorbable anchoring sutures from stomach to abdominal wall. The gastrostomy tube is connected directly to straight drainage. The infant is kept in a semi-upright position with about 45-degree elevation of his head to decrease potential reflux from the stomach.

Once the gastrostomy tube is in place, the patients can be grouped into two specific treatment categories. If the baby is a full-term, vigorous infant with minimal pulmonary contamination, a primary repair of the tracheoesophageal fistula is performed as a scheduled elective procedure. The other group consists of premature infants, all infants with significant pulmonary sepsis, and all infants with significant associated congenital anomalies, especially those with congestive heart failure as a result of cardiovascular anomalies. This higher risk group is treated by a staged repair.

In the combined institutional study of tracheoesophageal fistula reported by Holder et al. (1964), the number of premature infants saved by immediate emergency repair of tracheoesophageal fistula was discouragingly low. From this study came a recommendation that premature infants be seriously considered for staged repair, that is, gastrostomy and division of the fistula as one procedure and re-operation for anastomosis of the esophagus as a second.

A premature infant does not fight infections well because his own reticuloendothelial system and other immune mechanisms are not yet fully mature. Any pulmonary contamination that is present constitutes a much greater threat than in the mature newborn, and the superimposed trauma of an operative procedure and anesthesia may be more than his defenses can tolerate. In addition, the miniature structures of a full-term newborn seem relatively large by comparison with the tiny esophageal segments in a 1200- to 2000-Gm. premature infant. The technical aspects of such a miniature anastomosis are fraught with difficulty, one of the most significant complications being an anastomotic leak with secondary mediastinal or pleural infection.

The tracheoesophageal communication must be divided as soon as possible, because the threat of reflux from the stomach remains. We have preferred to approach such premature infants with an extrapleural division of the fistula and then return, transpleurally, for a primary anastomosis of the esophageal segments when the child reaches 3500 to 4000 Gm. Another temporizing approach in desperately ill babies is to transect the stomach, thus preventing reflux but avoiding a thoracotomy (Randolph, 1968).

A full-term infant with significant pulmonary sepsis is best treated with a gastrostomy as an emergency procedure and aggressive specific therapy for his pulmonary infection. This involves careful bacteriologic studies of the tracheal aspirate and the institution of appropriate antibacterial therapy. As soon as there is evidence of clearing of the pulmonary infection, usually by four to seven days, the full-term infant can be taken to the operating room and will tolerate general anesthesia and a thoracic procedure for repair of his fistula. Generally, these babies also have been operated on through an extrapleural approach, with division of the fistula and a primary anastomosis performed at the same time. In the full-term infant, the immune mechanisms are much more nearly mature, and with the assistance of specific antibiotics, satisfactory healing is to be expected.

In infants with tracheoesophageal fistula associated with significant cardiovascular anomalies, a delay is indicated for specific therapy of congestive failure. This can be brought under control within four to seven days if at all. Thereafter the child is handled in the same way as any other full-term or premature infant, with either a primary repair or a staged repair of the tracheoesophageal fistula. Certainly no infant in congestive failure with superimposed pneumonitis can be expected to tolerate general anesthesia and a thoracic procedure.

Operative Technique. There is a difference of opinion regarding indications for an extrapleural approach versus a transpleural approach to the tracheoesophageal fistula. Advocates of the extrapleural approach emphasize the advantage of localization of infected material if an anastomotic leak should occur. A local-

ized purulent process is a much less severe systemic insult, especially to a premature infant. Advocates of the transpleural approach feel that it is faster and gives somewhat better exposure. We prefer to try the extrapleural approach in all infants, but especially in the premature infant who is undergoing the staged repair of tracheoesophageal fistula. We use a transpleural approach for the secondary operative procedure in such cases.

An adequate endotracheal airway is established for general anesthesia, and an intravenous catheter is inserted for fluid and blood administration and for the monitoring of central venous pressure. We have found the external jugular vein to be most satisfactory for full-term infants and the internal jugular vein for the premature infant (Talbert and Haller, 1966) (Fig. 5-6*A*).

The anomaly is approached through a posterior lateral incision, which enters the extrapleural plane through the bed of the unresected fourth rib (Fig. 5-6*B*). With gentle blunt and sponge dissection, the pleura is separated from the endothoracic fascia until the apex of the chest is well visualized (Fig. 5-6*C*). The azygos vein is doubly ligated and divided, and the relationships of the two esophageal segments to the trachea are carefully visualized. The usual anatomic relationships seen at operation are shown in Figure 5-7, the prototype of tracheoesophageal fistulas. A braided silk is then passed around the distal esophageal segment near the fistula, and with this for traction, this segment is sharply mobilized as far as its junction with the membranous portion of the trachea. The fistula is then divided flush with the membranous posterior wall of the trachea, and the tracheal opening is closed with interrupted sutures of fine silk. It is important to emphasize that the fistula is *divided,* not ligated. A simple ligature usually cuts through and results in recurrence of the fistula.

At this point the operator must decide whether a primary anastomosis is a reasonable next step. In most cases, as already stated, it is better to carry out a primary anastomosis at the first operative procedure. Accordingly, the blind proximal pouch lying behind the apical pleura is identified and a mattress suture of silk placed in its tip for traction. The pouch is mobilized by sharp dissection until it can be pulled into apposition with the distal esophageal segment. In most cases these two ends can be brought together with moderate traction, but in some cases they are brought together only with great difficulty. An anastomosis may be carried out even if mobilization of the distal esophagus must be carried halfway down the posterior mediastinum.

Many types of anastomoses have been described. Basic surgical principles of minimal traction on the anastomosis, avoidance of trauma to tissues, and use

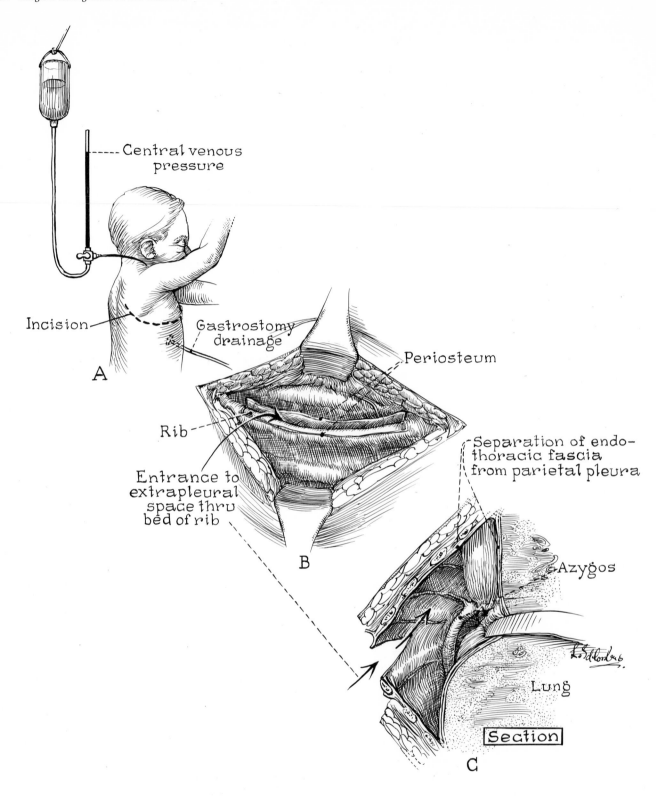

FIG. 5-6. Repair of tracheoesophageal fistula. *A,* Insertion of central venous monitoring catheter. Stamm gastrostomy may be performed under local anesthesia prior to chest procedure or may be added as last step in complete repair of this anomaly. *B,* With child positioned for right lateral thoracotomy, extrapleural dissection is begun in bed of 4th rib *C,* Parietal pleura is bluntly dissected from endothoracic fascia and azygos vein is divided. (From Haller, J. A., Jr., and White, J. J.: *In* Operative Surgery: Principles and Techniques. Edited by Paul F. Nora.)

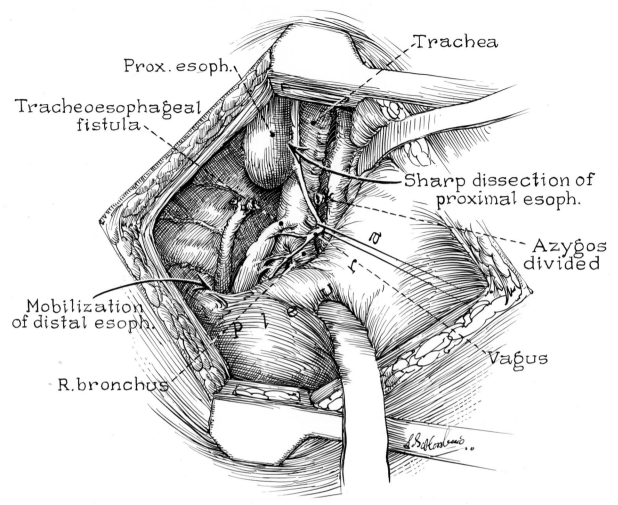

FIG. 5-7. Vagus nerve is carefully mobilized to expose both proximal pouch and fistula. (From Haller, J. A., Jr., and White, J. J.: *In* Operative Surgery: Principles and Techniques. Edited by Paul F. Nora.)

of delicate suturing techniques are important. We have preferred the Haight type anastomosis (1944), in which the mucosa of the proximal pouch is anastomosed to the full thickness of the distal esophageal segment with interrupted catgut sutures, and a second row of silk sutures is used to approximate the outer wall of the blind proximal pouch to the distal esophageal segment. This results in a telescoping anastomosis (Fig. 5-8). Recent experience with a single-layer anastomosis is quite encouraging, and may prove preferable.

A single catheter is left in the extrapleural pocket and the chest closed in layers. In the transpleural approach two chest catheters are often used, one lying low in the pleural space and the other near the site of the anastomosis. These catheters are connected to gentle underwater suction, and the child is returned to an intensive care unit, in an Isolette, with his head elevated 45 degrees and his gastrostomy tube open to drainage (Fig. 5-8G).

In a premature infant and in infants with associated anomalies in whom simple division of the fistula is to be carried out, no attempt is made to approximate the two segments of the esophagus as this will usually result in increased scarring and make the secondary anastomotic procedure more difficult. We have preferred to use a transpleural approach for the second operation in such staged procedures.

In premature infants and full-term infants with extensive sepsis, we have found the use of a pharyngostomy tube quite helpful in the control of secretions from the blind proximal pouch during the staged operative repair of tracheoesophageal fistula (Talbert and Haller, 1965). A rubber or plastic catheter is inserted through the lateral pharyngeal wall and positioned as a sump drain in the blind pouch (Fig. 5-9). This catheter can be changed by the nursing staff and can be used in lieu of repeated nasopharyngeal suction, since nasopharyngeal tubes can be traumatic to the nares,

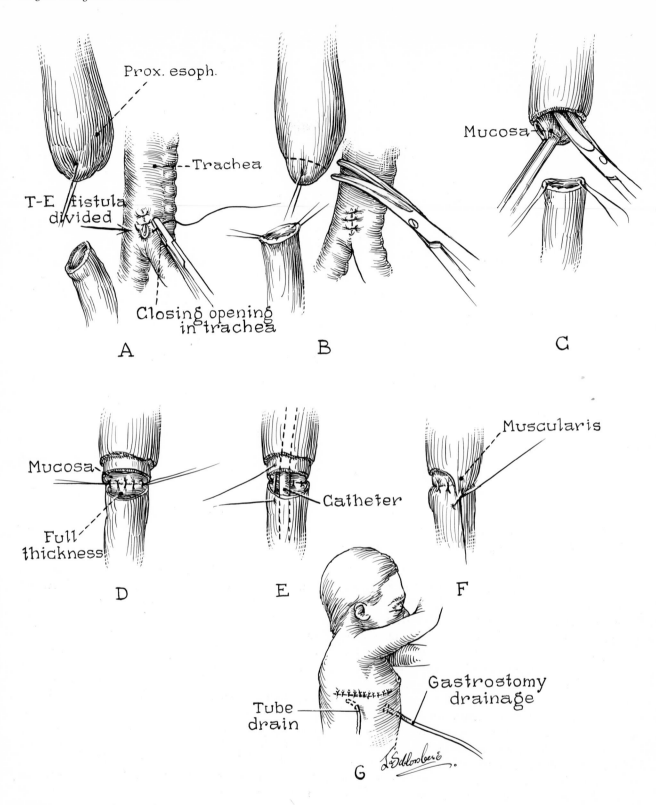

FIG. 5-8. *A,* Division of fistula and closure of tracheal opening with fine sutures. *B, C, D,* and *F,* Haight anastomosis, which consists of two layers, proximal mucosa to distal full thickness, followed by proximal muscularis to distal muscularis. *E,* Rubber catheter passed into pouch helps in its initial identification and may be helpful in separating anterior and posterior walls of esophagus during anastomosis. *G,* Chest catheter is left in extrapleural space through separate intercostal stab wound. (From Haller, J. A., Jr., and White, J. J.: *In* Operative Surgery: Principles and Techniques. Edited by Paul F. Nora.)

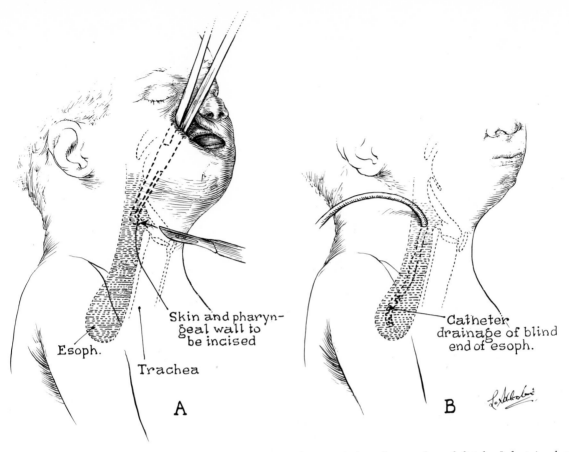

Fig. 5-9. Temporary tube pharyngostomy for staged repair of congenital tracheoesophageal fistula. Infant is placed in supine position; neck is extended and head turned to left. Right neck is prepped and small right-angle clamp is introduced through mouth until tip can be palpated externally through anterolateral pharyngeal wall at level of hyoid bone, *A.* Short transverse skin incision is then made over point and clamp is pushed gently through soft tissues of neck by blunt dissection. No. 14 French urethral catheter with additional side holes is grasped and pulled into pharynx for distance of approximately 3 to 4 cm. Catheter tip is then positioned in proximal esophageal pouch, either under direct vision with laryngoscope or with guidance of finger inserted through mouth, *B.* Catheter is secured externally with umbilical tape tied about infant's neck. Suction is instituted at 60 to 80 mm. Hg, a range that appears to cause minimal discomfort and still provides adequate continuous evacuation of secretions.

Catheter can be readily replaced by attaching new catheter to external end of old one and removing latter under direct vision through mouth. Tip of new catheter, which now lies within oropharynx, can be directed again into proximal esophageal pouch as previously described. After 48 hours, satisfactory tract is established, allowing direct insertion of fresh tube. New tube is easily directed into proximal esophageal pouch either under direct vision or with gloved fingers introduced into mouth. Catheter may be kept in place until after definitive esophageal anastomosis has been completed.

pharynx, and larynx in small babies. We have found this technique especially helpful in the tiny premature infant.

In more complicated cases of tracheoesophageal fistula in which there is no distal esophagus, or practically none, some part of the gastrointestinal tract eventually must be brought upward for replacement. The immediate treatment of such children is to bring out the cervical esophagus as an esophagostomy and to place a semi-permanent gastrostomy tube. In this way the infant can be managed until he is older and some type of bowel interposition procedure can be carried

out. If the decision is made to use a cervical esophagostomy, it is wise to wait until the child is 18 to 24 months of age before bringing a colon segment into the neck, because the substernal thoracic outlet is very tight in small babies.

We have preferred to use the transverse colon as an interposition segment between the stomach and the cervical esophagus (Gross, 1967). Others have used the jejunum or other parts of the colon. Waterston and associates at the Great Ormond Street Hospital in London have advocated use of a colon interposition for a one-stage repair of tracheoesophageal fistula and

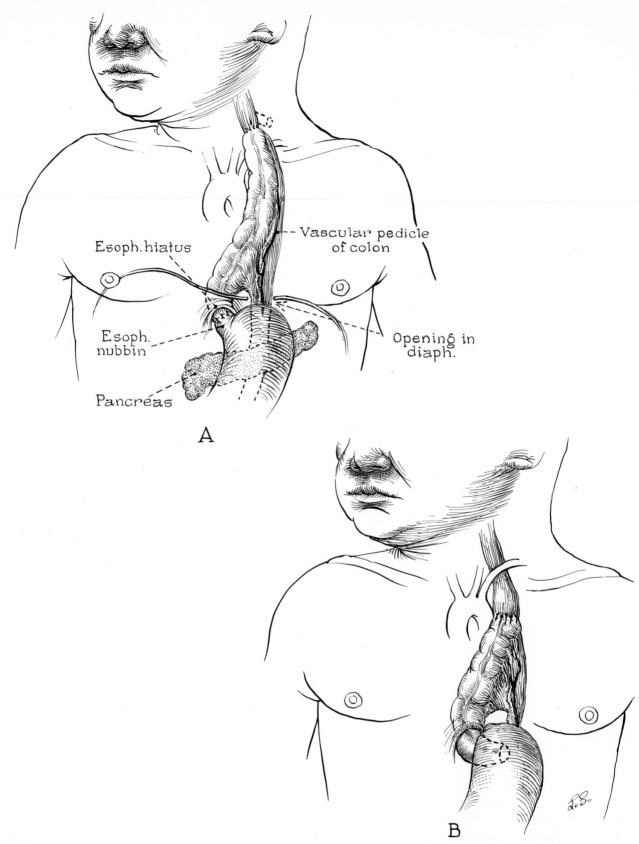

FIG. 5-10. Waterston procedure. *A,* If prior cervical esophagostomy is present, colon segment is pulled through base of neck and anastomosis is made in neck at that level. Distal anastomosis may be made to distal esophageal nubbin. *B,* If proximal pouch is still available through chest, anastomosis is made at level of aortic arch. Distal anastomosis to posterior stomach is shown here.

for esophageal atresia (Waterston, 1962). They prefer to bring the left colon transpleurally through the left hemithorax into the neck for a primary repair (Fig. 5-10). Although their early results with this more aggressive technique are encouraging, it has not been widely applied in this country. Our preliminary experience with the transthoracic colon interposition is generally more satisfactory than our earlier retrosternal pull-through into the neck in small babies.

Postoperative Complications. The two most significant postoperative complications are: (1) acute leakage from the anastomosis, and (2) chronic stricture formation at the anastomosis. Although hazardous at any age and particularly dangerous to a premature infant, leakage from an anastomosis need not be a lethal complication if it is properly managed. The basic principle of this management is immediate and adequate drainage from the site of the leak. In those procedures carried out in the extrapleural plane, a chest catheter in the extrapleural pocket is usually adequate for drainage, and a localized area of purulence is controlled. There is often little evidence of systemic response to this type of local leakage and drainage.

On the other hand, if there is widespread soilage of the pleural space, evidence of septicemia is usually noted as a result of the empyema. Adequate and immediate drainage is the keystone of successful therapy. If feedings have been instituted by mouth, these are immediately stopped and all further feeding is carried out through the gastrostomy with the child in an upright position.

A more serious associated complication is that of recurrence of the tracheoesophageal fistula in addition to leakage of the anastomosis. This may be a difficult diagnosis to make, because it usually occurs within the first ten days following the repair. If the child coughs and sputters after every attempt at oral feeding, this catastrophe should be strongly suspected.

If its presence can be proved, the only curative treatment is re-operation and re-closure of the fistula. In a gravely ill child, and in an area of edema and infection, this is a difficult technical undertaking. Fortunately, most anastomotic leaks are not associated with recurrence of the fistula and usually respond to adequate and immediate external drainage and defunctionalization of the proximal esophagus.

Anastomoses that leak ultimately show some evidence of stricture formation. No attempt at dilatation of an acute stricture should be carried out during the early phases of healing following anastomotic leakage. It is probably wise to wait at least two weeks following the last evidence of anastomotic drainage before proceeding with any attempt at dilatation of a progressive stricture at that site.

Mild-to-moderate stenosis at the site of anastomosis is a frequent minor complication of repair of esophageal atresia. Unlike esophageal strictures associated with caustic burns, in which there is dense scar tissue over a relatively long segment of esophagus, anastomotic strictures usually can be dilated easily and successfully. In some medical centers, esophageal anastomoses are routinely dilated on the seventh to tenth day. We have recommended dilatation only in patients who develop symptoms of dysphagia and whose postoperative x-ray studies show a significant stricture. Mild-to-moderate strictures are successfully dilated with a soft filiform bougie under direct vision or with retrograde dilatation with Tucker bougies through the gastrostomy. If the baby is being observed carefully in his postoperative period, a severe stricture should not be allowed to develop.

Prognosis. The late follow-up on patients surviving operative procedures for tracheoesophageal fistula indicate an excellent prognosis. Mild-to-moderate strictures usually respond to one or two dilatations and do not require prolonged chronic dilatation. Most of these children have normal growth and development and have no further difficulty with swallowing.

It is of considerable interest, however, that perhaps one in ten children with successful repair of tracheoesophageal fistula will have some type of dysphagia for many years. Barium swallow studies on these children usually reveal no stricture at the site of anastomosis, or a very slight stenosis. These dysphagia problems are usually diagnosed as functional, but careful recent cinefluoroscopic studies of children with dysphagia following esophageal repair suggest that this group may have significant neuromuscular abnormalities in the distal esophageal segment (Kirkpatrick et al., 1961; Lind, 1965; Sieber, 1964; Haller et al., 1966). Fortunately, this type of dysphagia, unassociated with an anastomotic stricture, does not usually produce a problem in nutrition. Most of the patients have normal growth and development. The dysphagia, however, can be a chronic problem, and unless its cause is understood, it may be a headache to both parents and family physician.

ESOPHAGEAL ATRESIA

Isolated esophageal atresia occurs more rarely than in combination with tracheoesophageal fistula. Respiratory distress and excessive oral secretions closely mimic a tracheoesophageal fistula, but the more serious aspects of reflux and aspiration of gastric juice are not present.

The blind cervical esophageal pouch is similar to that associated with tracheoesophageal fistula, and the distal esophageal segment may vary widely in length. Usually the distal esophageal segment is quite short, but often an esophagogastric junction is present.

Emergency treatment consists of a Stamm feeding gastrostomy and either a nasopharyngeal tube or a lateral pharyngostomy tube for suction on the blind pouch. Standard definitive treatment is to construct a cervical esophagostomy and, in later childhood, to bring an interposition colonic segment into the neck to reconstitute oral feedings. Recent experience with immediate left colon interposition through the left chest (Waterston, 1962) (see Fig. 5-10), which is discussed under tracheoesophageal fistula, gives promise of early total correction of esophageal atresia. Further experience is needed to determine its exact place and indication in the management of isolated esophageal atresia.

TRACHEOBRONCHIAL OBSTRUCTION

Tracheobronchial obstruction presents in the newborn as stertorous or crowing respirations and with varying degrees of chest retraction on inspiration due to partial obstruction of the airway. Characteristically, infants assume certain positions in which the partial obstruction is less severe and breathing is facilitated. The congenital lesions responsible for tracheobronchial obstruction may be intrinsic to the larynx and trachea, or may result from external compression of these structures.

Tracheomalacia. *Intrinsic obstruction* of the tracheobronchial tree is usually referred to as laryngomalacia and tracheomalacia, depending on the level of the major obstruction. These terms apply loosely to poorly understood abnormalities in the cartilaginous support of the larynx and trachea, respectively. These conditions result in an unstable airway, which tends to collapse on inspiration and cause partial obstruction. Flexion of the head seems to aggravate this difficulty, whereas stridor is decreased and patency of the airway is improved if the head is extended and the mandible lifted upward and forward.

Rarely is any surgical treatment necessary for laryngomalacia, since positioning of the head is usually satisfactory. With further growth and development, the condition rectifies itself. Tracheomalacia may be more troublesome, and occasionally it is necessary to perform a tracheostomy to establish and maintain a tracheal airway. The Silastic tracheostomy tubes have been particularly useful in this condition, since their soft, nonirritating material decreases injury to the delicate trachea and allows for safe mobility of the unsupported infant's head and neck. Both tracheomalacia and laryngomalacia improve with further growth and development of the infant, and thus treatment consists

usually of temporizing until adequate stability of these structures has occurred.

Vascular Rings. The most common cause of external compression of the tracheobronchial tree, resulting in inspiratory obstruction of the newborn, is a vascular ring. A vascular ring results from abnormal fetal development in which the complete branchial arches, encircling the trachea and esophagus, do not become incorporated into the normal branches of the aortic arch. They may persist as a complete vascular ring. These rings take a variety of forms, depending on the exact nature of the developmental defect. They all have the same feature in common: encirclement and compression of the trachea and esophagus by a vascular corset.

The characteristic feature of vascular ring compression of the tracheobronchial tree is inspiratory stridor and retraction, which is also partially relieved in certain positions, particularly by hyperextension of the head. Often these infants are misdiagnosed as having recurrent bronchiolitis or aspiration pneumonia, which is secondary to their partial esophageal obstruction and difficulty in swallowing.

Most significant vascular rings are complete, that is, they completely encircle the trachea and esophagus. These include the very common double aortic arch and the right aortic arch with persistent ligamentum or ductus arteriosus.

Once suspected, the diagnosis is easily confirmed by a thin barium swallow study, which reveals the striking indentation of the posterior wall of the esophagus. The exact nature of the anomaly may be verified by angiocardiography, but if the baby is in severe distress, this technique may be omitted because the operative approach is the same for all the vascular rings with esophageal obstruction.

If the baby's condition will permit, any associated pneumonia should be allowed to subside before a thoracotomy is undertaken. Endoscopy is not necessary and may be hazardous because the already compromised airway may become completely obstructed owing to mucosal edema following instrumentation. If endoscopy is carried out to exclude other abnormalities, it should be done in the operating room with full preparations to go ahead with a definitive thoracotomy if there is significant increase in respiratory difficulty on removal of the bronchoscope.

The preferred operative approach is a left lateral thoracotomy through the third or fourth interspace. If the anomaly has not been specifically defined by angiocardiography, the most important initial operative step is to identify all of the branches of the aortic arch. When the anatomic defect is clearly defined, division of the appropriate part of the vascular ring is the final step. Compression of the tracheobronchial tree will not be relieved by simple division of the vascular component of the ring. It is imperative that all associated adventitial and pericardial extensions be sharply divided and the vascular arch widely mobilized from the esophagus and trachea. Otherwise, residual and often troublesome symptoms persist.

Two partial variants of complete vascular ring exist. One consists of compression of the trachea alone without esophageal obstruction. This is a rare lesion described initially by Gross (1955) and more recently discussed in detail by Fearon (1963). Anterior compression of the trachea is nearly always due to anomalous origin of an aberrant innominate artery, which arises from the aortic arch to the left of the trachea and then swings back across in front of the trachea to assume its normal exit from the chest. This anomalous course results in anterior compression of the trachea and tracheal obstruction.

It may be recognized on the lateral film of the chest, which shows the compression of the tracheal air column. It can be verified by either angiocardiography or a cinetracheogram. If the symptoms of tracheal obstruction are severe, operative correction is indicated. A median sternotomy approach is preferred. The thymus is totally excised. The innominate artery is then easily visualized and can be widely mobilized from the underlying trachea. Care must be taken to leave adventitial tissue on the innominate artery, so that it may be used to suture this vessel to the sternum. Definitive treatment consists of two to three tacking sutures to the adventitia of the innominate artery, through the sternum, to pull it anteriorly and lift it off the trachea.

A final group consists of the rare compression of the posterior part of the esophagus, almost always by an aberrant, retro-esophageal right subclavian artery. Persistent dysphagia may result in recurrent aspiration pneumonia. Division of this anomalous vessel relieves the obstruction.

Mediastinal Masses. Newborn tracheobronchial obstruction may result from nonvascular mediastinal masses. Mediastinal masses in children represent a wide variety of conditions and diseases, but they usually are asymptomatic in the newborn. Posterior mediastinal masses are predominantly neurogenic in origin and rarely cause respiratory symptoms. Masses responsible for tracheobronchial obstruction occur either in the middle or anterior mediastinum. Few, if any, respiratory symptoms are related to enlargement of the thymus in spite of older references defining compression of the tracheobronchial tree. A short course of steroids may cause rapid involution of a thymic mass and help in the differential diagnosis of an anterior tumor mass.

By far, the most common cause of extrinsic compression of the tracheobronchial tree by a nonvascular lesion is a bronchial or duplication cyst. This lesion represents a partial duplication of a portion of the tracheobronchial tree which, because of its adjacent location, causes compression and obstruction to the airway.

The diagnosis should be considered in any newborn infant with inspiratory stridor in whom tracheobronchial distortion is noted on x-ray examination. Once the more common vascular ring has been excluded by barium swallow and/or angiocardiography, a cinetracheo-bronchogram may be helpful in defining the external compression.

These are treacherous lesions to diagnose by bronchoscopy, since the severely compromised airway may become completely obstructed from edema secondary to endoscopy. For this reason, if the baby is to undergo bronchoscopy, this procedure should be carried out in the operating room, where full preparation has been made for a definitive thoracotomy. If, following bronchoscopy, significant obstruction results, the bronchoscope or an endotracheal tube may be reinserted and the thoracic procedure completed.

Since bronchial cysts usually lie in the middle mediastinum, they are more easily approached through a lateral thoracotomy than through a median sternotomy. Specific therapy consists of thoracotomy and excision of the cyst.

INTRAPLEURAL TENSION PROBLEMS

Newborn infants are particularly susceptible to alterations in intrapleural pressure. In an adult, any localized increase in intrathoracic pressure is buffered by a relatively stable mediastinum. In a neonate, however, the mediastinum is more mobile and may be readily displaced by an expanding intrapleural lesion. It is imperative, therefore, that any intrapleural tension problem in these babies be promptly diagnosed and treated, because of the potential for bilateral compression of the lungs and impairment of venous return to the heart. A delay of only a few minutes may prove fatal!

Extrapulmonary Space-Occupying Lesions

Tension Pneumothorax. Air entrapment, either within or outside the lung, is the most frequent source of intrapleural tension problems in the newborn infant. Air leakage into the pleural cavity of mediastinum usually results from overdistention and rupture of the baby's fragile alveoli. Overzealous resuscitation of the apneic or hypoxic newborn infant by mechanical insufflation is a common cause (Srouji, 1967). As emphasized by Chernick and Avery, however, spontaneous alveolar rupture also may occur as a result of the unique mechanical stresses exerted by the baby during his first few efforts to breathe. Alveolar expansion in the newborn infant normally requires development of a transient pressure differential between the lung and intrapleural space approximating 40 to 80 cm. water (occasionally obtaining levels of 100 cm.). As the lung inflates and fills the pleural cavity, the natural mechanical advantage of the muscles of inspiration is proportionately decreased. In all infants, this process occurs somewhat unevenly and is impeded by the viscosity of fluid within the airway, the forces of surface tension, and the elasticity of the lung parenchyma. Aspiration of meconium, blood, or mucus during birth exaggerates these natural factors and may result in partial obstruction and incomplete aeration. In such circumstances, the forces of expansion are concentrated within the fragile alveoli of the aerated lung, and if unrelieved, spontaneous rupture may ensue. Air can then leak directly into the pleural cavity, or by dissecting along the perivascular sheath into the mediastinum, it may secondarily rupture into the pleural space. The frequency of this occurrence is attested by a high incidence of minor degrees of mediastinal emphysema and/or intrapleural air in newborn infants.

Later in the neonatal period, pneumothorax may develop as a sequel to hyaline membrane disease, mechanical ventilation, or rupture of a staphylococcal pneumatocele. A pneumothorax should be suspected in any baby with previous evidence of mild-to-moderate respiratory distress who suddenly exhibits gasping respirations and deep cyanosis.

An immediate roentgenogram of the chest is the key to diagnosis and treatment of any infant with evidence of cyanosis or respiratory distress. For minor degrees of pneumothorax and pneumomediastinum, the baby may just be kept under cautious observation if his clinical condition otherwise remains stable. Intrapleural and mediastinal air is rapidly absorbed in these babies, particularly if they breathe increased oxygen concentrations. In cases of underlying pulmonary disease from pneumonia or respiratory distress syndrome, however, the additional insult imposed by even minor degrees of pneumothorax may prove intolerable and may require prompt relief.

Tension pneumothorax is the ultimate outcome of any persistent intrapleural air leak. As air accumulates and pressure increases within the affected pleural cavity, the adjacent lung tissue is compressed, the mediastinum is displaced, and aeration of the contralateral lung is impeded. The diagnosis is suggested by hyperresonance and loss of breath sounds over the air-filled pleural cavity and shifting of cardiac dullness toward the opposite side. On roentgenogram the intrathoracic volume is seen to be increased, the intercostal spaces widened, the hemidiaphragm depressed, and the peripheral lung markings symmetrically absent on the affected side (Fig. 5-11).

Immediate needle aspiration may prove lifesaving in the desperately ill baby. For maximum safety in seriously ill patients or in instances of persistent air leak, a thoracostomy tube should be inserted as depicted in Figure 5-12 and attached to underwater seal suction (Krueger et al., 1968). Lung re-expansion is usually prompt, and if the tube has been properly positioned, the air leak seals within a few days. Any sudden deterioration in the patient's condition may signal recurrence of the pneumothorax or development of a similar process within the contralateral pleural cavity. This latter possibility always must be recognized as a potential complication of treatment. Pneumomediastinum rarely requires operative management, but needle aspiration or decompression through a suprasternal collar incision in the neck may be necessary in severe cases.

Pleural Effusions and Chylothorax. The series of physiologic disturbances that characterizes a tension pneumothorax in the newborn infant may also result occasionally from pleural effusions of chyle, blood, or pus. The exact type of effusion is readily determined by needle thoracentesis.

Intrapleural bleeding develops immediately following delivery as a result of birth trauma. Empyema appears later, most frequently as a complication of pneumonia. The young infant is particularly susceptible to the ravages of staphylococcal pneumonia, a condition that produces a characteristic radiographic picture of multiple cyst-like, emphysematous blebs interspersed throughout an area of pulmonary infiltrate. These blebs develop as a result of interstitial trapping of air within the pulmonary parenchyma, and progressive expansion of individual lesions can lead to formation of giant pneumatoceles. Any large pneumatocele poses a potential threat of rupture into the pleural cavity and development of a tension pyopneumothorax. Antibiotic therapy usually results in complete resolution of staphylococcal pneumonia, despite the forbidding radiographic appearance. Thoracotomy is rarely required for closure of persistent air leaks or for removal of a constricting fibrothorax.

Pleural effusions in newborn infants most frequently represent chylothorax resulting from birth trauma or congenital malformation of the mediastinal or pulmonary lymphatics (Yancy and Spock, 1967). The diagnosis is suggested by respiratory distress in association with dullness to percussion and diminished breath

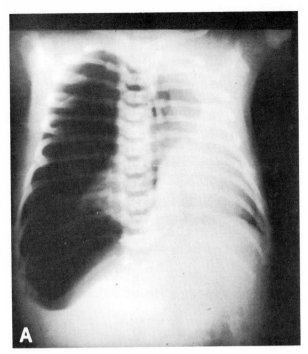 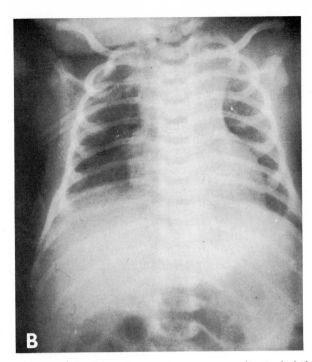

FIG. 5-11. Tension pneumothorax of newborn infant, *A*, relieved by tube drainage, *B*. Note extreme mediastinal shift, *A*, which may result from increased intrapleural pressure at this age. (From Ballinger, W. F. (Ed.): Management of Trauma. Philadelphia, W. B. Saunders Co., 1968.)

sounds over the affected hemithorax. Progression of the process eventually produces the typical changes of increased intrapleural pressure (i.e., shifting of the mediastinum, bilateral compression of the lungs, and interference with venous return to the heart).

Chylothorax may be present at birth and is usually evident (in 75 per cent of the affected infants) by the age of one week. Initially the fluid may be clear, but once milk feedings are instituted, the fluid assumes a characteristic opaque appearance with the addition of fat droplets.

Needle thoracentesis on one or two occasions may suffice for management of some cases of chylothorax, but repeated thoracentesis poses an increased risk of pneumothorax and empyema. In instances of persistent or massive effusion, closed tube thoracostomy is preferred. Open thoracotomy occasionally is required for management of refractory cases. Identification of the site of leakage may be facilitated at operation by subcutaneous thigh injection of methylene blue dye (0.5 mg./kg. body weight). The dye is subsequently transported by the lymphatic system to the thoracic duct and usually marks with a blue stain the point of leakage in the chest (Randolph and Gross, 1957).

Congenital Diaphragmatic Hernia. Any mass, such as a giant duplication cyst or intrathoracic tumor, can potentially encroach on the pleural space and produce signs and symptoms suggestive of increased intra-

pleural pressure. The most frequent cause of this type of problem in a newborn infant is herniation of abdominal viscera through a posterolateral diaphragmatic defect into the pleural cavity. These congenital hernias through the foramen of Bochdalek are usually left-sided. Since a hernial sac rarely is present, in most instances the abdominal viscera have free access to the left pleural cavity (Allen and Thomson, 1966). On the right side, the buttressing effect of the liver may prevent herniation.

Signs and symptoms of a congenital diaphragmatic hernia may be evident at birth, or may appear later as the displaced intrapleural intestine fills with ingested air and secretions. In general, the earlier respiratory distress becomes evident, the more serious is the problem and the greater is the urgency for surgical correction (Gross, 1964). Since the physiologic threat is that of increasing intrapleural pressure through intestinal distention and progressive herniation of abdominal viscera into the pleural cavity, immediate surgical intervention is required in all cases (Fig. 5-13).

Although a thoracic approach has been utilized, an abdominal incision provides major advantages. The concomitant occurrence of intra-abdominal abnormalities is relatively high in these babies, especially anomalies of intestinal rotation, and identification and treatment of these problems are facilitated with an abdominal approach. In addition, it is technically easier to extract

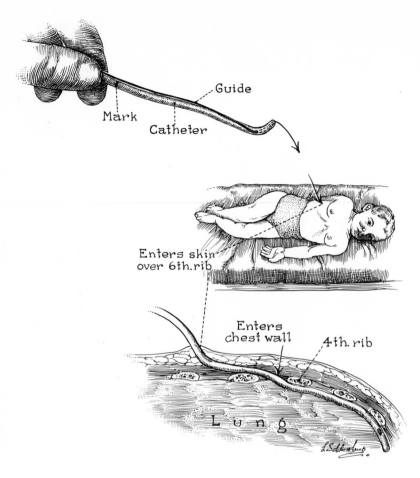

Guide
Mark
Catheter
Enters skin over 6th.rib
Enters chest wall
4th. rib
Lung

FIG. 5-12. Technique for chest tube insertion in infant. Short skin incision is made over 6th rib in midaxillary line following infiltration with 0.5 per cent procaine. Subcutaneous tract is then dissected bluntly with small curved clamp over superior margin of 5th rib and through intercostal muscles into pleural cavity. Malleable probe is then inserted as stylet into proximal side-hole of small French catheter (Nos. 10 to 12). Tip of stylet is curved in order to facilitate introduction of catheter through skin incision and subcutaneous tract into chest cavity. Catheter has been marked previously at optimum depth of insertion in order to prevent excessive penetration into thorax and possible injury to apical or mediastinal structures. Use of stylet facilitates placement of drainage tube in optimum position along lateral thoracic wall. Once positioning is achieved, probe may easily be withdrawn. Lateral insertion site is preferable in infants, even in treatment of pneumothorax. Introduction of catheter through second intercostal space anteriorly, as recommended in adults, is excessively difficult and hazardous in view of limited pleural space and close proximity of vital structures. In infants, direct insertion of catheters into chest, rather than tunneling through subcutaneous tissues, as described, may result in significant delay in healing of tube tract. (From Ballinger, W. F. (Ed.): Management of Trauma. Philadelphia, W. B. Saunders Co., 1968.)

the viscera from below than to push them out of the thorax from above. The abdominal incision also provides the surgeon with an option for leaving a ventral hernia (i.e., closing only the subcutaneous tissue and skin) in those cases in which replacement of the abdominal viscera into the peritoneal cavity would create an intolerable degree of intra-abdominal pressure. Since the newborn infant is primarily a diaphragmatic breather, increased intra-abdominal pressure seriously restricts ventilatory exchange, and eventually, can impede venous return through the inferior vena cava.

Closure of a diaphragmatic hernia is readily achieved through the abdomen, since the abdominal viscera are quite mobile and can be easily reduced and retracted for exposure. Direct suturing of the margins of the defect is possible in most instances, although insertion of a prosthetic mesh is rarely required. The rare instance of bilateral diaphragmatic hernia also can be excluded through abdominal exploration (Levy, 1969). Finally, insertion of a gastrostomy tube minimizes

postoperative distention and facilitates feeding (Fig. 5-14).

Valuable assistance in achieving survival of these babies is provided by serial monitoring of circulating blood volume, blood gases, and pH. Placement of a central venous catheter in the superior vena cava via the jugular vein facilitates such studies. Concomitant use of an inferior vena caval catheter, with monitoring of pressure both in the superior vena cava and the inferior vena cava, may assist in determining whether closure of the abdominal incision has created excessive intra-abdominal tension. Obviously, routine use of the inferior vena cava for pressure monitoring and fluid administration is contraindicated because of artifacts that result from changes in intra-abdominal pressure.

Special care must be taken by the anesthesiologist to avoid overdistention of the unexpanded ipsilateral lung during operative repair of the diaphragmatic defect. This lung may be hypoplastic as a result of prolonged compression in utero by the displaced abdominal viscera. A residual intrapleural space usually remains for the first few days following operation. Gradual expansion of the lung is safer than abrupt mechanical distention by positive pressure insufflation, since overinflation is likely to produce rupture, persistent air leakage, and possible tension pneumothorax if the tube becomes occluded. If a thoracostomy tube is inserted and connected to underwater seal drainage without suction, complete obliteration of the residual pleural space normally results within three to four days.

In those rare instances in which pulmonary hypoplasia occurs bilaterally as a result of in utero displacement of the mediastinum and encroachment on both pleural cavities by ectopic viscera, the resulting defi-

ciency in functional lung volume may prove incompatible with survival.

Eventration of the Diaphragm. Although the term eventration of the diaphragm properly designates an anomaly of muscular development of the diaphragm, the resultant clinical picture in a newborn infant is similar to that produced by unilateral paralysis of the phrenic nerve (Fig. 5-15). The only distinguishing characteristic between the two conditions may be the association of phrenic paralysis with brachial plexus palsy from birth trauma.

Because of the relative infrequency with which paralysis of the diaphragm produces symptoms in adults, it has not been generally appreciated that the similar condition may be accompanied by a significant mortal-

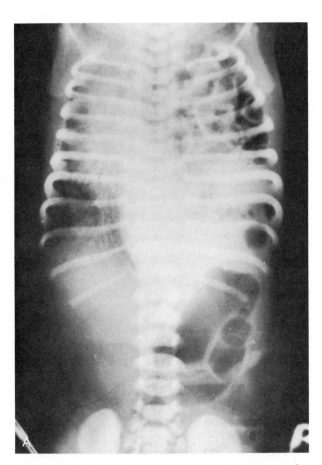 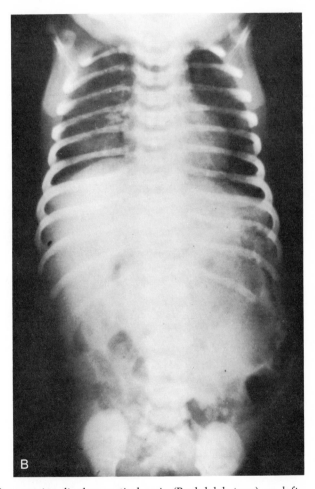

FIG. 5-13. *A.* Typical roentgenogram of newborn infant with posterior diaphragmatic hernia (Bochdalek type) on left. Note air- and fluid-filled loops of intestine in left hemithorax and relative absence of gas-filled loops of bowel in abdomen. Severe shift of mediastinum to right has caused distortion of tracheobronchial tree and seriously compressed right pulmonary parenchyma. Physiologic consequences of this mediastinal shift are discussed in text. *B,* Postoperative chest roentgenogram on same baby on 8th postoperative day following successful repair of left posterior diaphragmatic defect. Unlike many infants with diaphragmatic hernias, ipsilateral lung was normal in this baby and, as shown in roentgenogram, left lung has expanded normally, and chest tube left in pleural space postoperatively has been removed. Note return of mediastinum to normal position with full re-expansion of right lung.

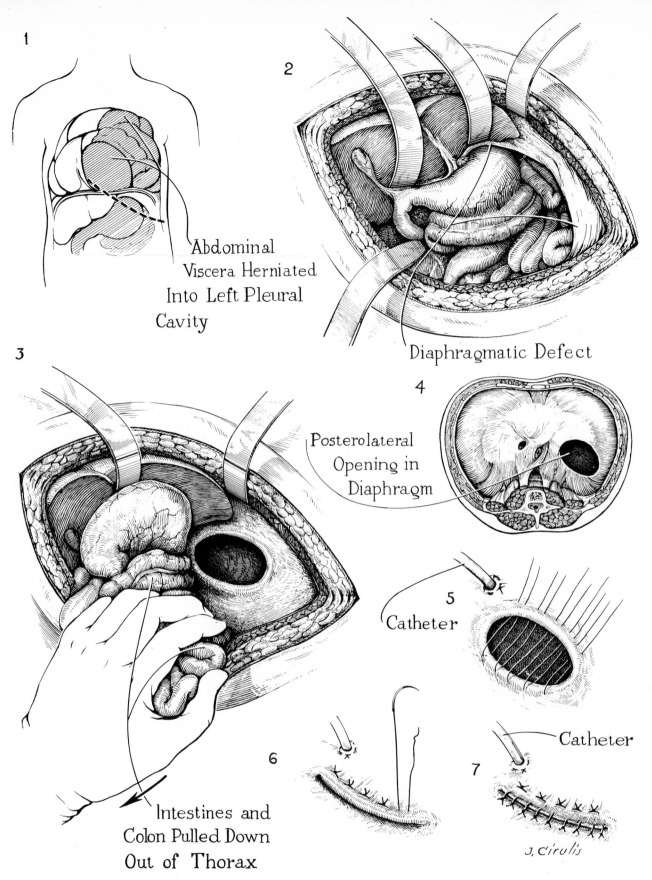

1

Abdominal
Viscera Herniated
Into Left Pleural
Cavity

2

Diaphragmatic Defect

3

4

Posterolateral
Opening in
Diaphragm

5

Catheter

6

7

Catheter

Intestines and
Colon Pulled Down
Out of Thorax

J. Cirulis

FIG. 5-14. Repair of diaphragmatic hernia. *1,* Nine out of 10 posterolateral diaphragmatic hernias occur on left side with abdominal viscera in left hemithorax and mediastinum shifted to right side. *2,* Abdominal incision is far superior to thoracic one (see text). Subcostal incision is shown, but left paramedian incision is equally satisfactory. *3,* Herniated viscera have been returned to abdomen and diaphragmatic defect is clearly visible. *4,* Note that there is practically always a posterior rim of diaphragm which permits direct primary repair. *5,* Intrapleural catheter may be placed either through diaphragm as shown or through intercostal stab wound. *6* and *7,* Two rows of interrupted sutures provide dependable strong closure of defect. (From Gross, R. E.: Atlas of Children's Surgery. Philadelphia, W. B. Saunders Company, 1970.)

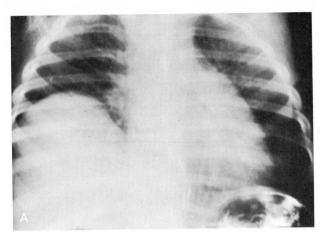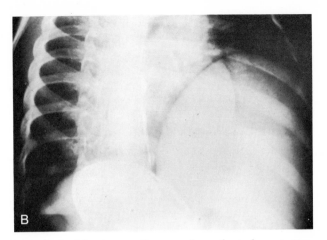

Fig. 5-15. Roentgenogram of patient with severe eventration of right leaf of diaphragm. Because of paradoxical respiration and dynamic shifting of mediastinum, a right thoracotomy was necessary and plication of diaphragm carried out with good postoperative functional result.

ity in newborn infants (Michelson, 1961). The two factors that appear to be of greatest clinical significance are (1) the increased mobility of the mediastinum and (2) the increased reliance on diaphragmatic movement for ventilatory exchange. On fluoroscopy, the affected diaphragm is seen to remain fixed in position or to move paradoxically on inspiration. Concomitantly, the mediastinum swings with a pendulum-like motion toward the contralateral pleural cavity. The net result is a significant decrease in effective air exchange and a demand for increased respiratory effort. The inevitable stasis of secretions, in turn, encourages complications of atelectasis and pneumonia, with escalation of respiratory distress. If uncorrected, this may eventually culminate in the death of the baby.

Whatever the underlying cause, correction is achieved by thoracotomy and plication of the diaphragm or, in cases with excessive thinning of the musculature, by a reinforced imbrication (Bishop and Koop, 1958; Thomas, 1968). Even when diaphragmatic motion is absent, fixation results in stabilization of the mediastinum and improved ventilation. As the patient grows older, the mediastinum achieves a greater degree of fixation and the clinical threat of eventration of the diaphragm is correspondingly diminished, even in those few cases in which the condition recurs following surgical repair (Jewett and Thomson, 1964).

Intrapulmonary Space-Occupying Lesions

Expanding intrapulmonary space-occupying lesions can produce the same clinical picture described previously for extrapulmonary problems. In most instances, the offending mass results from air entrapment within anomalous or damaged lung.

The role of neonatal staphylococcal pneumonia in

producing pneumatoceles and pneumothorax has been noted. Pulmonary hamartoma and congenital lobar emphysema are additional causes of neonatal respiratory distress.

Neonatal Pulmonary Hamartoma. A spectrum of cystic congenital tumors results from anomalies in bronchopulmonary-foregut development (Gerle et al., 1968; Izzo and Rickham, 1968). The final relationship of the cystic lesion to the mature bronchopulmonary system and gastrointestinal tract is determined by the phase of normal bronchopulmonary-foregut budding, during which it arises as an anomalous outpouching. The resulting malformation may be located either within or outside the lung and may retain an attachment to either the tracheobronchial tree or the intestinal tract. In one form of the anomaly, so-called extralobar sequestration of the lung, interference with closure of the pleuroperitoneal canal probably accounts for a 30 per cent incidence of associated congenital diaphragmatic hernia (Gerle et al., 1968).

Congenital Lung Cyst. There are two types of isolated congenital lung cysts: (1) the bronchogenic cyst, which has been described previously and is usually located within the mediastinum in close proximity to the major bronchi, and (2) the more common type of cyst, which occurs in the periphery of the lung and may not communicate directly with the bronchial tree. The wall of a congenital lung cyst is characteristically lined by respiratory epithelium and may contain cartilage, connective tissue, and, rarely, muscle. Once infection occurs, it is difficult to differentiate congenital from acquired lesions.

Congenital lung cysts produce symptoms in the newborn infant by increasing intrathoracic pressure, either as a result of overaeration of a peripheral lesion or through partial occlusion of a proximal bronchus, resulting in a "ball-valve" type of obstruction, which allows passage of air into the peripheral lung but prevents its escape. If uncorrected, this latter process eventually produces the typical picture of intrapleural tension (Eraklis et al., 1969).

Chest roentgenograms may demonstrate a mediastinal mass with atelectasis or hyperaeration of the distal lung or a circumscribed radiolucent lesion. Expiratory wheezing characterizes those patients with bronchial narrowing. Preoperative differentiation of a bronchogenic cyst is best achieved by an esophageal contrast study, which demonstrates posterior displacement of the esophagus and anterior displacement and narrowing of the trachea by an intervening mediastinal lesion. As emphasized before, bronchoscopy and bronchography are dangerous in these babies, and neither procedure proves as informative as a barium swallow study. The peripheral lung cyst is differentiated from lobar emphysema on roentgenogram of the chest by an absence of bronchovascular markings within the lesion. Lobectomy is curative for this last condition.

Adenomatoid Malformation of the Lung. This condition, sometimes termed *congenital cystic disease of the lung,* is characterized by the presence of multiple cysts, which impart a honeycomb appearance to the affected lung. The x-ray picture may be confused with congenital diaphragmatic hernia, but the presence of normal air-filled intestine beneath the diaphragm provides an essential clue for distinguishing between the two conditions. In addition, air-fluid levels rarely are seen in congenital cystic disease at birth. It is essential, therefore, that the initial radiographic study include both the abdomen and the chest for adequate diagnosis. Characteristically, these cysts are lined by respiratory epithelium and produce symptoms in the neonate through progressive expansion and encroachment on the pleural space. Later in life, retention of secretions and secondary infection are the most frequent cause of symptoms, and, then, air-fluid levels are characteristic of this lesion.

Intralobar Sequestration. This is a congenital lesion, which is rarely symptomatic in newborn infants. Although the associated cysts have been attributed to secondary inflammatory changes, the lesion probably represents a variant of congenital cystic disease of the lung and is characterized by an anomalous arterial supply from the descending aorta (Fig. 5-16) (Slim et al., 1968).

Congenital Lobar Emphysema. This condition presents as progressive overinflation of an upper or middle lobe of the lung, occurring most frequently in a male infant. The majority of cases are seen within the first few weeks of life and produce symptoms that are indistinguishable from other causes of intrapleural tension

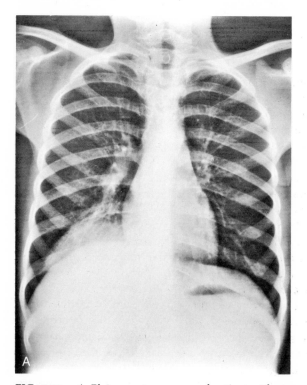
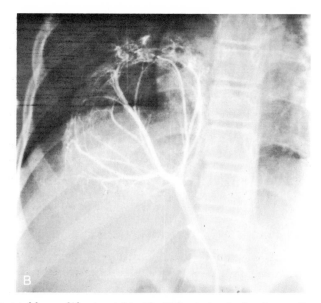

FIG. 5-16. *A,* Plain roentgenogram of patient with sequestration of lower lobe on right side. Patient also had soft systolic bruit heard over lower part of chest. Increased radiodensity in right lower lung field suggested abnormality. *B,* Aortogram clearly defines systemic origin of blood supply from descending aorta to sequestered segment.

(Murray, 1967). Clinical distinction is usually achieved by physical examination and chest roentgenogram.

Massive air trapping within the abnormal lobe results in hyperresonance and diminished breath sounds over the affected hemithorax and displacement of the mediastinum toward the contralateral side. A chest roentgenogram identifies a hyperlucent area within which, on careful scrutiny, bronchovascular markings can be defined (Fig. 5-17). The remaining ipsilateral and the contralateral lung are compressed as the involved lobe progressively expands. Particular care must be taken to ensure that congenital lobar emphysema is not confused with primary atelectasis of the lung with compensatory hyperinflation of the uninvolved segments. As noted by Hendren and McKee, total atelectasis of one lung is capable of producing a significant mediastinal shift in the infant, but the resultant compensatory hypertrophy usually involves the entire contralateral lung, rather than limiting itself to a single lobe. In almost all instances of congenital lobar emphysema, compressed ipsilateral lung is apparent either on chest roentgenogram or on radioactive pulmonary scan (Mauney and Sabiston, 1970).

Although bronchial stenosis is assumed to be the primary cause of this condition, an anatomic obstruction has been defined in only 50 per cent of cases. In 25 per cent of babies, bronchial cartilaginous dysplasia has been noted. In 15 per cent the obstruction has been endobronchial and in 8 per cent it has resulted from extrinsic compression of the bronchus (Hendren and McKee, 1966). One case of obstructive emphysema from bronchial obstruction by a mucous plug has been reported (Murray, Talbert, and Haller, 1967).

In most instances, immediate thoracotomy is required for relief of severe respiratory distress. The affected lobe is characteristically hyperinflated, and remains fixed in expansion even when the bronchus is transected. The lung presents a smooth, pale pink surface and imparts a spongy feeling with crepitus on palpation. When a normal degree of elasticity and compressibility of pulmonary tissue is identified, the possibility of a proximal bronchial mucous plug or an extrinsic mediastinal cyst must be excluded.

As noted above, congenital lobar emphysema occurs most frequently in males (2:1) and usually involves an upper lobe, occasionally the middle, and with extreme rarity, the lower lobes of the lung. Bilateral occurrence is infrequent.

Emergency thoracotomy with lobectomy is curative and can almost always be undertaken on the basis of the clinical picture and plain chest roentgenogram. Bronchoscopy and bronchography are unnecessary and may be dangerous, since rapid distention of the affected

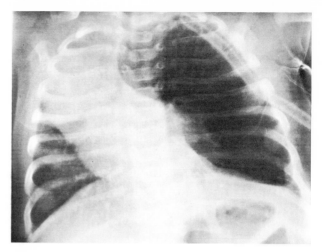

FIG. 5-17. Characteristic roentgen finding of intralobar emphysema. Hyperaerated segment is much more radiolucent than remaining lung and has shifted that portion of adjacent mediastinum away from side of increased pressure. This patient responded to intratracheal suctioning and apparent dislodgment of mucous plug, which was partially obstructing bronchus to hyperaerated segment.

lobe may ensue. If these procedures are utilized for clarification of obscure cases, they should be performed in an operating room with instruments immediately available for emergency thoracotomy. With appropriate management, the long-term prognosis of these infants is excellent, and there is usually no tendency for recurrence of the disease in the remaining lung.

REFERENCES

Allen, M. S., and Thomson, S. A.: Congenital diaphragmatic hernia in children under one year of age: a 24-year review. J. Pediat. Surg., 2:157, 1966.

Apgar, V.: A proposal for a new method of evaluation of the newborn infant. Anesth. Analg., 32:260, 1953.

Apgar, V.: The newborn (APGAR) scoring system. Pediat. Clin. N. Amer., 13:645, 1966.

Ayres, W. W., Delaney, A. J., and Backer, M. H.: Congenital neurofibromatous macroglossia associated in some cases with von Recklinghausen's disease. Cancer, 5:721, 1952.

Behrman, R. E., et al.: Treatment of the asphyxiated newborn infant. J. Pediat., 74:981, 1969.

Bill, A. H., Jr., and Sumner, D. S.: A unified concept of lymphangioma and cystic hygroma. Surg. Gynec. Obstet., 120:79, 1965.

Bishop, H. C., and Koop, C. E.: Acquired eventration of the diaphragm in infancy. Pediatrics, 22:1088, 1958.

Boeckman, C. R.: Teratoid tumors of the nasopharynx in children. J. Pediat. Surg., 3:735, 1968.

Booth, J. B., and Berry, C. L.: Unilateral pulmonary agenesis. Arch. Dis. Child., 42:361, 1967.

Burford, T. H., and Ferguson, T. B.: Congenital lesions of the lungs and emphysema. *In* Surgery of the Chest. Edited by J. H. Gibbon, D. C. Sabiston, and F. C. Spencer. Philadelphia, W. B. Saunders Co., 1969.

Capitanio, M. A., and Kirkpatrick, J. A., Jr.: Roentgen examination in the evaluation of the newborn infant with respiratory distress. J. Pediat., 75:896, 1969.

Chamberlain, J. W.: Congenital epulis (granular cell myoblastoma). J. Pediat. Surg., 2:158, 1967.

Chernick, V., and Avery, M. E.: Spontaneous alveolar rupture in newborn infants. Pediatrics, 32:816, 1963.

Dawes, G. S.: Foetal and Neonatal Physiology. Chicago, Year Book Medical Publishers, Inc., 1968.

Douglas, B.: A further report on treatment of micrognathia with obstruction by a plastic procedure. Plast. Reconstr. Surg., 5:113, 1950.

Eraklis, A. J., Griscom, N. T., and McGovern, J. B.: Bronchogenic cysts of the mediastinum in infancy. New Eng. J. Med., 281:1150, 1969.

Fearon, B., and Shortreed, R.: Tracheobronchial compression by congenital cardiovascular anomalies in children. Ann. Otolaryng., 72:949, 1963.

Ferguson, C. F.: Treatment of airway problems in the newborn. Ann. Otol., 76:762, 1967.

Fost, N. C., and Esterly, N. B.: Successful treatment of juvenile hemangiomas with prednisone. J. Pediat., 72:351, 1968.

Galofre, M., Judd, E. S., Perez, P. E., and Harrison, E. G., Jr.: Results of surgical treatment of cystic hygroma. Surg. Gynec. Obstet., 115:319, 1962.

Gerle, R. D., Jaretzki, A., III, Ashley, C. A., and Berne, A. S.: Congenital bronchopulmonary-foregut malformation. New Eng. J. Med., 278:1413, 1968.

Gross, R. E.: Thoracic surgery for infants. J. Thorac. Cardiov. Surg., 48:152, 1964.

Gross, R. E., and Firestone, F. N.: Colonic reconstruction of the esophagus in infants and children. Surgery, 61:955, 1967.

Gross, R. E., and Ware, P. F.: Arterial malformations which cause compression of trachea and esophagus. Circulation 11:124, 1955.

Haight, C.: Congenital atresia of the esophagus with tracheoesophageal fistula: reconstruction of esophageal continuity by primary anastomosis. Ann. Surg., 120:623, 1944.

Hajdu, S. I., Faruque, A. A., Hajdu, E. O., and Morgan, W. S.: Teratoma of the neck in infants. Amer. J. Dis. Child., 111:412, 1966.

Haller, J. A., Jr., et al.: Esophageal function following resection: studies in newborn puppies. Ann. Thorac. Surg., 2:180, 1966.

Hendren, W. H., and McKee, D. M.: Lobar emphysema of infancy. J. Pediat. Surg., 1:24, 1966.

Holder, T., Cloud, D. T., and Lewis, E. J.: Esophageal atresia and tracheoesophageal fistula. Pediatrics, 34:542, 1964.

Hurlbut, H. J., Webb, H. W., and Moseley, T.: Cervical teratoma in infant siblings. J. Pediat. Surg., 2:424, 1967.

Izzo, C., and Rickham, P. P.: Neonatal pulmonary hamartoma. J. Pediat. Surg., 3:77, 1968.

Jewett, T. C., Jr., and Thomson, N. B., Jr.: Iatrogenic eventration of the diaphragm in infancy. J. Thorac. Cardiov. Surg., 48:861, 1964.

Key, F. M., Jr., and Mendel, E. B.: Bilateral choanal atresia. Obstet. Gynec., 32:58, 1968.

Kirkpatrick, J. A., Cresson, S. L., and Pilling, G. P.: Motor activity of esophagus in association with esophageal atresia and tracheoesophageal fistula. Amer. J. Roentgenol., 86:884, 1961.

Koop, C. E., and Moschakis, E. A.: Capillary lymphangioma of the tongue complicated by glossitis. Pediatrics, 27:800, 1961.

Krueger, C., Mostafa, S., and Reagan, L. B.: Spontaneous pneumothorax in newborn infants. Surgery, 2:498, 1968.

Levy, J. L., Jr., Guynes, W. A., Jr., Louis, J. E., and Linder, L. H.: Bilateral congenital diaphragmatic hernias through the foramina of Bochdalek. J. Pediat. Surg., 4:557, 1969.

Lind, J. F.: Personal communication. 1965.

Lister, J., and Zachary, R. B.: Cystic duplications in the tongue. J. Pediat. Surg., 3:491, 1968.

Mauney, F. M., Jr., and Sabiston, D. C., Jr.: The role of pulmonary scanning in the diagnosis of congenital lobar emphysema. Amer. Surg., 36:20, 1970.

McEvitt, W. G.: Micrognathia and its management. Plast. Reconstr. Surg., 41:450, 1968.

Mehrizi, A., Folger, G. M., and Rowe, R.: Tracheoesophageal fistula associated with congenital cardiovascular malformations. Bull. Johns Hopkins Hosp., 118:246, 1966.

Michelson, E.: Eventration of the diaphragm. Surgery, 49:410, 1961.

Murray, G. F.: Congenital lobar emphysema. Surg. Gynec. Obstet., 124:611, 1967.

Murray, G. F., Talbert, J. L., and Haller, J. A., Jr.: Obstructive lobar emphysema of the newborn infant. J. Thorac. Cardiov. Surg., 53:886, 1967.

Packard, G. B., Williams, E. T., and Wheelock, S. E.: Congenital obstructing goiter. Surgery, 48:422, 1960.

Parodi-Hueck, L. E., and Koop, C. E.: Subhyoid midline ectopic thyroid tissue in the absence of normal thyroid gland. J. Pediat. Surg., 3:710, 1968.

Polgar, G.: The nasal resistance of newborn infants. J. Pediat., 67:557, 1965.

Randall, P.: Micrognathia and glossoptosis with airway obstruction: the Pierre Robin syndrome. *In* Reconstructive Plastic Surgery. Edited by J. M. Converse. Philadelphia, W. B. Saunders Co., 1964.

Randolph, J. G., and Gross, R. E.: Congenital chylothorax. Arch. Surg., 74:405, 1957.

Randolph, J. G., Tunell, W. P., and Lilly, J. R.: Gastric division in the critically ill infant with esophageal atresia and tracheoesophageal fistula. Surgery, 63:496, 1968.

Reid, L.: The embryology of the lung. *In* Development of the Lung. Edited by A. V. S. de Reuck and R. Porter. London, J. and A. Churchill, Ltd., 1967.

Scarpelli, E. M.: Respiratory distress syndrome of the newborn. Ann. Rev. Med., 19:153, 1968.

Sieber, W., and Shepard, R.: Evaluation of esophageal function in postoperative esophageal atresia and tracheoesophageal fistula. Paper presented at Academy of Pediatrics, New York, 1964.

Slim, M. S., Sahyoun, P., and Balikian, J.: Congenital bronchiolar cysts simulating intralobar sequestration. J. Pediat. Surg., 3:60, 1968.

Srouji, M. N.: Pneumothorax and pneumomediastinum in the first three days of life. J. Pediat. Surg., 2:410, 1967.

Talbert, J. L., and Haller, J. A., Jr.: Temporary tube pharyngostomy in the staged repair of congenital tracheoesophageal fistula. Surgery, 58:737, 1965.

Talbert, J. L., and Haller, J. A., Jr.: Technic of central venous pressure monitoring in infants. Amer. Surg. 32:767, 1966.

Thomas, T. V.: Nonparalytic eventration of the diaphragm. J. Thorac. Cardiov. Surg., 55:586, 1968.

Waterston, D. J., Carter, R. E. B., and Aberdeen, E.: Esophageal atresia: tracheoesophageal fistula. Lancet, 1:819, 1962.

Yancy, W. S., and Spock, A.: Spontaneous neonatal pleural effusion. J. Pediat. Surg., 2:313, 1967.

6

Cardiovascular Emergencies

Congenital Heart Abnormalities with Cyanosis

Severe respiratory distress at birth may be associated with cyanotic congenital heart anomalies, especially transposition of the great vessels, tricuspid atresia, and hypoplastic right ventricle. By far the most common anomaly causing cyanosis at birth is transposition of the great vessels. Babies with this condition usually are well developed because their anomaly does not interfere with adequate intrauterine growth and development, inasmuch as fetal blood is oxygenated by the placenta and then pumped by either or both ventricles into the systemic circulation. It is only after the placental oxygenator is severed at birth that caval blood, which is pumped into the aorta in transposition, produces severe cyanosis.

The many causes of cyanotic congenital heart disease include chromosomal abnormalities as well as uterine environmental influences. The incidence of cyanotic congenital heart disease resulting from viral infections in the mother during the first trimester of pregnancy is being increasingly documented. The outstanding example of this etiologic factor is maternal-fetal rubella, which may result in a variety of heart deformities as well as other anomalies.

The functional derangement that is common to almost all cyanotic congenital heart abnormalities is inadequate blood flow to the lungs or a right-to-left intracardiac shunt or both. An exception is transposition of the great vessels with poor admixture, in which there may be *no* pulmonary stenosis, but rather *increased* pulmonary flow. As a result of decreased pulmonary flow and the mixture of unoxygenated blood from the right-to-left shunt, a severe degree of hypoxemia may be present in the immediate newborn period. Chronic hypoxia often results in varying degrees of compensated metabolic acidosis, but the buffering ability of an infant's electrolyte system is limited and eventually acidosis combines with hypoxia to produce severe tissue anoxia. This hypoxic state may be tolerated by a newborn infant for a short period of time, but ultimately the characteristic response to prolonged hypoxemia occurs. This is a so-called cyanotic spell, which must be differentiated from apnea or dyspnea resulting from newborn intracranial damage and hemorrhage. This differentiation may be difficult at first, but becomes obvious when an infant with primary cyanotic heart disease responds to treatment for his hypoxia. A baby with intracranial damage usually does not survive this stage of his disease.

Treatment is directed toward increasing the oxygenation of arterial blood and improving myocardial function. The baby should be placed immediately in an environment of high oxygen concentration; a face mask may be necessary. For reasons that are not entirely clear, sedation with morphine sulfate (0.1 mg./kg.) has a dramatic influence on cyanotic spells and is an important drug in the management of such spells. In addition, intravenous calcium gluconate (100 to 200 mg.) has an immediate effect on cardiac slowing as a result of its direct inotropic effect on the myocardium. Thus, oxygen, morphine, and calcium gluconate form a therapeutic triad for cyanotic spells.

As soon as the baby's condition permits, appropriate diagnostic studies must be carried out before definitive therapy can be initiated. Accurate diagnosis of the anatomic defect in newborn infants requires a high degree of sophisticated technical skill in cardiac catheterization. These are usually fragile babies who are suffering from severe cerebral depression and varying degrees of metabolic acidosis, as a result of their hypoxemia. For this reason even brief procedures are poorly tolerated and must be carried out expeditiously and precisely. Ideally, the metabolic acidosis and hypoxemia should be corrected prior to cardiac catheterization, but in actual practice this is often impossible. Intravenous sodium bicarbonate has been the most useful drug in the temporary adjustment of acidosis, but it treats only the effect and not the cause.

A newborn infant who has a severe cyanotic spell probably will not survive more than a few hours, unless a palliative or corrective surgical procedure can be carried out. If survival is impossible without operative intervention, it has been our policy to recommend aggressive surgical management, despite the risks. It is our philosophy that no baby with a correctable anomaly should succumb to it without an honest surgical attempt to relieve his condition.

The differential diagnosis of four common causes of cyanotic spells in newborn infants may be made from their electrocardiograms, results of cardiac catheterization, and typical features of angiocardiography.

Transposition of the Great Vessels (Fig. 6-1). In transposition of the great vessels the systemic (right) ventricle pumps unoxygenated venous blood out of the aorta with progressive hypoxemia. The left ventricle pumps oxygenated blood into the pulmonary artery and it returns to the same ventricle. Unless there is some means of admixture of these two blood pools, babies

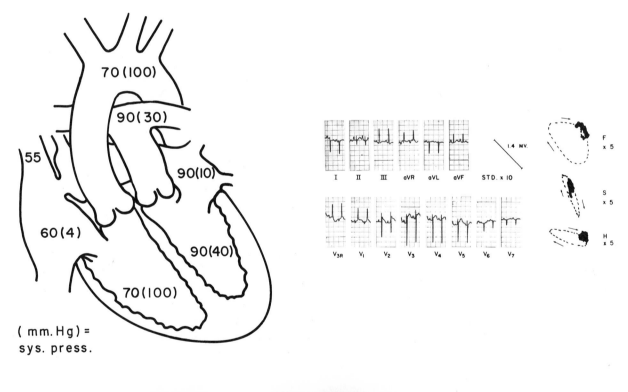

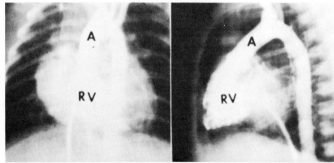

FIG. 6-1. Composite diagnostic features for transposition of great vessels. Plain figures in catheterization diagram represent oxygen per cent saturation. Figures in parentheses represent systolic pressure in millimeters of mercury.

with transposition do not survive their first few minutes of life.

Although total functional repair (Mustard operation) has been attempted in newborn infants, results in small babies have not been satisfactory to date, owing largely to the problems of prolonged extracorporeal circulation in newborn infants and to the technical difficulties of total repair in tiny hearts. The recent reports of Dillard and associates of successful total repair of transposition in infants using deep hypothermia are very exciting, but this experience is limited and preliminary (Dillard, 1970). The operative approach to transposition of the great vessels is, therefore, a palliative one in newborn infants. Basically the operation is an attempt to increase mixing between the arterial and venous sides of the heart by creating an atrial septal defect.

Rashkind (1966) recently introduced a nonsurgical approach in which a balloon-tipped catheter is passed through the foramen ovale and inflated in the left atrium. When the inflated balloon is withdrawn through the foramen, the septum is torn and an atrial septal defect is created. Theoretically this technique is appealing because it obviates general anesthesia and a major thoracotomy in a desperately ill child. Some excellent results of this procedure, as well as numerous failures, have been reported. Its exact place in the management of transposition of the great vessels has not yet been determined. It is our primary attempt at therapy in the catheterization laboratory. If a definite increase in left-to-right shunting results from the Rashkind procedure, and the systemic arterial oxygen saturation is significantly elevated, operative creation of an atrial septal defect is withheld. If the baby is not improved by an attempted Rashkind procedure, or if the condition of the baby subsequently deteriorates, an atrial septal defect is surgically created.

The two methods currently in use for the creation of a large atrial septal defect are the open heart and the closed heart techniques. A closed heart operation is more commonly used and is a modification of the original Blalock-Hanlon procedure (Blalock, 1950) (Fig. 6-2). The basis for this technique is the anatomic relationship of the right pulmonary veins to the back of the right atrial wall. If this common wall is excised, a communication that functions as an atrial septal defect is created. With special instruments, some of which have been recently modified, it is possible to carry out this procedure without interrupting the normal circulation. It is reasonably well tolerated by a sick infant if it is performed quickly and if adequate mixing of the two blood pools results (Cornell, 1966). The mortality associated with the operative procedure remains relatively high in these desperately ill babies, approximately 30 to 40 per cent in a recent report of Hallman and Cooley (1964).

Creation of an atrial septal defect by an open heart, nonpump technique is usually carried out under moderate hypothermia (28° to 32°C.), with inflow occlusion of the two cavae and a right atrial incision. Under direct vision the atrial septum is seized at the foramen ovale and excised. A major hazard associated with this procedure is air embolization because it is difficult to eliminate all air from the right atrium and right ventricle, which in this case empty into the aorta.

Eighty or 90 per cent of infants with transposition of the great vessels die before the age of six months unless some type of palliative procedure is carried out (Rowe, 1968). Some infants with transposition of the great vessels have associated congenital anomalies which permit natural mixing, namely ventricular septal defects and atrial septal defects. These infants have another basis for respiratory difficulty. They may have an increased flow of blood to the lungs, especially with an associated ventricular septal defect. Occasionally a banding procedure of the pulmonary artery is combined with creation of an atrial septal defect. The pulmonary artery band both prevents pulmonary congestion and decreases pressure in the pulmonary artery. In this way banding may prevent irreversible pulmonary vascular changes. Now that we have an operative procedure that functionally corrects transposition of the great vessels (Mustard operation) (Mustard, 1964), it is imperative that the pulmonary vascular bed is not allowed to become severely damaged in infancy. Unless the pulmonary vascular changes associated with a large VSD can be prevented, these children with transposition never become candidates for total repair.

Appropriate timing for total repair of transposition of the great vessels has not been determined, since experience is still limited. The Mustard operation is shown in Figure 6-3 (Haller, 1969). Some very fine results have been reported in children as young as two and three years of age. Aberdeen has reported a large series of total repairs, which include many young children (Aberdeen, 1970). Most of the total repairs have been carried out in children weighing 10 kg. or more, and in those with an intact ventricular septum. Recently McGoon and associates reported excellent results in a small group of older children with VSD-transposition combinations, but with normal pulmonary vasculature (Rastelli, 1969).

Tetralogy of Fallot (Fig. 6-4). The four components of the tetralogy of Fallot—pulmonic stenosis, ventricular septal defect, overriding of the aorta, and right ventricular hypertrophy—rarely result in severe cyanotic spells at birth unless there is extreme pulmonic stenosis or atresia. Even with pulmonary atresia, a patent ductus arteriosus usually allows sufficient pulmonary blood flow to prevent cyanotic spells. The most common history for a tetralogy of Fallot is increasing cyanosis

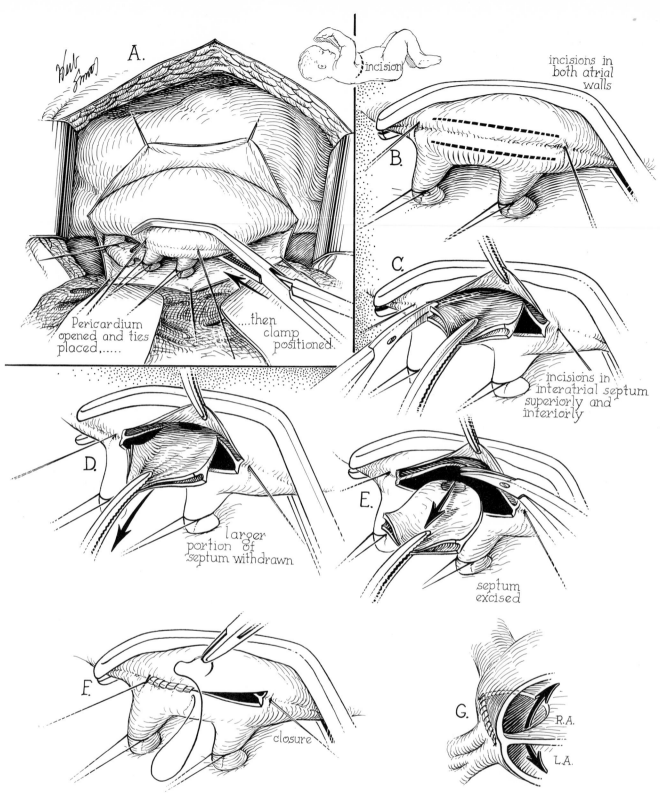

FIG. 6-2. Creation of atrial septal defect. (*Inset*) Lateral position. Incision in right fifth intercostal space. *A,* Pericardium opened anterior to phrenic nerve. Control ligatures looped doubly about right pulmonary artery and superior and inferior pulmonary veins. *B,* Sutures placed through septum at superior and inferior limits of proposed area of incision. Control ligatures tightened about right pulmonary artery and veins. Curved vascular clamp applied to anterior surface right atrium and posterior surface left atrium. Dotted lines indicate sites of incision into left and right atria on either side of septum. *C,* Incisions made into both atria. Intervening septum grasped with hemostat. Incisions carried onto septum inferiorly and superiorly. *D,* Vascular clamp loosened allowing greater portion of septum to be withdrawn from heart. *E,* Septum excised down to foramen ovale. *F,* Anterior and posterior margins of atrial tissue approximated with preplaced sutures. *G,* Oblique cut-away view showing orientation of septal defect. (From Cooley, D. A., and Hallman, G. L.: Surgical Treatment of Congenital Heart Disease.)

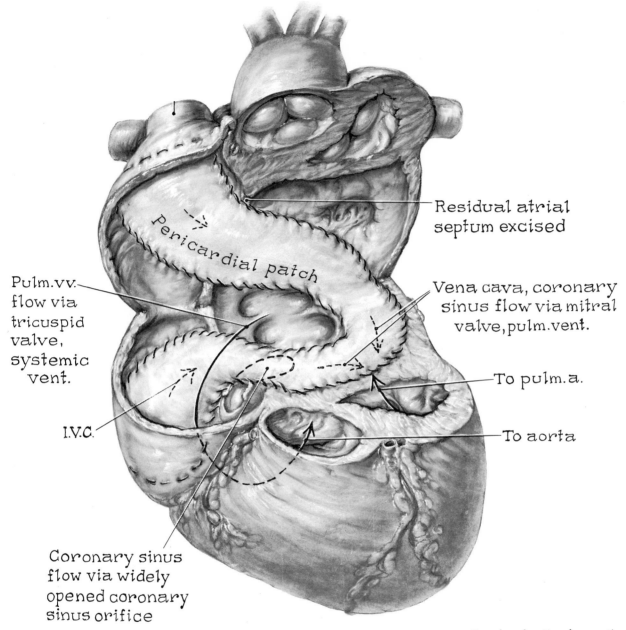

Residual atrial septum excised

Pulm.vv. flow via tricuspid valve, systemic vent.

Pericardial patch

Vena cava, coronary sinus flow via mitral valve, pulm.vent.

To pulm.a.

To aorta

I.V.C.

Coronary sinus flow via widely opened coronary sinus orifice

FIG. 6-3. Three-dimensional view shows rerouted caval and pulmonary venous streams. Complete functional correction has been achieved in Mustard operation. (From Haller, J. A., Jr., Crisler, C., Brawley, R., and Cameron, J.: Mustard operation for transposition of the great vessels. J. Thorac. Cardiov. Surg., *58*:269, 1969.)

and spells after the first several weeks or month of life.

In those rare cases with pulmonary atresia and inadequate flow through a ductus arteriosus, it becomes necessary to increase pulmonary blood flow with some type of artificial ductus operation in the first few hours or days of life. Because the subclavian artery is too small for a Blalock-Taussig operation at birth (Blalock, 1945), some type of modified Potts operation (an aorta to pulmonary artery anastomosis) is preferable.

The Potts operation (Potts, 1946), a side-to-side anastomosis of the descending aorta to the left pulmonary artery, is a proved cardiac procedure. It has given excellent palliation for infants with pulmonary stenosis and VSD since its introduction in 1946 (Fig. 6-5). A major hazard of this operation is making the anastomosis too large, with the resultant development of either intractable congestive failure or severe pulmonary hypertension. With the development of techniques for total correction of the tetralogy of Fallot,

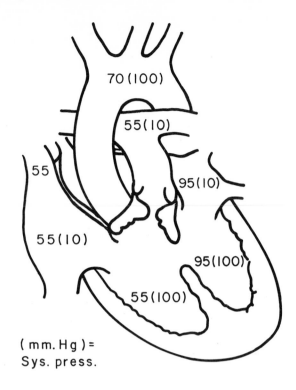

70 (100)

55 (10)

55

95 (10)

55 (10)

95 (100)

55 (100)

(mm. Hg) =
Sys. press.

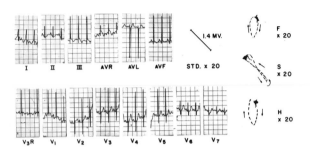

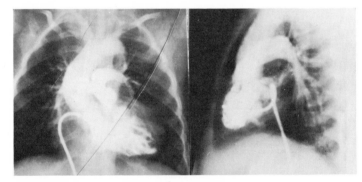

FIG. 6-4. Composite diagnostic features for tetralogy of Fallot. Plain figures in catheterization diagram represent oxygen per cent saturation. Figures in parentheses represent systolic pressure in millimeters of mercury.

a second contraindication to this operation has developed. The technical difficulty in isolating and repairing the Potts aortopulmonary anastomosis presents a formidable hazard. In addition, distortion and kinking of the left pulmonary artery at the anastomotic site may make reconstruction extremely difficult. Because of these technical problems in the total repair of tetralogy of Fallot with a Potts anastomosis, we prefer a bilateral thoracotomy and circumferential ligation of the anastomosis as popularized by Cooley (Cooley, 1966).

To obviate the difficulty of taking down a Potts anastomosis during total repair, a so-called central shunt (Waterston shunt) was introduced at The Great Ormond Street Hospital in London, England

(Waterston, 1962). This consists of a side-to-side anastomosis between the ascending aorta and right pulmonary artery. The limiting factor in this operative procedure is the size of the pulmonary artery. The modified technique used by Cooley is shown in Figure 6-6 (Cooley, 1966). The major theoretic advantage of the central shunt is that the anastomosis may be repaired at the time of total correction by cross-clamping the aorta and closing the anastomosis through an aortotomy. Further experience with this operative procedure is required before its applicability is defined and its ease of management during total repair has been determined.

Few surgeons in the United States electively use

transventricular infundibulectomy as first described by Brock (Brock, 1948), but it has been used extensively in Great Britain. The basis for the operation is removal of a part of the infundibular or valvular obstruction in the outflow tract of the right ventricle. The major hazard in this operative procedure is the difficulty in defining exactly how much infundibulum to resect. If too much is resected, a left-to-right shunt at the ven-tricular level occurs with overflow into the pulmonary vascular bed. If too little is removed, the incidental injury to the right ventricular myocardium may cause ventricular failure owing to the additional load of unrelieved obstruction.

Tricuspid Atresia (Fig. 6-7). Tricuspid atresia, with or without a hypoplastic right ventricle, usually results in severe respiratory difficulty with profound cyanosis

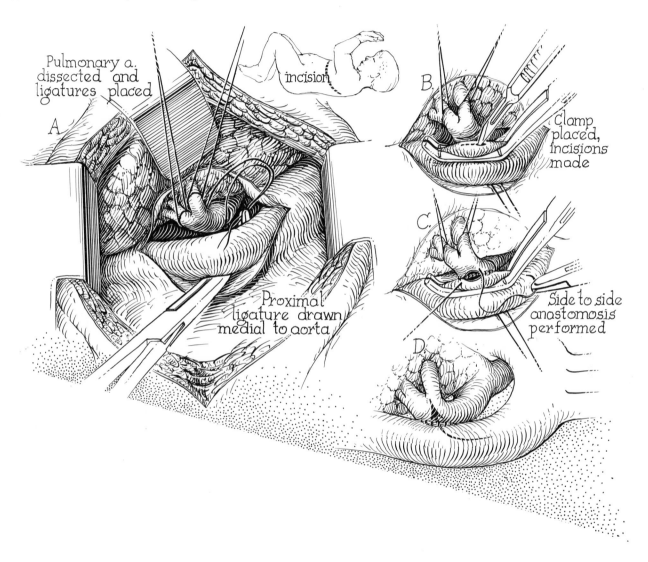

FIG. 6-5. Creation of Potts aortopulmonary shunt. (*Inset*) Lateral position. Incision through left fourth interspace. *A,* Mediastinal pleura incised over aorta. Left pulmonary artery dissected and first segmental branch and artery distal to this doubly encircled with heavy silk control ligatures. Another ligature placed proximally on pulmonary artery and drawn with right-angle clamps medial to aorta. *B,* Control ligatures tightened. Five-millimeter incision made in anterior surface of aorta within partial occluding clamp. Adjacent pulmonary artery incised. *C,* Incisions joined by continuous suture. First suture passes from outside-in on superior portion of anterior wall of pulmonary artery. Suture then passes inside-out on superior part of aortic incision. Suture passes outside-in on posterior wall pulmonary artery. Posterior suture line then made, sewing inside vessels passing needle from surgeon's right to left (aorta to pulmonary artery). Suture passed to outside through distal potion of aortic incision and held. Anterior portion of anastomosis made with another suture. *D,* Anterior suture completed. Control ligatures and clamp removed. Blood flows from aorta to pulmonary artery. (From Cooley, D. A., and Hallman, G. L.: Surgical Treatment of Congenital Heart Disease.)

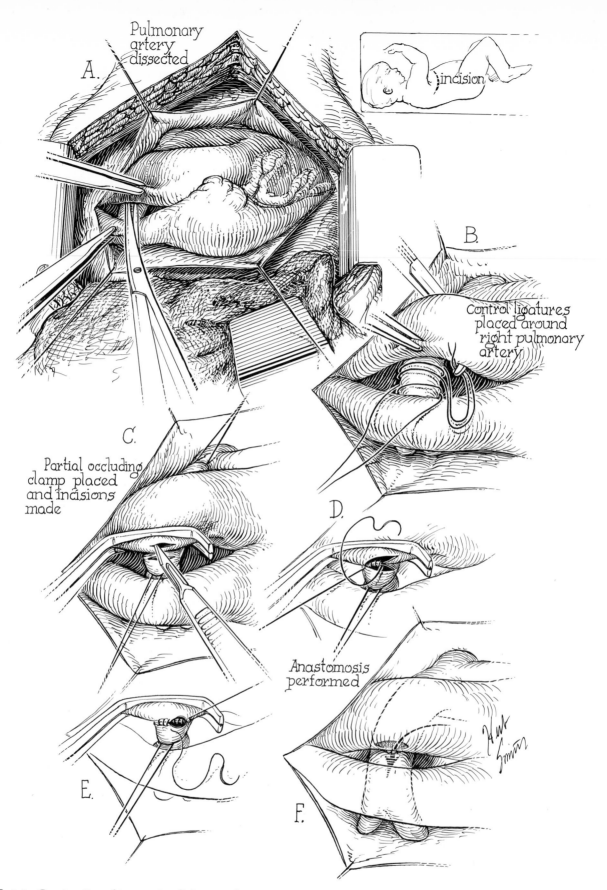

FIG. 6-6. Construction of intrapericardial aortopulmonary anastomosis (Waterston operation). (*Insert*) Anterolateral incision through fourth interspace. *A,* Lung retracted posteriorly. Pericardium incised anterior to phrenic nerve. Right pulmonary artery dissected posterior to aorta. *B,* Control ligatures placed about pulmonary artery. Lateral ligature just medial to superior vena cava. Medial ligature drawn medial to aorta by right-angle clamps. *C,* Partial occluding clamp placed on aorta and 5-mm. incisions are made in aorta and pulmonary artery. *D,* Posterior suture line placed. *E,* Anterior suture line placed. *F,* Anastomosis completed. Clamp and control ligatures removed. (From Cooley, D. A., and Hallman, G. L.: Surgical Treatment of Congenital Heart Disease.)

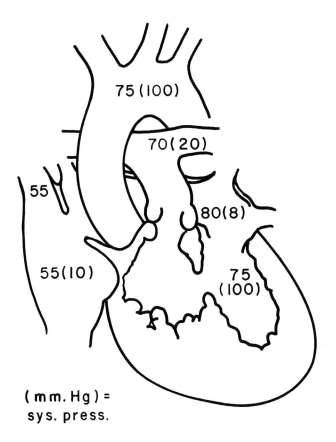

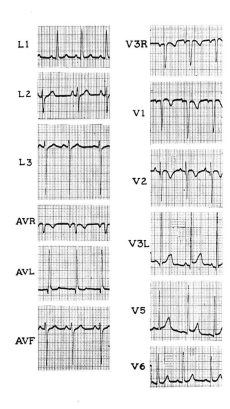

75(100)

70(20)

55

80(8)

55(10)

75 (100)

(mm. Hg) = sys. press.

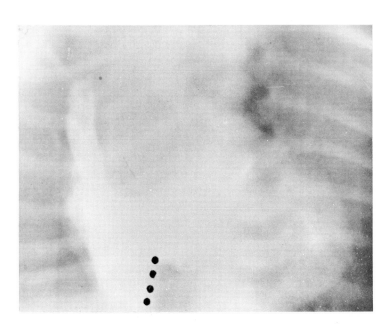

FIG. 6-7. Composite diagnostic features for tricuspid atresia. Plain figures in catheterization diagram represent oxygen per cent saturation. Figures in parentheses represent systolic pressure in millimeters of mercury.

in the immediate newborn period, especially if pulmonary atresia is also present. The major functional abnormality in this condition is a mandatory right-to-left shunt at the atrial level because of absence of a tricuspid valve. In the most common form of this anomaly, mixed left atrial blood is finally delivered to the pulmonary artery through a high ventricular septal defect, which connects to an infundibular chamber in the outflow tract of a hypoplastic right ventricle. For such a gross congenital anomaly no repair is possible at present, although several experimental operations have been reported (Haller, 1966).

From a functional standpoint the most logical operation is the Glenn procedure, in which the superior vena cava is connected to the right pulmonary artery (Glenn, 1954), allowing approximately half of the returning venous blood to bypass the right-to-left shunt within the heart and flow directly into the pulmonary artery. The major and often catastrophic difficulty associated with the Glenn procedure in a newborn infant is the inability of a tiny right pulmonary artery to accept the total blood flow of the superior vena cava. The superior vena caval pressure rises, stagnation occurs, and thrombosis at the site of the anastomosis is a constant threat. In a tiny infant, the increased pressure in an obstructed superior vena cava produces a rising intracranial pressure, causing cerebral edema, spreading of the boney sutures, and enlargement of the baby's head. Cerebral complications and venous stagnation have been responsible for a high mortality rate in infants under 6 months of age.

Because of the high mortality rate of the original Glenn operation in the newborn, several modifications have been proposed (Haller, 1966; Edwards, 1968). In older children it is an excellent palliative procedure and has resulted in dramatic relief of both cyanosis and hypoxic spells. The Glenn procedure is shown in Figure 6-8. Edwards has suggested leaving the azygos vein unligated initially to allow partial decompression of the superior vena cava. After 24 to 48 hours the baby undergoes a second operation, and the azygos is secondarily divided. More recently we have placed an untied ligature around the azygos vein, brought it through the chest wall, and tied it over a gauze pledget 48 hours later. Edwards has also emphasized the necessity of monitoring a central venous pressure in these Glenn procedures via the inferior vena cava, since the divided superior cava no longer is a reflection of filling pressure in the right heart. This is an important point, since much water and colloid may be trapped in the edematous upper half of the body with a resultant hypovolemia and increasing metabolic acidosis due to incipient shock (Edwards, 1968).

Others (Cooley, 1966) have championed a central

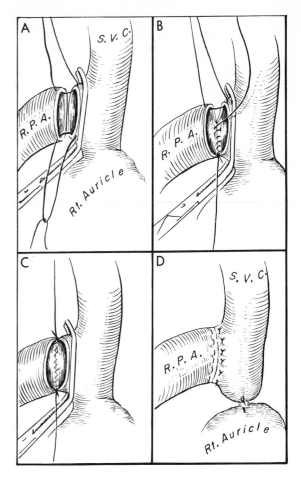

FIG. 6-8. Cavo-pulmonary anastomosis (Glenn operation): Technique for anastomosis of distal end of right main pulmonary artery to side of superior vena cava. *A,* Exclusion clamp placed on lateral aspect of superior vena cava. Distal end of right main pulmonary artery detached from its central trunk. *B* to *D,* Anastomosis completed with usual vascular suture technique. *D,* Note ligation of superior vena cava at its point of entry into right atrium. This makes shunt into right main pulmonary artery obligatory. (From Benson, C. D., et al. (Eds.): Pediatric Surgery. Chicago, Year Book Medical Publishers, 1962, Vol. I.)

shunt (Waterston operation) to palliate tricuspid atresia in the newborn (see Fig. 6-6). Our experience with a central shunt is still too limited to evaluate its efficacy in such patients. Theoretically it is not as satisfactory a palliative procedure as the venous shunt, since it does not decrease the volume of the right-to-left shunt. It does, however, prevent the serious complication of superior vena caval hypertension and its often lethal sequelae.

Valvular Pulmonic Stenosis with Intact Ventricular Septum (Fig. 6-9). Valvular pulmonary stenosis with an intact ventricular septum is a relatively uncommon cause of respiratory difficulty in a newborn infant. The associated cyanosis results from a right-to-left shunt through a patent foramen ovale. This shunt, in turn, is due to a high right atrial mean pressure, which results from failure of the right ventricle to empty itself against the severe pulmonary valvular stenosis. Unfortunately infants who have extreme difficulty in the first few hours or days of life usually have severely deformed pulmonary valves. Of greater consequence is a frequent association of either severe hypertrophy of the right ventricular musculature with an inadequate right ventricular chamber or primary hypoplasia of the right ventricle. Even if the valvular obstruction is re-

lieved by valvulotomy, many of these infants do not survive because of poor right ventricular function. The diagnosis can be made with a single contrast injection in the right ventricle.

The operative treatment of choice for these desperately ill infants is a transventricular pulmonary valvulotomy, which was first described by Brock (1948). We prefer to carry out this procedure at normal temperatures and with intermittent caval occlusion. The overloaded right ventricular myocardium is extremely irritable in these infants, and serious arrhythmias may occur if the operative procedure is prolonged or if the temperature is allowed to fall to very low levels. If the

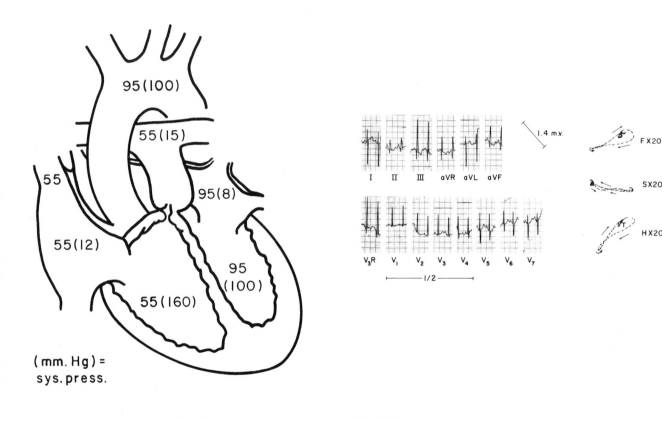

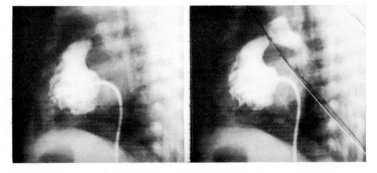

FIG. 6-9. Composite diagnostic features for pulmonary stenosis with intact ventricular septum. Plain figures in catheterization diagram represent oxygen per cent saturation. Figures in parentheses represent systolic pressure in millimeters of mercury.

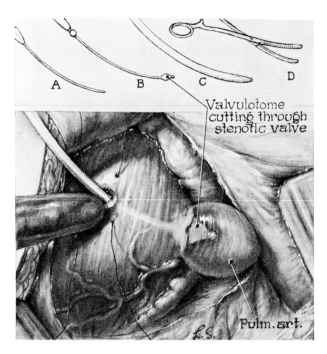

A   B   C   D

Valvulotome
cutting through
stenotic valve

Pulm. art.

L.S.

FIG. 6-10. Transventricular pulmonary valvulotomy with flat Brock valvulotome. Other instruments have been developed which greatly facilitate operation. (From Blalock, A., and Kieffer, R. F., Jr.: Valvulotomy for the relief of congenital valvular pulmonic stenosis with intact ventricular septum. Ann. Surg., *132*:496, 1950.)

right ventricle is severely hypoplastic with pulmonary atresia, a systemic-to-pulmonary shunt may be the only choice for the baby.

The operative technique we employ is shown in Figure 6-10. An attempt is made to open the valve to the full limit of the diameter of the annulus, but no attempt is made to achieve an arbitrary pressure in the right ventricle. The intermittent caval occlusion decreases blood loss from the ventriculotomy during instrumentation. Those babies who survive the operative procedure and the postoperative adjustment in hemodynamics have an excellent prognosis, and follow-up catheterization studies have shown a dramatic improvement in ventricular function and in growth and development of the right ventricle. Some of these children may require further valve surgery in later life, but the immediate threat to life can usually be relieved by the Brock operation.

Congenital Heart Abnormalities without Cyanosis

Acyanotic congenital heart anomalies that require emergency treatment in infancy consist of large left-to-right shunts with secondary pulmonary congestion. These babies, therefore, present a differential diagnosis of acute congestive heart failure. The earliest symptoms of congestive failure in an infant are tachypnea and difficulty in feeding; the earliest signs are usually a rapid respiratory rate and an enlarged liver, which may or may not be tender. Even with primary left ventricular failure and secondary right heart failure, liver enlargement in infants is an earlier sign of myocardial decompensation than is pulmonary edema, although usually tachypnea is present. The immediate problem is that of management of the congestive failure.

Basically the management of cardiac decompensation in infants is the same as in adults, but there are quantitative differences. A rapid-acting *digitalis* preparation should be administered immediately, according to the dosage schedule shown in Table 6-1. Infants require more digitalis than adults for an initial response, and they need larger maintenance doses for adequate chronic digitalization. Concomitant with initiation of digitalis therapy, an appropriate diuretic should be administered. We have found mercurial diuretics at a dosage of 0.1 to 0.3 cc. to be dependable. The newer ethocrynic acid derivatives at a dosage of 1 mg./kg. are quite effective and are less toxic to the kidney tubules. Potassium must be monitored and cautiously administered because there is a concomitant excessive

TABLE 6-1. Digoxin Dosage Table for Infants						
	Premature		Term		Neonate	
	Oral (µg/kg.)	Parenteral (µg/kg.)	Oral (µg/kg.)	Parenteral (µg/kg.)	Oral (µg/kg.)	Parenteral (µg/kg.)
Digitalizing	45	30–50	70	30–50	60–80	40–60
Maintenance	10	10	15	15	15	15

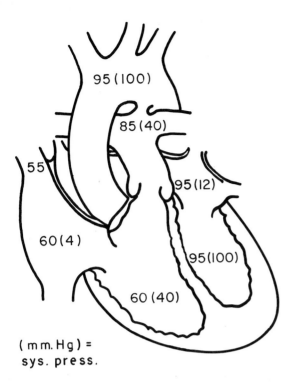

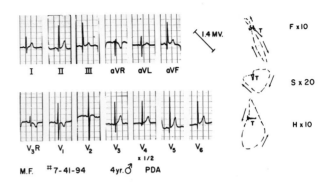

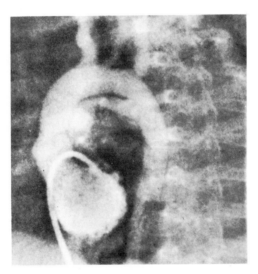

FIG. 6-11. Composite diagnostic features for patent ductus arteriosus. Plain figures in catheterization diagram represent oxygen per cent saturation. Figures in parentheses represent systolic pressure in millimeters of mercury.

washout of K+ in the urine. The intake of *sodium chloride* should be limited to decrease edema formation. Mild to moderate *sedation* is helpful in decreasing anxiety and its associated increased metabolic rate, which results in an increased utilization of oxygen. *Oxygen* is administered either in the Isolette or, in severe failure, by face mask. Great care should be taken to avoid intratracheal concentrations of oxygen greater than 40 per cent, for there is increasing evidence that higher concentrations of oxygen produce injurious effects on the pulmonary parenchyma (Shermeta, 1970). In premature infants, high intra-arterial oxygen concentrations may result in retrolental fibroplasia and permanent blindness.

As soon as an appropriate response to intensive management of congestive failure has occurred, the baby should be taken forthwith to a cardiac catheterization laboratory for a definitive diagnostic study. It is a serious error to wait until the child has had a full response to management of his congestive failure, for this may not occur, and if it does, he may begin to deteriorate again. Invaluable time will have been lost in the interim.

In acyanotic congenital heart disease catheterization usually entails left as well as right heart catheterization. Once catheterization has been completed, a definitive decision can be made regarding further therapy. It is wise to alert the surgical team at the time a baby is taken to the catheterization laboratory because the nature of the anomaly may require immediate operative intervention. Indeed, it may be imperative to transfer the baby directly from the cardiac catheterization laboratory to the operating room. Another reason for notifying the surgical staff is that complications associated with arterial catheterization may occur in small infants and require the services of a vascular surgeon (Cahill, 1967). However, left heart catheterization is usually possible in newborn infants via the saphenous vein route and through the foramen ovale into the left side of the heart.

If the baby continues to respond to the management of his congestive heart failure, no operative intervention may be immediately necessary and a diagnosis has been established. If he does not respond to these measures, operative management is instituted. Fortunately, many congenital anomalies of an acyanotic nature respond to intensive treatment of congestive failure. A definitive operative procedure can be carried out when the child is older and presents a less serious problem in anesthesia management and postoperative care.

Patent Ductus Arteriosus (Fig. 6-11). If the fetal ductus arteriosus fails to close, a left-to-right shunt remains in the newborn infant. Factors responsible for obliteration of the ductus are still under intense investigation (Rowe, 1968). Currently, normal oxygenation of arterial blood is thought to be the most potent factor in functional closure of the ductus arteriosus. As a corollary to this, any condition that causes hypoxemia may be associated with prolonged patency of the ductus arteriosus.

If a ductus is large and the pulmonary vascular resistance is relatively low, a tremendous flow of blood may come from the aorta into the pulmonary artery. This effect is similar to that of an arteriovenous fistula and produces two functional problems. One result is to decrease effective cardiac output because of the loss of shunted blood into the pulmonary circulation. This causes a decrease in peripheral flow to distal tissues, i.e., muscle and adipose tissues that may become ischemic.

The second effect is a hemodynamic problem. The shunt greatly increases pulmonary blood flow and overloads the capillary pulmonary bed. The increased pulmonary venous flow may also overload the left heart with a resulting rise in left atrial pressure. The increased pulmonary flow and the back-up left atrial pressure together catch the intervening lung in a squeeze. Pulmonary edema is the result. The edema is initially occult, with roentgenographic evidence of congestion. More rarely, it may be floridly present with rales and overt edema fluid.

Unless complicated by associated congenital heart anomalies, many patent ducti gradually decrease in

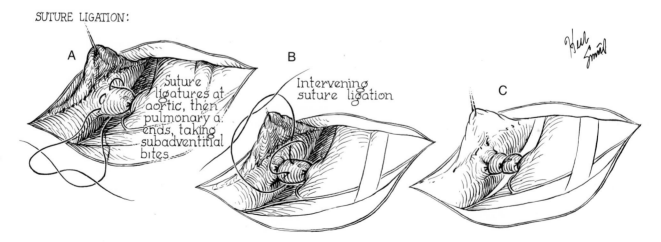

FIG. 6-12. *A,* Technique of suture ligation used in small infants. Circumferential sutures placed at aortic and pulmonary artery ends of ductus taking superficial subadventitial bites. *B,* Intervening suture ligature placed. *C,* All sutures have been tied. Flow through ductus interrupted. (From Cooley, D. A., and Hallman, G. L.: Surgical Treatment of Congenital Heart Disease.)

size. Most infants, therefore, respond to intensive therapy for congestive failure resulting from a patent ductus and ultimately become hemodynamically stable. These babies do not require immediate operative repair. However, some infants with large ductus shunts do not respond to anticongestive measures, and operative intervention becomes necessary. A patent ductus in a newborn baby may not be associated with the typical machinery murmur because of the high resistance and pressure in the pulmonary artery.

Positive pressure anesthesia helps to control pulmonary congestion. Therefore light anesthesia, often with muscle relaxants, is usually well tolerated. A left posterolateral thoracotomy is carried out through the fourth intercostal space and the mediastinal pleura is incised posterior to the vagus nerve. We prefer to encircle the aorta proximal to the ductus with braided silk, although we do not widely mobilize the aorta. The pericardial reflection on the ductus is then dissected toward the pulmonary artery from the aorta until the ductus is clearly isolated and the recurrent nerve carefully exposed.

Unless the ductus is the site of subacute bacterial endocarditis, either triple suture ligation or division of the ductus is a satisfactory technique. If the history is suggestive of endocarditis, division of the ductus is mandatory to avoid recurrence. We prefer to divide a large, short ductus and to triply ligate a small ductus. The technique for triple suture ligation is that described by Blalock and by others (Blalock, 1946) (Fig. 6-12). The division technique is a modification of that first described by Gross in 1944 (Fig. 6-13).

On rare occasions the hemodynamic alterations typical of a large ductus arteriosus are present on close examination, but an opening from the ascending aorta to the pulmonary artery is found. This is the aorticopulmonary window or aorticopulmonary fistula. Several differential features are helpful in recognizing this condition. A large left-to-right shunt is always present with severe pulmonary plethora. In addition, the murmur is usually located nearer the middle of the mediastinum than is the typical ductus murmur. The definitive differential diagnosis is made by cineangiocardiography. Since almost all newborn infants with intractable congestive failure require cardiac catheterization for definitive diagnosis, a preoperative diagnosis of aorticopulmonary window is usually made. This lesion is demonstrated by the appearance of contrast medium in the pulmonary artery as the ascending, not the descending, aorta is opacified.

If an infant does not respond to intensive treatment for congestive failure, operative intervention is clearly necessary. Although closed heart techniques have been used successfully for repair of aorticopulmonary window defects (Scott et al., 1953), extracorporeal circulation has greatly simplified the repair of this lesion. Since the window defect often lies near the bifurcation of the pulmonary artery, it is technically difficult to partially occlude these vessels. The heart-lung machine allows a much easier repair. Once on cardiopulmonary bypass, the aorta may be cross-clamped and an aortotomy used for exposure and direct closure of the defect. Another method is to cross-clamp the aorta and open the pulmonary artery. In this way both the aortic side and pulmonary arterial side can be individually sutured. We prefer the latter approach. The perfusion time is short and generally the results have been satisfactory for this lesion in older children, but in newborn infants extracorporeal perfusion contributes to a higher mortality rate.

Coarctation of the Aorta (Fig. 6-14). Profound left ventricular failure with pulmonary congestion and hepatomegaly can be associated with tight coarctation of the thoracic aorta. Isolated postductal coarctation rarely necessitates operative intervention in the first few days of life, but this anomaly may require intensive anticongestive treatment. A more serious situation accompanies preductal coarctation of the aorta, in which the hemodynamic alterations more severely affect the myocardium and the lungs (Keith, 1958). Preductal coarctation usually is associated with anomalies of the aortic valve (primarily bicuspid aortic valves) or hypoplasia of the aortic arch or ventricular endocardial abnormality (fibroelastosis). Preductal coarctation carries a formidable mortality primarily because of these serious associated defects.

The differential diagnosis includes the various conditions causing profound congestive failure in a newborn infant. The immediate step is prompt and aggressive management of congestive failure. As soon as this is initiated, an emergency cardiac catheterization must be carried out. A definitive diagnosis is usually quickly determined. Operative intervention is indicated when the baby does not improve progressively with intensive management of congestive failure (Glass, 1960; Keith, 1967).

With better techniques for effecting anesthesia in the infant and better operative and postoperative care for newborn infants, a trend toward earlier operative intervention for coarctation has developed. Much of the impetus toward early operation results from the high mortality associated with nonoperative treatment of infants in congestive failure from coarctation. This nonsurgical mortality (Keith, 1967) has been reported as high as 40 to 50 per cent.

For operative repair a left lateral thoracotomy is performed through the fourth intercostal space. The transverse aorta distal to the left common carotid ar-

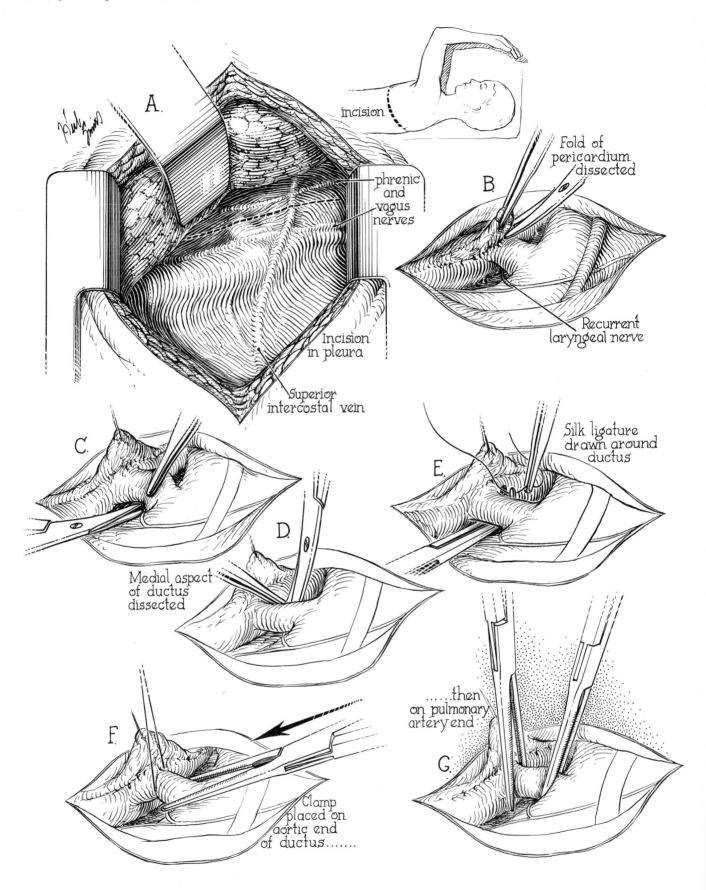

A.

incision

phrenic
and
vagus
nerves

Incision
in pleura

Superior
intercostal vein

B.

Fold of
pericardium
dissected

Recurrent
laryngeal nerve

C.

Medial aspect
of ductus
dissected

D.

E.

Silk ligature
drawn around
ductus

F.

Clamp
placed on
aortic end
of ductus.......

G.

......then
on pulmonary
artery end

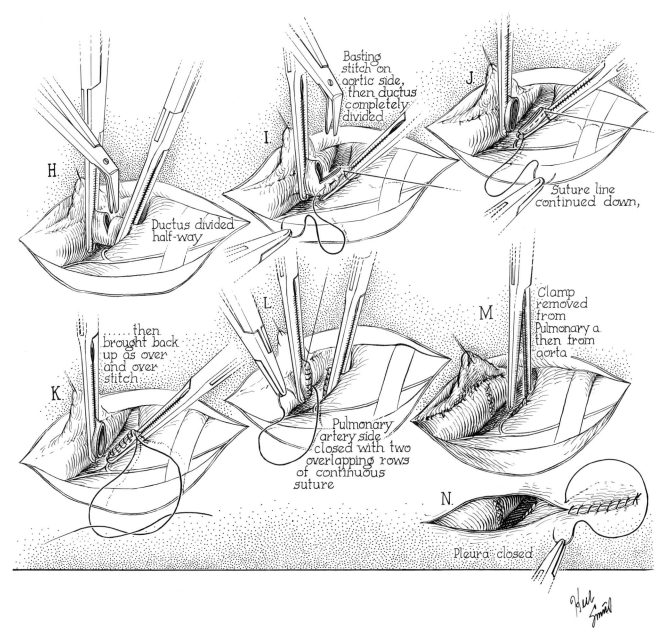

FIG. 6-13. Division of patent ductus arteriosus (*Inset*) Posterolateral incision through left fourth intercostal space. *A,* Lung retracted forward. Mediastinal pleura incised between vagus and phrenic nerves (dotted line). *B,* Recurrent laryngeal nerve identified. Ductus dissected. Fold of pericardium dissected from lateral aspect of ductus. *C* and *D,* Medial aspect of ductus dissected with forceps for gentle manipulation of ductus. *E,* Right-angle clamp passed and silk traction ligature drawn around ductus. *F,* Traction exerted on ligature as vascular clamp is placed on aortic end of ductus, avoiding recurrent laryngeal nerve. *G,* Vascular clamp placed on pulmonary artery end of ductus. *H,* Ductus partially divided with Potts scissors. *I,* Basting suture begun on aortic end of ductus. Ductus completely transected. *J,* Basting stitch completed medially. *K,* Suture brought laterally over-and-over supplementing previous basting stitch. *L,* Pulmonary artery end of ductus closed with continuous suture technique in two overlapping rows (over-and-over). *M,* Clamp removed from pulmonary artery. Clamp then removed cautiously from aorta. Supplementary sutures placed if necessary. *N,* Mediastinal pleura sutured. (From Cooley, D. A., and Hallman, G. L.: Surgical Treatment of Congenital Heart Disease.)

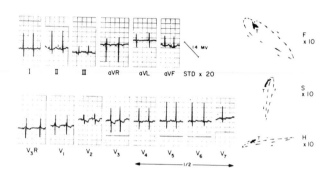

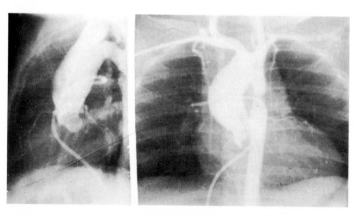

FIG. 6-14. Composite diagnostic features for coarctation of aorta. Plain figures in catheterization diagram represent oxygen per cent saturation. Figures in parentheses represent systolic pressure in millimeters of mercury.

tery, the left subclavian artery, and the descending aorta are widely mobilized and carefully inspected. In a postductal coarctation an adequate proximal segment of descending aorta is usually present for a primary end-to-end anastomosis following resection of the coarcted segment. If a patent ductus arteriosus is also present, it is divided with resection of the coarctation (Haller, 1968). It is not necessary to use a prosthetic bridge for coarctation in infants, since the vessels are elastic and can be approximated. If hypoplasia of the descending aorta is present, or if an atretic or hypo-

plastic transverse aortic arch is present, the specific anatomy dictates the best management of the lesion.

The anastomosis should be constructed with interrupted sutures so that growth can occur and a relative stenosis will not result with further growth of the patient (Fig. 6-15). Unless there are associated intracardiac abnormalities, the results of operative repair of ductal and postductal coarctation of the aorta in infants have been excellent (Haller et al., 1968). The technical repair for preductal coarctation is similar, but most of these infants have more serious pulmonary vascular changes as well as a higher incidence of intra-cardiac anomalies. When a large VSD is also present, banding of the pulmonary artery is combined with resection of the coarctation. The operative mortality is correspondingly higher in the preductal group.

A more formidable problem is presented by severe hypoplasia of the transverse aortic arch. Attempts to carry out prosthetic bridging from the ascending to the descending aorta have met with disappointing failures (Baffes, 1963). In this anomaly the ductus arteriosus contributes the main blood flow to the descending aorta, and the pulmonary vascular resistance is so high that division of the ductus often results in sudden right ventricular dilatation and acute cor pulmonale. In addition, hypoplasia of the transverse arch is commonly associated with aortic and mitral valve abnormalities, which contribute to a high mortality rate. A dependably satisfactory operative repair of this lesion has yet to be developed.

Ventricular Septal Defect (Fig. 6-16). A large ventricular septal defect produces a significant left-to-right shunt and congestive failure in infancy. As in all acyanotic newborn heart disease, the differential diagnosis focuses on causes of congestive failure. Once treatment of congestive failure is well under way, definitive cardiac catheterization is carried out and a specific diagnosis is determined. If the pulmonary vascular resistance is low and the VSD is large, it may be impossible to control the congestive failure with nonoperative measures. At the present time we believe that this situation indicates a palliative operation, which decreases pulmonary blood flow by banding the pulmonary artery. If a baby can be managed with anticongestive therapy until he reaches a weight of 4 or 5 kg., we prefer open heart correction of the VSD. Because great risk is attached to the mechanics of extracorporeal circulation in a desperately ill newborn, a palliative banding procedure is often employed for intractable failure due to a large VSD in infants under 5 kg.

Pulmonary Artery Banding (Fig. 6-17). We use a median sternotomy incision rather than a left thoracotomy with a small opening in the superior pericardium for banding the pulmonary artery in small babies. A median sternotomy is preferable because it obviates handling of the lung, which is edematous and stiff from pulmonary hypertension and congestion in these infants. A left anterior thoracotomy through the third or fourth intercostal space is a satisfactory approach for pulmonary artery banding, but the left lung must be retracted out of the way. The main pulmonary artery is surrounded with a banding ribbon (currently we are using a ribbon of knitted Teflon approximately 1 cm. wide). This band is cinched down to create a surgical pulmonary stenosis just distal to the pulmonary valve.

There is no precise means of determining the extent of stenosis desired. One must avoid too much stenosis or a right-to-left shunt through the ventricular septal defect may result. This produces a functional, surgical tetralogy of Fallot! Currently, the most widely used monitoring technique for this procedure consists of simultaneous measurement of distal pulmonary artery and proximal right ventricle pressures as the band is made snug. Prior to banding, the pulmonary artery and aortic pressures are nearly equal. Generally, an attempt is made to bring the pulmonary artery pressure to between one-half and two-thirds of the systemic (aortic) pressure. This degree of stenosis should produce a strong, palpable systolic thrill in the distal pulmonary artery and still allow adequate emptying of the right ventricle. We have come to rely more on this palpable thrill and the visible function of the right ventricle than on pressure measurements.

We prefer a technique of cinching down on the band with two hemostats or a right-angled clamp as shown in Figure 6-17. If a trial period of stenosis is well tolerated and the new pressures are satisfactory, this degree of banding is made permanent with several mattress sutures of silk. The banding ribbon must be sutured to the adventitia or epicardium near the pulmonary annulus, so that distal migration of the band cannot occur. Otherwise, the band may slide out to the bifurcation of the pulmonary artery. This migration seriously interferes with removal of a band at the time of total repair of the ventricular septal defect, because the area of stenosis includes the right and left pulmonary arteries.

As a general rule we have banded the pulmonary artery in all babies under 5 kg. with ventricular septal defects and intractable failure. We have individualized treatment for infants between 5 and 10 kg. (open heart repair vs. banding) and, for those over 10 kg., have carried out open heart repair of the ventricular septal defect (Sloan, 1967).

UNUSUAL CARDIAC PROBLEMS

A number of unusual congenital anomalies that cause profound congestive failure in infancy can be seen in any large cardiac center for children. Of these rarer abnormalities, truncus arteriosus, total anomalous pulmonary venous drainage, left coronary artery arising ectopically from the pulmonary artery, and aortic stenosis have surgical implications. As in other conditions in the acyanotic category, the major effect of these conditions is profound congestive failure. The first step

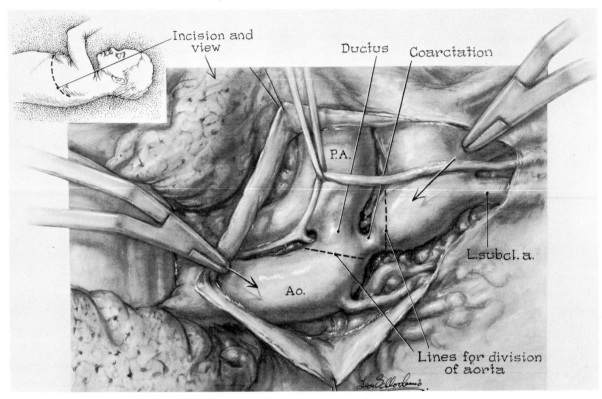

Incision and view

Ductus

Coarctation

P.A.

L.subcl. a.

Ao.

Lines for division of aorta

A

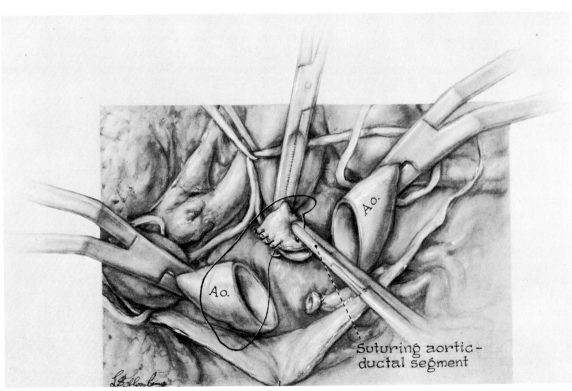

Ao.

Ao.

Suturing aortic-ductal segment

B

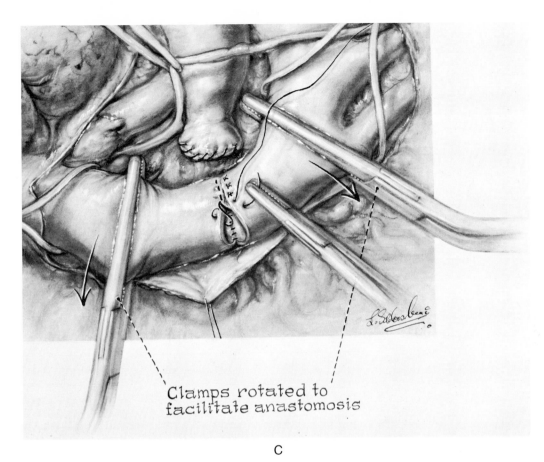

Clamps rotated to facilitate anastomosis

C

FIG. 6-15. *A,* Operative exposure for division of ductus arteriosus and resection of coarctation. Preductal coarctation of type often seen in infants is shown. *B,* Division of ductus arteriosus using coarcted segment for closure of pulmonary end. This maneuver has been most careful in large short ducti. *C,* Aortic anastomosis performed with interrupted sutures. Placement of vascular clamps as described (see surgical management) greatly facilitates placement of sutures. (From Haller, J. A., Jr., Luke, M. J., Greenfield, L., and Donahoo, J. S.: Immediate and long-term evaluation of operative treatment for combined coarctation of the aorta and patent ductus arteriosus. J. Cardiov. Surg., *9:*428, 1968.)

in management is treatment of heart failure. To initiate intelligent definitive therapy, cardiac catheterization is necessary. Babies with these unusual abnormalities are particularly fragile, and their catheterization should be in the most skilled hands.

Truncus Arteriosus. The most common form of truncus arteriosus is a single pulmonary trunk arising from the ascending aorta and giving off two pulmonary arteries. Until the recent reports of Wallace et al. (1969) and Weldon (1968), no total repair of this condition had been reported. With potential repair available, it is increasingly important that a diagnosis be made and an attempt to decrease pulmonary blood flow be carried out. Banding the common trunk of the pulmonary artery has been fraught with operative and postoperative complications and a very high mortality. For the present, an attempt at decreasing flow into the pulmonary bed by banding is all that is available, and the results have been very discouraging. Rarely a truncus

arteriosus responds temporarily to intensive management of congestive failure alone.

Total Anomalous Pulmonary Venous Drainage. In this condition the pulmonary veins drain into the right atrium through either a supracardiac vein or the coronary sinus, or rarely through an infradiaphragmatic vein. This abnormality carries a high mortality if an associated atrial septal defect is absent or too small to permit adequate mixing. Infants with a tiny foramen ovale may die within the first few hours of life. Those with better mixing may respond to intensive treatment of their congestive failure. A Rashkind balloon used to stretch or tear the foramen ovale may give acceptable palliative results. Total correction of the defect can then be carried out at a later date.

When treatment of congestive failure brings no response, operative repair has been successful in babies with drainage into the coronary sinus. The surgical procedure is usually carried out under moderate hypo-

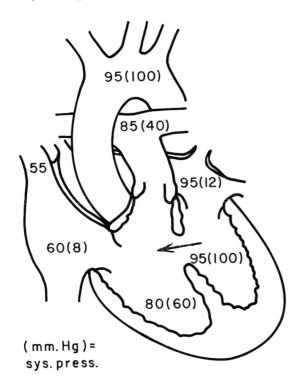

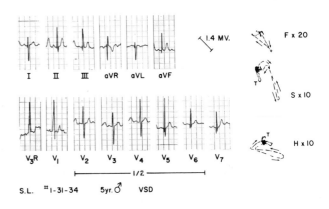

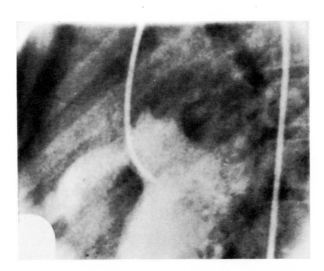

FIG. 6-16. Composite diagnostic features for ventricular septal defect. Plain figures in catheterization diagram represent oxygen per cent saturation. Figures in parentheses represent systolic pressure in millimeters of mercury.

thermia (28 to 30°C.) with caval inflow occlusion (Fig. 6-18). The coronary sinus is incised to open into the left atrium and the atrial septal defect is closed with a patch. This procedure is more easily carried out when extracorporeal circulation is used, but problems of perfusion in a desperately ill newborn are manifold. The combined use of deep hypothermia and perfusion

may be the proper approach (Dillard, 1970; Barratt-Boyes, 1971).

In infants with supracardiac drainage of the pulmonary venous return, the operative repair requires extracorporeal circulation. Because of the problems of perfusion in a young infant, successful repairs of this form of the anomaly have been recorded primarily in older children (Ryan, 1963). In the repair an anastomosis is carried out between the supracardiac vessel and the left atrium. This is followed by ligation of the supracardiac vessel and closure of the atrial septal defect. These operative maneuvers are shown in Figure 6-19.

Aortic Stenosis. Severe valvular aortic stenosis may produce profound congestive failure in a newborn infant. If the infant does not respond to treatment of heart failure there are usually significant, associated abnormalities which result in the infant's demise. In babies with isolated valvular stenosis, however, who do not respond adequately to nonoperative management, a short extracorporeal perfusion and direct commissurotomy have produced dramatic results. Usually the valve is bicuspid (Spencer, 1960). The two commissures must be opened to within approximately 1 mm. of the aortic annulus to ensure residual support

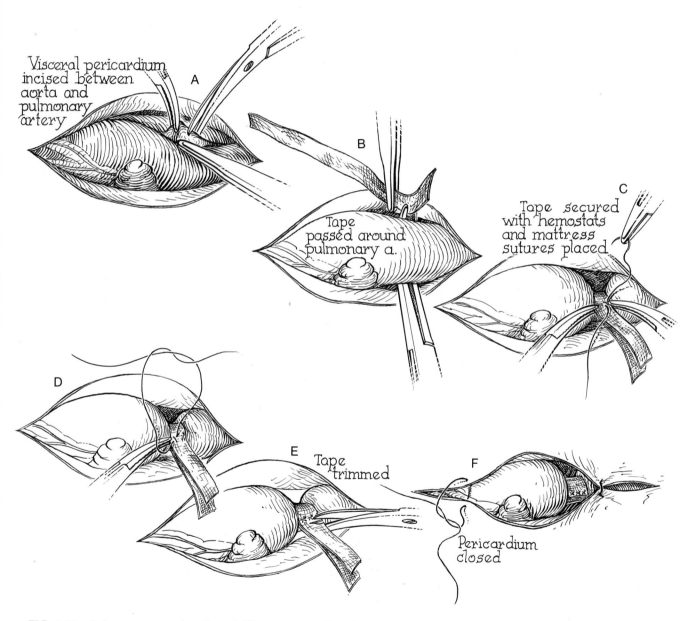

FIG. 6-17. Pulmonary artery banding. *A,* Visceral pericardium between aorta and pulmonary artery grasped with hemostat and incised. *B,* Right-angle clamp passed around pulmonary artery and Teflon tape grasped and drawn about this vessel. *C,* Tape secured with hemostats. One mattress suture placed. *D,* Other mattress sutures placed to maintain desired degree of constriction. *E,* Excess tape cut away. *F,* Pericardium closed loosely. (From Cooley, D. A., and Hallman, G. L.: Surgical Treatment of Congenital Heart Disease.)

FIG. 6-18. Correction of cardiac type of TAVR in which pulmonary veins drain into the coronary sinus. *A*, Ostium of coronary sinus is greatly enlarged. Foramen ovale is patent, but its valve is incompetent. *B*, Atrial septum between foramen ovale and coronary sinus excised. Valve of foramen ovale removed. *C*, Superior wall of coronary sinus incised, so that blood from it can drain into left atrium. *D*, Dacron patch anchored to margins of foramen ovale and coronary sinus by means of continuous suture. *E*, Insertion of Dacron patch has been completed. *F*, Pattern of venous flow after patch inserted. All blood from pulmonary vein and coronary sinus drains into left atrium behind patch. (From Cooley, D. A., and Hallman, G. L.: Surgical Treatment of Congenital Heart Disease.)

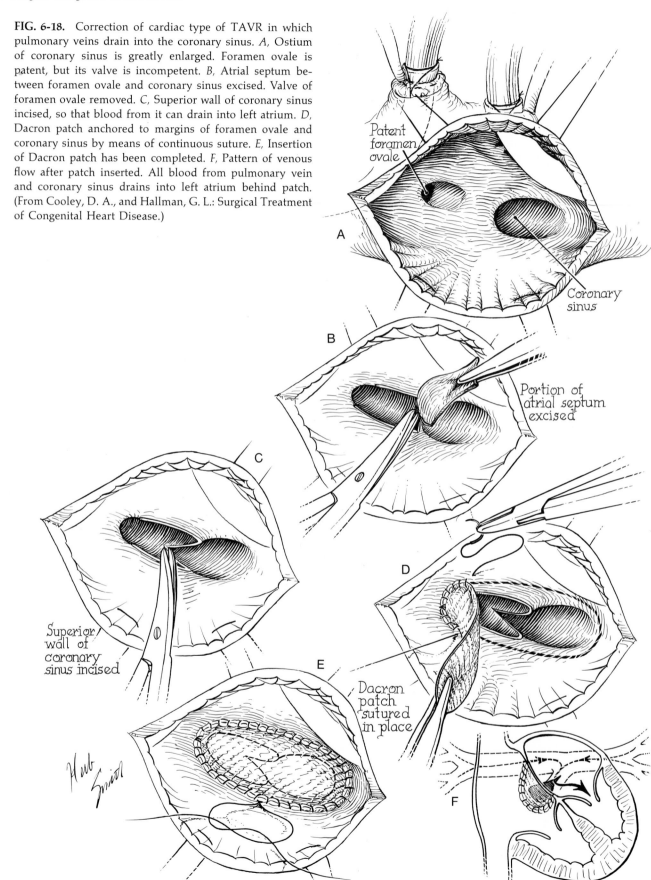

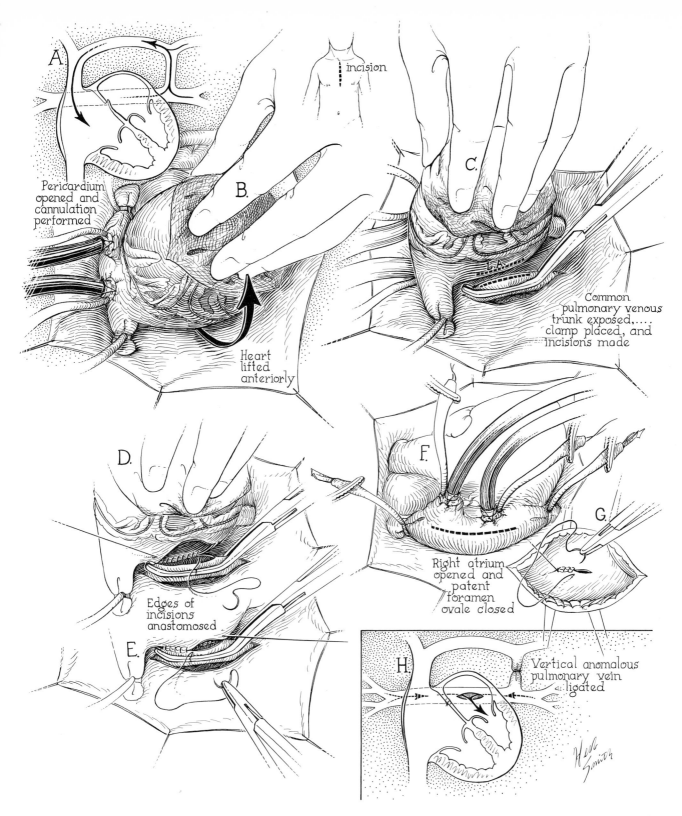

FIG. 6-19. Correction of supracardiac type of TAVR with vertical anomalous pulmonary vein ("persistent left superior vena cava"). (*Inset*) Median sternotomy incision. *A*, Pattern of venous connections. *B*, Cannulation done. Ascending aorta clamped. Heart retracted anteriorly with gauze square or traction suture. *C*, Retrocardiac transverse pulmonary venous trunk dissected and partially occluding vascular clamp applied. Incision made in pulmonary vein and posterior aspect of adjacent left atrium (dotted lines). *D*, Edges of incision united by continuous suture technique. Posterior row placed. *E*, Anterior row placed. Heart returned to pericardial sac. *F*, Longitudinal incision in right atrium exposes patent foramen ovale or atrial septal defect. *G*, Patent foramen ovale closed with continuous suture. Clamp removed. Cardiopulmonary bypass discontinued. *H*, Pattern of flow after completion of repair and ligation of vertical anomalous pulmonary vein. (From Cooley, D. A., and Hallman, G. L.: Surgical Treatment of Congenital Heart Disease.)

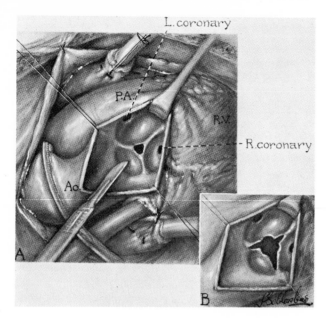

FIG. 6-20. Valvular aortic stenosis exposed with incision in ascending aorta. Aorta is occluded distally with patient on cardiopulmonary bypass. (From Spencer, F. C., Neill, C. A., Sank, L., and Bahnson, H. T.: Anatomical variations in 46 patients with congenital aortic stenosis. Amer. Surg., 26:204, 1960.)

of the valve tissue and avoid aortic insufficiency (Fig. 6-20). Aortic insufficiency from commissurotomy that is too extensive is a major complication of the operative procedure (Morrow, 1963). The ultimate fate of these abnormal aortic valves has not yet been documented, but it seems likely that they will undergo calcification and require valvular replacement.

Ectopic Origin of Coronary Artery from Pulmonary Artery. This is a rare and interesting anomaly in which the left coronary artery arises from the pulmonary artery. The clinical features are severe congestive failure, with electrocardiographic evidence of myocardial ischemia and occasionally an infarct pattern. Normal low pressure in the pulmonary artery results in a runoff of oxygenated blood from the coronary artery into the pulmonary artery. This produces a dangerous decrease of perfusion pressure within the myocardial vascular bed.

A definitive diagnosis, following treatment of the congestive failure, is obtained by injecting radiopaque dye into the ascending aorta and determining the origin of the coronary vessels. It is often possible to see contrast medium from the coronary artery spill over into the pulmonary artery. This finding confirms the retrograde flow from the left coronary artery to the pulmonary artery. Infants with this anomaly do not respond to medical management alone and should be

operated on as soon as the diagnosis is made and their condition will permit (Sabiston, 1960).

The operative procedure is carried out through a median sternotomy, which permits adequate visualization of the origin of the left coronary artery from the posterior wall of the pulmonary artery. Temporary occlusion of the coronary artery at the pulmonary artery takeoff is carried out to determine if this will be tolerated. The coronary artery is then permanently ligated. The operative procedure is shown in Figure 6-21. Occlusion is usually tolerated in infants. In a few older children, attempts at revascularization have been carried out to augment the deficient myocardial perfusion (Cooley and Hallman, 1966).

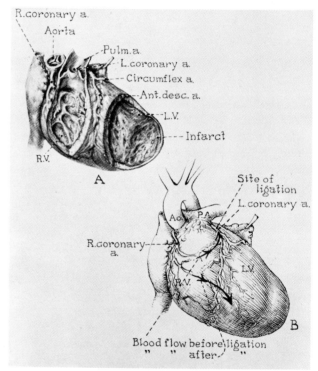

FIG. 6-21. *A*, Specimen obtained at time of postmortem examination. Left coronary artery arises anomalously from pulmonary artery. Dilated left ventricle with aneurysmal area of infarction is seen. *B*, Diagrammatic illustration of blood flow in anomalous left coronary artery before and after ligation at its origin. Prior to ligation blood flowed from aorta under systemic arterial pressure (with complete oxygen saturation) into right coronary artery and through collateral vessels into left coronary artery, with ultimate drainage into pulmonary artery in retrograde manner. Following ligation of anomalous left coronary at its origin, arterial blood from right coronary artery is directed peripherally into branches of left coronary artery where it reaches myocardial vascular bed. (From Sabiston, D. C., Jr., Pelargonio, S., and Taussig, H. B.: Myocardial infarction in infancy. J. Thorac. Surg., 40:321, 1960.)

REFERENCES

Barratt-Boyes, B. G.: Personal communication.

Blalock, A.: Operative closure of the patent ductus arteriosus. Surg. Gynec. Obstet., 82:113, 1946.

Blalock, A., and Hanlon, C. R.: The surgical treatment of complete transposition of the aorta and pulmonary artery. Surg. Gynec. Obstet., 90:1, 1950.

Blalock, A., and Taussig, H. B.: The surgical treatment of malformations of the heart in which there is pulmonary stenosis or atresia. J.A.M.A., 128:189, 1945.

Brock, R. C.: Pulmonary valvulotomy for the relief of congenital pulmonary stenosis. Brit. Med. J., 1:1121, 1948.

Bromberger-Barnes, B., Rowe, R. D., and Bor, I.: Vascular tone in ductus arteriosus. Circulation, 32:59, 1965.

Cahill, J. L., et al.: Arterial complications following cardiac catheterization in infants. J. Pediat. Surg., 2:134, 1967.

Cooley, D. A., and Hallman, G. L.: Intrapericardial aorto-right pulmonary artery anastomosis. Surg. Gynec. Obstet., 122:1084, 1966.

Cooley, D. A., and Hallman, G. L.: Surgical Treatment of Congenital Heart Disease. Philadelphia, Lea & Febiger, 1966.

Cornell, W. P., Maxwell, R. E., Haller, J. A., and Sabiston, D. C.: Results of the Blalock-Hanlon operation in 90 patients with TGV. J. Thorac. Cardiovasc. Surg., 52:525, 1966.

Dillard, D. H., Mohri, H., and Merendino, K. A.: Correction of heart disease in infancy utilizing deep hypothermia and total circulatory arrest. J. Thorac. Cardiovasc. Surg., 61:64, 1970.

Edwards, S., and Bargeron, L. M.: The superiority of the Glenn operation for tricuspid atresia in infancy and childhood. J. Thorac. Cardiovasc. Surg., 55:60, 1968.

Glass, I. H., Mustard, W. T., and Keith, J. D.: Coarctation of the aorta in infants. Pediatrics, 26:109, 1960.

Glenn, W. W. L., and Patine, J. F.: Circulatory bypass of the right heart. Yale J. Biol. Med., 27:147, 1954.

Gross, R. E.: Complete surgical division of the patent ductus arteriosus. Surg. Gynec. Obstet., 74:36, 1944.

Haller, J. A., Adkins, J. C., Worthington, M., and Ravenhurst, J.: Experimental studies on permanent bypass of the right heart. Surgery, 59:1128, 1966.

Haller, J. A., Jr., Crisler, C., Brawley, R., and Cameron, J.: Mustard operation for transposition of the great vessels. J. Thorac. Cardiovasc. Surg., 58:296, 1969.

Haller, J. A., Jr., Luke, M. J., Greenfield, L., and Donahoo, J. S.: Immediate and long-term evaluation of operative treatment for combined coarctation of aorta and PDA. J. Cardiovasc. Surg., 9:428, 1968.

Hallman, G. L., and Cooley, D. A.: Complete transposition of great vessels. Arch. Surg., 89:891, 1964.

Keith, J. D., Rowe, R. D., and Vlad, P.: Heart Disease in Infancy and Childhood. 2nd Ed. New York, The Macmillan Co., 1967.

Morrow, A. G., Goldblatt, A., and Braunwald, E.: Congenital aortic stenosis. Circulation, 27:450, 1963.

Mustard, W. T.: Successful two-stage correction of transposition of great vessels. Surgery, 55:469, 1964.

Potts, W. J., Smith, S., and Gibson, S.: Anastomosis of the aorta to a pulmonary artery. J.A.M.A., 132:627, 1946.

Rashkind, W. J., and Miller, W. W.: Creation of an atrial septal defect without thoracotomy. J.A.M.A., 196:991, 1966.

Rastelli, G. C., and McGoon, D. C., and Wallace, R. B.: Anatomic correction of TGV with ventricular septal defect and sub-pulmonary stenosis. J. Thorac. Cardiovasc. Surg., 58:545, 1969.

Rowe, R. D., and Mehrizi, A.: The Neonate with Congenital Heart Disease. Philadelphia, W. B. Saunders Co., 1968.

Ryan, N. J., et al.: Total anomalous pulmonary venous drainage. Amer. J. Dis. Child., 105:42, 1963.

Sabiston, D. C., et al.: The direction of blood flow in anomalous left coronary artery arising from the pulmonary artery. Circulation, 22:591, 1960.

Scott, H. W., and Sabiston, D. C.: Surgical treatment for congenital aortico-pulmonary fistula. J. Thorac. Surg., 25:26, 1953.

Shermeta, D. W., White, J. J., De Lemos, R., and Haller, J. A., Jr.: Pulmonary effects of lethal and sublethal oxygen exposure in lambs. Amer. Surg., 36:721, 1970.

Sloan, H. E., Sigmann, J. M., and Stern, A. M.: Early surgical correction of large ventricular septal defects. Pediatrics, 39:4, 1967.

Spencer, F. C., Neill, C. A., Sank, L., and Bahnson, H. T.: Anatomical variations in 46 patients with congenital aortic stenosis. Amer. Surg., 26:204, 1960.

Stark, J., Tynan, M., Tatooles, C. J., Aberdeen, E., and Waterston, D. J.: Banding of the pulmonary artery for transposition of great arteries (TGA) and ventricular septal defect (VSD). Circulation, Suppl., 39–40, 1969.

Wallace, R. B., et al.: Complete repair of truncus arteriosus defects. J. Thorac. Cardiovasc. Surg., 57:95, 1969.

Waterston, D. J.: Treatment of Fallot's tetralogy in infants under 1 year of age. Rozhl. Chir., 41:183, 1962.

Weldon, C. S.: Personal communication. 1968.

Ziegler, R. F., and Lam, C. R.: Indications for surgical correction of coarctation of the aorta in infancy. Amer. J. Cardiol., 12:60, 1963.

7

Gastrointestinal Emergencies

Just as in the older child and adult, gastrointestinal emergencies in the neonate are characterized by obstruction, perforation, or bleeding. In the newborn infant, however, the etiology, diagnosis, and treatment of these conditions differ significantly from those in the adult.

Intestinal Obstruction

Intestinal obstruction is the most frequent gastrointestinal emergency requiring surgical intervention in the newborn. Early recognition is essential for success, since the optimum time for surgical intervention is usually within the first few hours following birth, and any significant delay may increase the risk. Five major signs that suggest the diagnosis of intestinal obstruction are (1) maternal hydramnios, (2) excessive gastric aspirant, (3) bilious vomiting, (4) abdominal distention, and (5) obstipation (Talbert et al., 1970).

Maternal Hydramnios. Hydramnios is frequently associated with obstruction of the proximal gastrointestinal tract in the fetus, since amniotic fluid is continually ingested and absorbed from the small intestine. Normally, this fluid is then transferred to the maternal circulation via the placenta and is partially excreted in the urine of the mother (Lloyd, 1958). Obstruction of the upper gastrointestinal tract interrupts this cycle and results in the accumulation of an excess of amniotic fluid. This observation provides an early warning to the obstetrician and pediatrician which, if correctly interpreted, may significantly decrease the delay between birth and surgical intervention. Specific conditions that may be associated with hydramnios include those producing obstruction of the esophagus, stomach, duodenum, or proximal small bowel. Obstruction of distal small bowel or colon does not ordinarily produce hydramnios, since an adequate surface for absorption remains in the proximal gastrointestinal tract.

Excessive Gastric Aspirant. In many centers a nasogastric tube is routinely inserted in premature infants at the time of birth. Certainly, intubation should always be performed in the presence of maternal hydramnios. Gastric aspirant exceeding 15 to 20 cc. of fluid, particularly bilious fluid, provides presumptive evidence of intestinal obstruction. In the presence of upper gastrointestinal obstruction, a follow-up abdominal roentgenogram obtained in four to six hours almost invariably reveals distention of the proximal bowel by accumulated gas.

Bilious Vomiting. Surgical lesions produce vomiting in the newborn as a result of either intestinal obstruction or paralytic ileus. Since obstruction proximal to the point of entry of the biliary ducts is rare (except for esophageal atresia, which usually presents as respiratory distress), the color of the vomitus (i.e., bilious or clear) aids in distinguishing the usual postprandial regurgitation of infancy from pathologic vomiting. Healthy newborn infants may spit up, but no normal full-term infant ever vomits bile (Nixon, 1955). In normal premature infants, bilious vomiting occasionally may result from an immature and incompetent pyloric sphincter. Paralytic ileus may result in bilious vomiting, but is practically always associated with profound sepsis. Overwhelming sepsis is rare in the first 24 hours of life, and other signs of infection are present, including stupor and collapse.

Abdominal Distention. The newborn infant with intestinal obstruction or paralytic ileus develops abdominal distention as ingested air accumulates in the proximal gastrointestinal tract. This sign, therefore, develops late and is not immediately apparent at the time of birth. The configuration of the distended abdomen may suggest the level of obstruction. Protuberance of the epigastrium indicates obstruction of the stomach or duodenum, whereas generalized abdominal distention, usually apparent by 12 to 24 hours, suggests obstruction of the distal gastrointestinal tract. The frequent association of abdominal distention and paralytic ileus with peritonitis and sepsis must also be considered in the differential diagnosis.

Obstipation. Failure to pass meconium is another late sign of intestinal obstruction. A normal newborn may not have a meconium stool until 24 to 48 hours after birth. By this time, other signs of intestinal obstruction should be apparent if the infant has received reasonable surveillance. Occasionally small inspissated stools are passed, even in the presence of an obstructive lesion in the proximal gastrointestinal tract. Thus, *the passage of a meconium stool does not exclude the presence of an obstructive lesion requiring surgical correction.*

Serious problems that may develop later with obstruction include ischemic necrosis of bowel and perforation with generalized peritonitis. But the earliest

evidence of gastrointestinal obstruction is vomiting, with the degree of abdominal distention depending on the level of obstruction. The significant feature is *bilious vomiting,* which almost always indicates an abnormality that will require surgical intervention.

The earlier the diagnosis of intestinal obstruction is made in a baby, the better the prognosis. The reasons for this fact are: (1) the more rapid metabolic rate of an infant is associated with an increase in oxygen demand; if strangulation of the bowel is associated with the obstruction (for example, in volvulus of the intestine or incarceration of a hernia), viability of the bowel is probably lost much more rapidly in an infant because of a more rapid oxygen debt and ischemic necrosis; and (2) the small electrolyte and fluid pool that is available to a newborn infant is more rapidly compromised by losses that result from vomiting and from sequestration of fluid in obstructed loops of bowel.

X-RAY EXAMINATION

Abdominal x-rays usually provide confirmatory evidence of intestinal obstruction. In congenital esophageal atresia, a radiopaque catheter cannot be passed beyond the upper esophagus; the presence of a distal

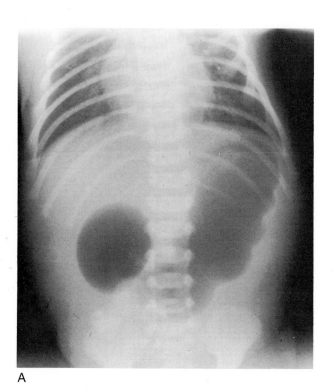

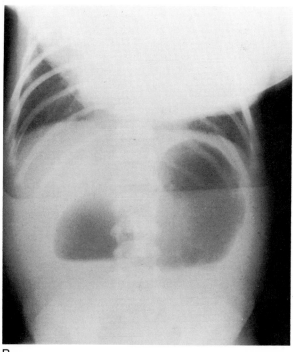

A   B

FIG. 7-1. *A,* Flat abdominal film, and *B,* upright film of abdomen, show typical features of complete obstruction of duodenum associated with duodenal atresia in newborn infant. Classic "double bubble sign" is shown best in upright film, *B,* with air-fluid level in stomach and air-fluid level in duodenum.

tracheoesophageal fistula is confirmed by the demonstration of air in the stomach. In gastric obstruction from a pyloric web, the stomach is distended and air is absent in the distal gastrointestinal tract. In duodenal obstruction, from either an annular pancreas or duodenal atresia, a characteristic "double bubble" results from two pockets of air distending the duodenum and stomach (Fig. 7-1). Complete high intestinal obstruction is manifested radiographically by distended, air-filled loops of jejunum and absence of gas in the remaining bowel (Fig. 7-2). Distal obstructions are more difficult to localize at this age because of an inability to distinguish between distended large and small bowel on plain roentgenograms of the abdomen. Diffuse bowel distention may result from a variety of obstructing lesions, i.e., ileal or colonic atresia, aganglionic megacolon, meconium plug syndrome, intussusception, volvulus, and imperforate anus. In meconium ileus, the

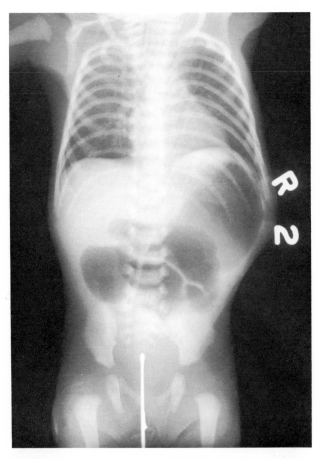

FIG. 7-2. Flat abdominal film diagnostic of jejunal atresia. Note dilated stomach, duodenum, and one or two loops of first portion of jejunum. Note complete absence of air in distal small intestine indicative of atresia rather than stenosis of first portion of jejunum.

roentgenogram may demonstrate minute bubbles of gas intermixed with meconium throughout the intestinal lumen, producing a granular "ground glass" appearance. Peritoneal and scrotal calcifications present at birth suggest intrauterine perforation and meconium peritonitis. An upper gastrointestinal radiographic study is rarely needed to diagnose newborn intestinal obstruction except in those instances in which the obstruction appears incomplete or the exact site is in doubt. A barium enema may be useful in distinguishing between the various types of lower bowel obstruction and excluding malrotation.

PREOPERATIVE PREPARATION OF NEWBORN INFANTS

In high intestinal obstruction, as caused by duodenal atresia and duodenal bands, the fluid loss is primarily gastric juice with a high concentration of hydrogen, chloride, and potassium ions. In such conditions *hypochloremic alkalosis* may rapidly develop and must be reversed prior to operative intervention. If the obstruction is at a more distal level of the intestine, as in meconium ileus and Hirschsprung's disease, acid and alkaline ions are lost in approximately equal amounts by vomiting or by isolation in obstructed loops. Typically, therefore, in lower obstructions, a generalized depletion of electrolytes and fluid results. With such conditions, babies may present with severe dehydration, marked oliguria, and mild metabolic acidosis, which may reflect inadequate peripheral circulation from hypovolemia rather than a specific imbalance of electrolyte losses. Balanced buffered salt replacement and re-hydration are necessary prior to operative intervention in such conditions.

It is our belief that the restoration of normal circulating blood volume is of greater importance in preoperative preparation than is specific electrolyte or water replacement. When adequate peripheral perfusion has been re-established, with concomitant oxygenation of tissues, operation may be undertaken. Correction of an electrolyte imbalance can be accomplished much more rapidly after an obstructing lesion has been corrected, for otherwise hidden losses are continuing during attempts at replacement. Accordingly, babies with significant electrolyte and fluid imbalances are managed best by the placement of a dependable central venous pressure monitor, as noted under general principles of care in Chapter 3. With the central venous pressure monitor and recording of serum proteins, intelligent replacement of colloid and electrolytes can be aggressively instituted to achieve a satisfactory level of central venous pressure. This ensures adequate cardiac output and peripheral perfusion if the heart is normal. When this condition is reached, the baby will tolerate general anesthesia and the operative procedures necessary for correction of the mechanical intestinal obstruction. We believe the correction of central venous pressure to high normal levels, i.e., 10 to 12 cm. water, is of greater consequence in preoperative preparation than the precise re-establishment of electrolyte figures (Haller, 1964).

GASTROSTOMY

Definitive operative treatment will be discussed under specific abnormalities, but a common component of operative management for all cases of newborn intestinal obstruction is a gastrostomy. The value of a gastrostomy in the postoperative care of an infant who presents with intestinal obstruction was pointed out by Gross and Holder (Holder, 1960), and subsequently has been emphasized by others. The primary purpose of a gastrostomy is appropriate decompression of the obstructed proximal bowel. Therefore, it is useful in all cases of intestinal obstruction distal to the stomach. The second purpose of a gastrostomy is postoperative nutrition by controlled gastrostomy feedings. In addition, we have found it a useful vent along which we insert a small Silastic feeding catheter through a high anastomosis, such as a duodeno-jejunostomy for duodenal atresia and a jejunojejunostomy for jejunal atresia. The Silastic catheter permits earlier distal feeding than is possible if we wait for the edematous anastomosis and the distended atonic bowel to become functional.

The technique for performance of a Stamm gastrostomy is illustrated in Figure 7-3. The two basic steps in this procedure are (1) placement of a double purse-string catgut suture about halfway down the greater curvature, and (2) suturing of the stomach to the anterior peritoneum with permanent suture material. We have found the No. 16 to 18 rubber mushroom catheters, with the nipple tip excised, to be satisfactory. Our preliminary experience with the newer Silastic tubes is encouraging. The gastrostomy tube may be supported on the abdominal skin by a gauze bolus.

Various devices also have been proposed for administering gastrostomy tube feedings and achieving simultaneous decompression while the feeding is progressing (an automatic burper). A simple and reliable approach is to attach a large glass syringe to the end of the gastrostomy tube. If the system is then elevated, the height of the fluid column within the tube represents the maximum pressure that can be exerted within the stomach itself. Feedings may be administered through the syringe while simultaneous decompression is achieved through the fluid column (Fig. 7-4).

Just as soon as oral alimentation is satisfactory, the gastrostomy tube is removed; but not before 7 to 10 days have elapsed to permit proper adherence of the stomach to the anterior abdominal wall. It is rarely necessary to perform secondary closure of a gastrostomy as it will close progressively by contracture.

We are opposed to the initial use of a Foley catheter for the gastrostomy, because the balloon may be caught by a strong peristaltic wave and pushed through the pylorus into the duodenum. This may cause serious gastric obstruction and result in regurgitation and aspiration pneumonitis. If catheter replacement is necessary because of leakage, a Foley catheter can be cautiously used, but it must be firmly fixed to the abdominal wall so that it cannot be carried through the pylorus.

GASTRIC OBSTRUCTION

Gastric obstruction is a rare cause of vomiting in a newborn infant. The vomitus is characterized by an absence of bile and therefore is similar to that of hypertrophic pyloric stenosis. Indeed, hypertrophic pyloric stenosis has been known to occur in newborn infants, but characteristically it is present at a somewhat later time. Therefore it will not be discussed here as a cause of gastric obstruction in the newborn.

Gastric obstruction may be due to a partial or complete membrane at the pylorus. If the membrane is incomplete, gastric dilatation and muscular hypertrophy result and may not be recognized for weeks after birth. If the veil or diaphragm is complete or practically complete, the vomiting is so severe that operative intervention is necessary within the first few days of life (Rowe, 1968).

This anomaly may occur in combination with other gastrointestinal defects and has been described in association with duodenal atresia (Haller and Cahill, 1968) (Figs. 7-5 and 7-6). An abdominal roentgenogram, as well as a contrast study of the stomach and duodenum, may be misinterpreted as duodenal obstruction, a more common anomaly. The differential feature of a gastric diaphragm is the absence of a true dumbbell-shaped gas bubble, which is diagnostic of duodenal atresia.

After adequate fluid and blood volume replacement, operative intervention should be carried out without delay. We prefer a generous transverse or right paramedian incision, because associated anomalies may be present further down the gastrointestinal tract and require treatment. Through a short anterior gastrostomy the pyloric membrane is easily identified and can usually be simply excised. If intramural fibrosis is associated with it, a pyloroplasty may be necessary to avoid secondary stenosis at the site of excision.

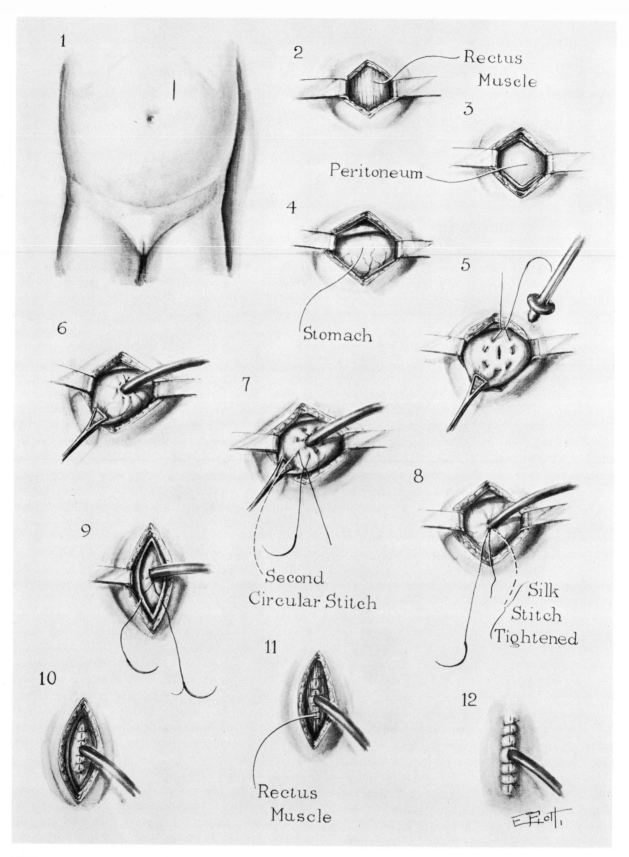

FIG. 7-3. Stamm gastrostomy. *1*, Position of short incision, midway between medial and lateral borders of rectus muscle. *2*, Anterior rectus fascia exposed. *3*, Anterior rectus fascia opened and rectus muscle split, exposing posterior rectus sheath. *4*, Peritoneum opening, exposing liver edge and greater curvature of stomach. *5*, Stomach pulled out through wound with Babcock clamp. Purse-string suture of silk placed. Stomach punctured. Mushroom catheter about to be inserted. *6*, Catheter in stomach, purse-string suture tied. *7*, Second purse-string of silk placed. *8*, Second purse-string tied. *9*, End of purse-string stitch carried through parietal peritoneum, for anchoring stomach to anterior abdominal wall. *10*, Peritoneum closed around catheter. *11*, Rectus muscle closed. *12*, Skin approximated. (From Gross, R. E.: An Atlas of Children's Surgery. Philadelphia, W. B. Saunders Co., 1970.)

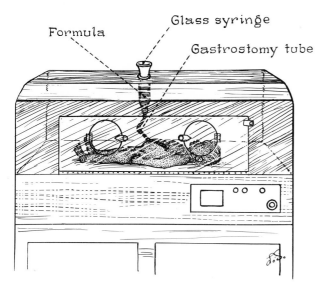

Formula — Glass syringe
Gastrostomy tube

FIG. 7-4. Method of handling gastrostomy tubes for management of baby in Isolette. Gastrostomy tube is brought through small opening in top of Isolette and attached to glass syringe which supports it. Between feedings this gastrostomy tube acts as "burp tube."

Three common causes of significant duodenal obstruction in the newborn are duodenal atresia, annular pancreas, and lateral peritoneal bands associated with incomplete rotation of the cecum. All three anomalies characteristically present with bilious vomiting, and each has an x-ray picture of tremendously dilated duodenum and stomach. If the baby is premature (less than 2500 Gm.), the cause of obstruction is probably an annular pancreas; if a mongol, the obstruction is probably duodenal stenosis or atresia; if a full-term baby, the obstruction is probably due to duodenal bands associated with malrotation of the colon (Dorst, 1970). Mongolism is commonly associated with duodenal atresia, but it is not related to an annular pancreas or duodenal bands. Since the degree of mental retardation associated with mongolism is impossible to evaluate accurately in a newborn infant, we must be certain, before we undertake operative correction of the duodenal atresia, that the parents recognize and accept the fact that we are not going to change the outcome of the baby's mongoloid state.

Duodenal Atresia. Unlike intestinal atresia below the ligament of Treitz, which results from a vascular catastrophe occurring in utero (Louw, 1955 and 1959), duodenal atresia may result from other causes. Obliteration

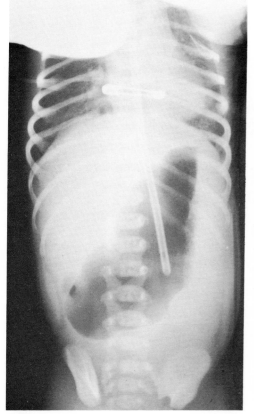

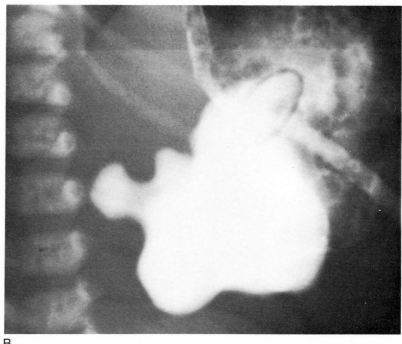

A   B

FIG. 7-5. A, Initial abdominal film at 30 hours of age in infant subsequently found to have both pyloric diaphragm and duodenal atresia. This was interpreted as showing distended stomach and gas bubble in first portion of duodenum. B, Gastrografin-filled stomach after first operation for duodenal atresia and before second operation, showing prolapse of gastric mucosal diaphragm through pylorus with complete obstruction in first portion of duodenum. Gastrostomy tube from first operation is also shown in position. (From Haller, J. A., Jr., and Cahill, J. L.: Combined congenital gastric and duodenal obstruction. Surgery, 63:503, 1968.)

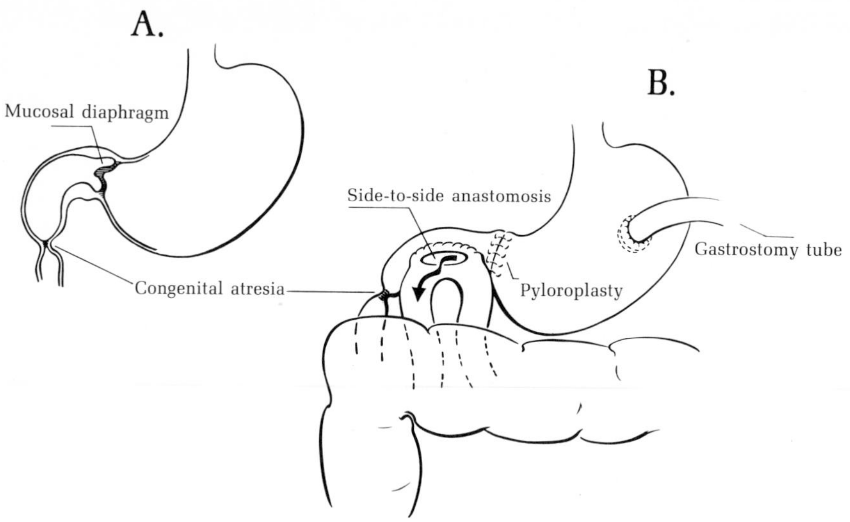

A.

Mucosal diaphragm

Side-to-side anastomosis

Congenital atresia

Pyloroplasty

B.

Gastrostomy tube

FIG. 7-6. *A,* Double obstruction due to duodenal atresia and pyloric diaphragm which was ultimately identified. *B,* Initial operative procedure was side-to-side duodenojejunostomy and gastrostomy; second operation was excision of pyloric diaphragm and pyloroplasty. Following second operative procedure patient has done well. (From Haller, J. A., Jr., and Cahill, J. L.: Combined congenital gastric and duodenal obstruction. Surgery, *63*:503, 1968.)

of the duodenal lumen during embryonic development from the proliferative stage of epithelial growth may not become recanalized (Tandler, 1902). Thus, the duodenal lumen may not be re-established. This process has been documented in the duodenum of human embryos, but has not been found to occur in the lower intestinal tract (Lynn, 1959).

Characteristically, the duodenum proximal to the site of obstruction, whether it be a complete atresia or severe stenosis, is both dilated and hypertrophied. There is reflux into the stomach, which is secondarily dilated and hypertrophied. Very little abdominal distention occurs with duodenal atresia because only a small part of the intestinal tract is dilated.

Once the diagnosis is established, the baby should be prepared rapidly for operative correction of his duodenal atresia. Because of a documented incidence of multiple areas of atresia and associated anomalies, we prefer a vertical paramedian or generous transverse incision. The procedure of choice for duodenal atresia is a side-to-side duodenojejunostomy between the distended duodenum and the first loop of jejunum. This is performed by bringing the proximal jejunum through the transverse mesocolon for the anatomosis as shown in Figure 7-7. Occasionally a side-to-side duodenoduodenostomy is possible. A gastrostomy is then carried out and a small Silastic feeding tube is passed via the gastrostomy through the anastomosis into the distal jejunal loop; if there are no associated anomalies, the prognosis is excellent.

Duodenal Bands. The major problem in the diagnosis of duodenal obstruction is in differentiating between duodenal atresia and duodenal bands associated with incomplete rotation of the cecum. This differential diagnosis is of great consequence because volvulus of

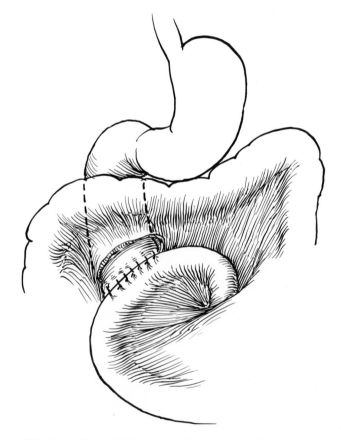

FIG. 7-7. Retrocolic jejunoduodenostomy is the usual operation for duodenal atresia, but occasionally side-to-side duodenoduodenostomy is possible. (From Haller, J. A., Jr., and White, J. J.: *In* Operative Surgery: Principles and Techniques. Edited by P. F. Nora.)

the midgut, which frequently coexists with incomplete rotation of the cecum, will cause early strangulation necrosis of the middle portion of the small intestine. Unless the infant is definitely mongoloid, it is safer to assume that the duodenal obstruction is due to duodenal bands, in which case immediate operation is mandatory. A barium enema will document the rotational state of the cecum and is useful in establishing this crucial differential diagnosis. Rapid reconstitution of blood volume and the initiation of electrolyte repletion are all that is necessary preoperatively.

Obstruction of the duodenum due to peritoneal bands is associated with failure of normal rotation of the cecum. The cecum establishes normal fixation to the parietal peritoneum in the right upper quadrant. The bands of attachment overlie the second and third portions of the duodenum and result in obstruction due to compression.

The proper management of duodenal bands is simple division with mobilization of the incompletely rotated cecum and replacement of the cecum into the lower quadrant. If the infant is in good condition and there are no other serious abnormalities, it is probably wise to perform an appendectomy because otherwise the appendix later assumes an abnormal position. The definitive procedure was originally described by Ladd and is shown in Figures 7-8 and 7-9.

Annular Pancreas. An annular pancreas results when the anterior and posterior anlagen of the pancreas become fused to form a circle of pancreatic tissue around the middle portion of the duodenum. This is associated with severe stenosis of the duodenum and

occasionally with atresia at this point. Attempts to divide the pancreatic ring have been disastrous because of the high incidence of pancreatic fistula. The proper treatment of intestinal obstruction due to an annular pancreas is a bypass procedure. The methods of choice are a duodenojejunostomy or a duodenoduodenostomy, similar to procedures used for correction of duodenal atresia. In the absence of other abnormalities, the prognosis is excellent.

JEJUNAL AND ILEAL OBSTRUCTION

Atresia of the jejunum and ileum is a more common cause of intestinal obstruction in the newborn infant than is midgut volvulus or strangulation due to internal hernias. However, the impending ischemic necrosis and perforation associated with volvulus and internal herniation make it imperative to handle as acute surgical emergencies all newborn infants with jejunal or ileal obstruction. With a history of vomiting bile and evidences of varying degrees of dehydration and abdominal distention, an abdominal film is all that is necessary to confirm the impression of jejunal or ileal obstruction. The air-filled distended proximal bowel and the absence of air-filled intestine beyond this point are indications for immediate operative intervention. Very little time can be allowed for preoperative preparation. These infants require reconstitution of adequate functioning blood volume as their primary preoperative preparation. The use of a central venous pressure monitor is invaluable in re-establishing an adequate circulating blood volume. As in all forms of congenital intestinal obstruction, an adequate abdominal incision

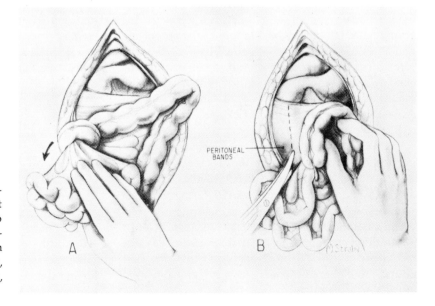

FIG. 7-8. Operative procedure for incomplete rotation of cecum and midgut volvulus. *A,* Unwinding of intestine to correct volvulus. *B,* Transection of peritoneal bands extending from cecum in right upper quadrant. (From Schwartz, S. I.: Principles of Surgery. New York, McGraw-Hill, 1969.)

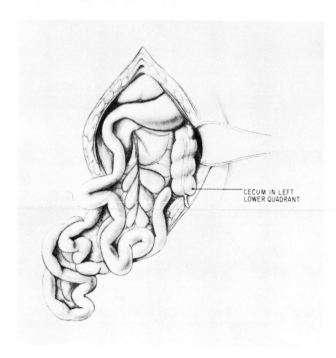

CECUM IN LEFT
LOWER QUADRANT

FIG. 7-9. Cecum relocated in left lower quadrant. (From Schwartz, S. I.: Principles of Surgery. New York, McGraw-Hill, 1969.)

is necessary to define the nature of the primary lesion and to investigate any associated congenital anomalies.

Volvulus of the Midgut. As noted in the discussion of duodenal obstruction due to aberrant cecal bands and incomplete rotation of the cecum, volvulus of the midgut is a commonly associated anomaly. Incomplete rotation of the cecum results from the failure of normal migration of the fetal cecum about the superior mesenteric vessels when it returns into the abdominal cavity from the umbilical stalk. Associated with this incomplete rotation may be a failure of fixation of the small intestine to the posterior abdominal wall. In other words, there is an absent posterior mesenteric attachment. As a consequence, the entire midportion of the small intestine hangs freely from the superior mesenteric vessels. The small intestine can easily twist upon itself, resulting in a midgut volvulus.

Approximately half of all patients requiring operation for incomplete rotation of the cecum have an associated midgut volvulus. Midgut volvulus occurring as an isolated entity is much rarer. As the volvulus continues, torsion on the superior mesenteric vessels results in strangulation and ischemic necrosis, in addition to the mechanical intestinal obstruction. It is this impending catastrophe of strangulated intestine that dictates rapid operative intervention for jejunal or ileal obstruction in the newborn.

At operation, the entire midgut must be delivered into the wound and the volvulus reduced by unwinding the intestinal mass. If there is no necrosis of the intestine, simple unwinding is enough. Surgical fixation of the small intestine is not required since handling and associated serosal injury from the volvulus are enough to produce adhesions, which prevent recurrence. It is necessary of course, to divide cecal bands if there is an associated duodenal obstruction.

If the small intestine is not viable, it must be resected. A conservative resection is imperative, since the period of rapid growth and development immediately ahead for a newborn infant will require an adequate absorptive surface of the small intestine. It is remarkable that as much as 70 to 80 per cent of the small intestine may be resected with subsequent normal growth and development, but extensive resection in a newborn infant always results in a major postoperative problem in management of both nutrition and fluid and electrolytes (Clatworthy, 1952). The recently introduced techniques of intravenous "hyperalimentation" have increased the survival rate of these unfortunate babies (Dudrick, 1968; Filler, 1969) (see Chap. 2).

It has been our policy to carry out a limited resection or none at all in those rare cases in which the entire small intestine appears gangrenous. We have generally reduced the volvulus and then returned the baby to the operating room within eight to ten hours for a "second-look" operation. If part or all of the questionably gangrenous bowel has regained viability, it can be preserved; otherwise, resection of a major portion of the small bowel is necessary for survival.

If perforation has occurred, resection is obviously necessary. Most of these infants do not develop the same toxic effects usually associated with generalized peritonitis because in a newborn infant the intestinal contents are sterile. Nevertheless, sterile peritonitis can result in significant loss of fluid into the abdominal cavity and this must be carefully replaced if an adequate circulating blood volume is to be maintained.

Atresia. Atresia of the intestine is the most frequent cause of newborn intestinal obstruction. The ileum is affected in approximately half the cases, with the duodenum and jejunum following in frequency. Multiple areas of atresia may be present although it is more common to have an isolated lesion.

As noted in the discussion of duodenal atresia, the classic explanation for the embryogenesis of atresia has been a failure of recanalization following a proliferative stage in the development of the intestine. Apparently this process is applicable only to the duodenum. Following the elegant experimental studies of Louw and Barnard (1955), which demonstrated that atresia of the small intestine could be produced by ligation of the mesenteric vessels of fetal puppies, many clinical examples of vascular catastrophes occurring in utero have been recorded. These vascular injuries may result from intrauterine intussusception (Parkkulainen, 1958), from volvulus (Louw, 1955), from strangulation during the period of physiologic herniation of the small intestine into the umbilical stalk (Nixon, 1955), from internal herniation, and perhaps from congenital anomalies in the blood vessels themselves. This embryogenesis of atresia has now been experimentally and clinically documented. The major cause of jejunal and ileal atresia is a vascular catastrophe occurring in utero. Atresia is rarely a genetically determined anomaly (Esterly and Talbert, 1969).

The signs and symptoms of intestinal atresia are identical to those for any other cause of mechanical obstruction. In low ileal or colonic obstruction, vomiting may be delayed for 24 to 36 hours following birth, but characteristically it occurs shortly after delivery. Vomiting of *bilious material* is the *sine qua non* of mechanical intestinal obstruction in the newborn. The degree of abdominal distention is related to the level of the lesion and the extent of effective decompression that occurs from vomiting.

Polyhydramnios is commonly associated with obstruction of the gastrointestinal tract of the fetus and should alert the physician to this possibility prior to delivery (see p. 86). Since early diagnosis and expeditious surgical intervention contribute materially to a lower mortality from atresia, a clinical hint provided by polyhydramnios may significantly lower the mortality associated with intestinal atresia.

Jejunal atresia may be confused with midgut volvulus. With midgut volvulus there is usually some gas distal to the obstruction and the jejunum is not dilated, but a large duodenum may be present. Ileal atresia is difficult to differentiate from meconium ileus on the basis of roentgenographic findings. A Gastrografin enema may differentiate the condition and occasionally may relieve the obstruction. Frequently in meconium ileus the roentgenogram reveals minute bubbles in the intestinal lumen in the regions where the meconium is mixed with gas, but this is not a consistent diagnostic feature.

Operative treatment of jejunal and ileal atresia requires decompression of the proximal dilated bowel and generous resection of the hypertrophied blind end. The distal collapsed bowel must be carefully distended with air or saline to ascertain the patency of the lower intestinal tract.

Following adequate resection, ideally an end-to-end or end-to-back anastomosis is carried out, as shown in Figure 7-10.

Generally, a primary anastomosis is best performed with a single layer of fine nonabsorbable suture, but a double-layer anastomosis also has yielded good results. Although side-to-side anastomoses are easier to perform, they are associated with a high incidence of later blind-loop obstruction and should be avoided (Figure 7-10*B*).

The necessity for generous resection of the proximal dilated pouch has not been adequately emphasized. This hypertrophied bowel must be resected since it lacks normal peristaltic activity. If retained, it represents a primary cause of failure of anastomotic function owing to a type of paralytic ileus.

In rare instances, when primary resection and anastomosis of the ileum are not feasible (as in perforated meconium ileus), an exteriorization operation may be performed as shown in Figure 7-11. The proximal and distal blind loops are sewn together along their antimesenteric surfaces and are brought out through a separate abdominal wound. After the wound has been carefully closed around this double barrel, the loops are opened to decompress the proximal bowel and to provide a portal for the injection of fluid into the distal intestine. After four to five days a small crushing clamp is inserted to obliterate the septum between the two limbs and provide a single stoma which can then be secondarily closed in ten days to two weeks (Randolph, et al., 1963).

The collected mortality for jejunal and ileal atresia reported by Gross in 1951 was 90 per cent, but a year later he was able to report a 70 per cent survival by using the exteriorization procedure (Gross, 1953). With recent advances in fluid and electrolyte replacement, anesthesia, and postoperative care, a comparable survival rate has been reported for primary resection and anastomosis. Nevertheless, the exteriorization procedure, a double-barrel ileostomy, is helpful in the management of unusual problems.

We prefer gastrostomy, not decompression by nasogastric tube in the postoperative period. In the case of jejunal anastomosis, a small catheter may be threaded alongside the gastrostomy tube through the anastomosis and into the distal small intestine. A small Silastic catheter has been most satisfactory in our hands. It can then be attached to a continuous infusion pump and a progressive formula delivered to the baby.

Internal Hernias and Adhesive Bands. Internal herniation of the intestine occurs through congenital defects in the mesentery of the small intestine. Hernias may result from a paraduodenal anomaly and hernial sac or may occur through an actual rent in the mesentery (Zimmerman, 1953). Examples of these two forms of internal herniation are shown in Figures 7-12 and 7-13.

The presenting features of such hernias are similar

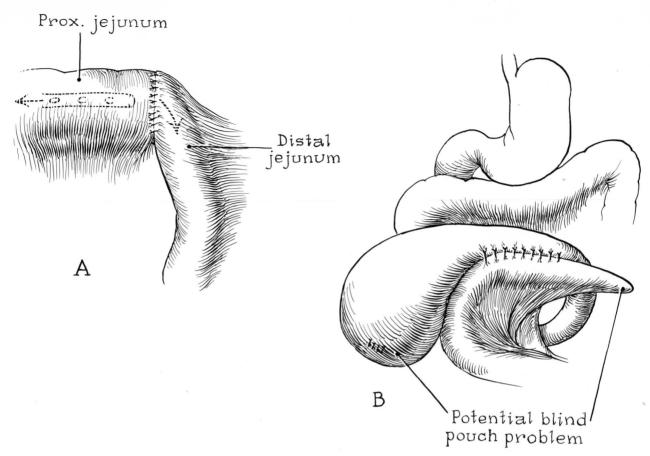

FIG. 7-10. *A*, End-to-side (end-to-back) anastomosis is preferred for jejunal and ileal atresia. The distended and atonic proximal pouch is resected back to more normal bowel, and postoperative decompression is used to help the bowel regain normal peristalsis. *B*, Side-to-side anastomosis should be practically obsolete because of high incidence of blind pouch dilatation with secondary obstruction. (From Haller, J. A., Jr., and White, J. J.: *In* Operative Surgery: Principles and Techniques. Edited by P. F. Nora.)

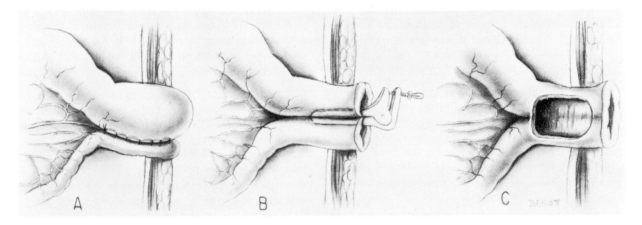

FIG. 7-11. Exteriorization procedure for ileal atresia or meconium ileus. *A*, Proximal dilated bowel and distal contracted bowel sutured together and brought out through abdominal wall; double-barrel colostomy is performed to decompress proximal intestine and permit irrigation of distal intestine. *B*, After 4 or 5 days, crushing clamp is inserted to crush septum between 2 limbs. *C*, Septum crushed and intestinal continuity established. Colostomy may be closed within 2 weeks. (From Schwartz, S. I.: Principles of Surgery. New York, McGraw-Hill, 1969.)

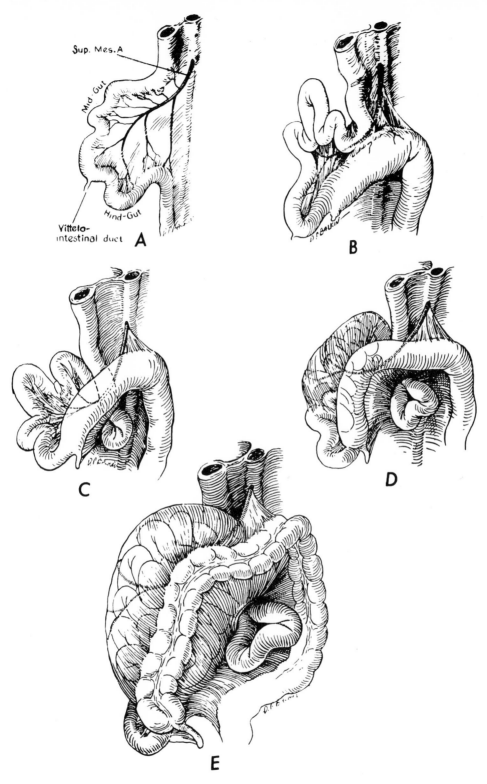

FIG. 7-12. Anomalous rotation of intestine resulting in right paraduodenal hernia. *A,* Original position of midgut. *B,* Rotation is delayed and small bowel loops return to peritoneal cavity before this occurs. *C,* Loops of small intestine are trapped behind the mesentery of the descending colon as rotation occurs. *D,* Completed rotation with almost entire small bowel behind mesentery of right colon. *E,* Characteristic position of small intestine in right paraduodenal hernia. (From Zimmerman, L. M., and Laufman, H.: Intra-abdominal hernias due to developmental and rotational anomalies. Ann. Surg., *138:*82, 1953.)

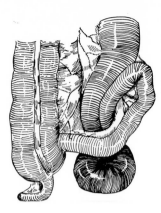

FIG. 7-13. Mesenteric hernia with intestine prolapsing through defect. (From Gross, R. E.: Surgery of Infancy and Childhood. Philadelphia, W. B. Saunders Co., 1953.)

to those of mechanical intestinal obstruction in general. It is uncommon to find this etiology for complete intestinal obstruction at birth. Internal hernias usually result in partial intestinal obstruction and are noted in later infancy and early childhood.

Operative correction consists of reduction of the hernia and resection of bowel if strangulation necrosis has occurred. If the herniated intestine is viable, the mesenteric defect can be repaired or the paraduodenal hernial sac closed with sutures. As in all cases of small intestinal obstruction in the newborn, we believe that a gastrostomy aids considerably in postoperative decompression and subsequent feeding of the infant.

Meconium Ileus. Meconium ileus accounts for approximately 10 to 20 per cent of the cases of lower intestinal obstruction in the newborn requiring surgical intervention. It occurs in about 10 per cent of proved cases of cystic fibrosis and is a manifestation of muco-viscidosis. Meconium ileus is probably associated with mucoviscidosis in at least 80 to 90 per cent of cases. The fact that infants with mucoviscidosis have other serious exocrine problems and associated pancreatic insufficiency is not, to us, a contraindication to the repair of mechanical intestinal obstruction. Ultimately, most of these infants with cystic fibrosis die of secondary pulmonary sepsis (Donnison, 1966). Better techniques for the management of the pulmonary problems are constantly being developed and, therefore, the relatively simple surgical lesion should be handled operatively.

The major functional abnormality associated with meconium ileus is obstruction of the distal ileum by inspissated meconium and a dilated proximal small intestine. Volvulus of the dilated, meconium-filled ileum, perforation, and meconium peritonitis are serious secondary complications of meconium ileus. Often it is possible to palpate several rubbery loops of intestine in a newborn baby. Meconium is rarely passed per rectum, and then in small quantities, in infants with meconium ileus.

If perforation of the intestine has occurred in utero and meconium peritonitis has developed prior to birth, calcific densities may be seen throughout the peritoneal cavity on the x-ray examination. These calcifications and bubbles of air within the inspissated meconium on an abdominal roentgenogram are strongly suggestive of meconium ileus.

Two major operative approaches have been employed for uncomplicated meconium ileus. The first was introduced by Gross as a type of Mikulicz resection in which the distended portion of the ileum, containing inspissated meconium, is excised and a double-barrel ileostomy is created similar to the one described for ileal atresia. The most commonly used procedure was introduced by Bishop and Koop (1957) and is shown in Figure 7-14. Following resection the distal normal bowel is brought through the abdominal wall through a separate stoma to create an ileostomy. The proximal normal intestine is anastomosed to the side of this loop of bowel approximately 4 to 5 cm. from the ileostomy. A small catheter is then inserted through the ileostomy into the distal bowel and solutions instilled to liquify the remaining meconium plugs.

The single most effective solution for clearing meconium from the obstructed intestine is acetylcysteine or Mucomist (Meeker, 1964). Other substances such as

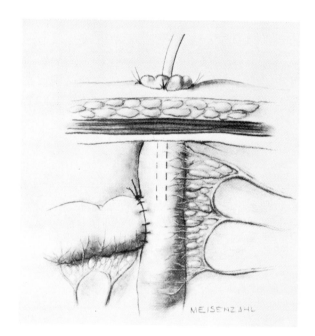

FIG. 7-14. Bishop-Koop procedure for meconium ileus. Resection of maximally distended ileum and end-to-side Roux-Y anastomosis between proximal and distal ileum, leaving one segment as a distal ileostomy. (From Schwartz, S. I.: Principles of Surgery. New York, McGraw-Hill, 1969.)

saline, hydrogen peroxide, and pancreatic enzymes have been used but are less effective. Postoperatively this solution is instilled into the distal ileostomy stoma until the remaining thick meconium is liquified and evacuated. A Gastrograffin enema may be useful in cleansing the distal colon. If the meconium obstruction has not been present too long in utero, it is possible to open the ileum and wash out the thick meconium with a Mucomist lavage. The ileotomies can then be closed and a gastrostomy carried out to complete the operative management.

Unfortunately, the overall mortality associated with meconium ileus is still in the range of 50 per cent. This high mortality results not only from the complications of volvulus, perforation, and peritonitis associated with meconium ileus, but also from the common occurrence of significant respiratory insufficiency in a newborn infant with mucoviscidosis. Kiesewetter (1971) has reported a 25 per cent long-term survival in babies who recover from an operation for meconium ileus. This discouraging long-term attrition rate is due to continuing loss of patients from pulmonary sepsis.

COLONIC OBSTRUCTION

Most congenital anomalies that result in colonic obstruction require the construction of a temporary colostomy as a part of the overall management of the newborn infant. The technical aspects of colostomy construction are unique in an infant.

Colostomy. The major indications for colostomy in infants and young children are imperforate anus and Hirschsprung's disease. Since both conditions ultimately require definitive pelvic operative procedures, the proper construction of a colostomy is important in both immediate and late treatment. A sigmoid or transverse colostomy may be used for both. In Hirschsprung's disease the colostomy must be placed in ganglion-containing bowel, the presence of ganglion cells being carefully checked by frozen section at the time of operation.

Since the colostomy is elective, an extensive incision to facilitate abdominal exploration is unnecessary. A transverse incision usually is preferred, and the abdomen is entered through a muscle-spreading, gridiron type dissection, in either the right upper quadrant for a transverse colostomy or the left lower quadrant for a sigmoid colostomy (Fig. 7-15A).

A loop colostomy is initially satisfactory, with subsequent division of the posterior wall if complete defunctionalization of the distal bowel is needed. The practice of inserting a glass rod for support of the colon loop in adults would be disastrous in an infant because his relatively increased intra-abdominal pressure can result in either paracolonic evisceration or significant prolapse of the colon, or both.

The selected loop of colon is freed of its peritoneal attachments until it can be brought easily through the abdominal wall without tension (Fig. 7-15B). The edges of the mesentery are then carefully sutured to the parietal peritoneum. The serosa of the colonic loop must be sutured, preferably with fine chromic catgut, to each layer of the abdominal wall: peritoneum, fascia, subcutaneous tissue, and skin (Fig. 7-15C). Usually it is possible to close the fascia with several sutures under the colostomy loop for added support. Many surgeons prefer to use, in addition, a rubber catheter for support of the loop colostomy (Fig. 7-16A, B, C).

The colostomy may be sutured immediately, especially in a newborn infant with an imperforate anus in whom there is practically no fecal bacterial problem (Fig. 7-16D). Even in an older infant immediate suturing is satisfactory, since the serosa will have been sutured to the subcutaneous tissues and this is well sealed before the colon is opened and its mucosa sutured directly to the skin edges.

Some surgeons prefer to close the skin under a colostomy loop to form a permanent skin bridge. Others prefer to suture the mucosa directly to the skin edges. The important principle in the creation of a colostomy in infants is that each layer be securely attached to the serosa of the colon to avoid evisceration and prolapse. The posterior wall of the loop colostomy may be divided with the cautery several days following the creation of the colostomy, just as with an adult colostomy.

With proper attention to detail, the postoperative management of a newborn with a colostomy should prove almost as easy as caring for a normal infant. The pediatrician must guard against the development of constipation or stenosis of the colostomy orifice. It is necessary to dilate the colostomy stoma periodically and/or add stool softeners such as Malsupex. Irritation of the skin around the colostomy orifice is caused by excessive moisture. This complication should be treated by applying an inexpensive, powdered cornstarch to the skin. If maceration develops, Karaya gum powder should be substituted for cornstarch. Certainly no adjustment is required of the patient in these cases, because the care of an infant's bowel function requires a diaper whether it be over the abdominal wall or at the usual anal orifice! The ultimate reconstruction of colonic continuity is discussed under the individual congenital defects. Reconstitution is usually completed at about 18 to 24 months of age, when normal toilet training becomes a consideration.

Meconium Plug Syndrome. Long tenacious plugs of inspissated meconium may stop up the distal colon and

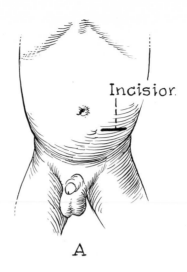

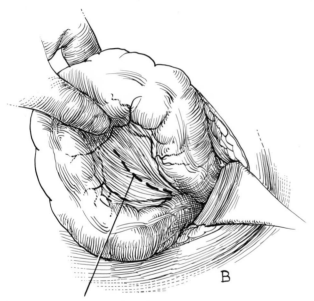

Incision in avascular
area of mesosigmoid

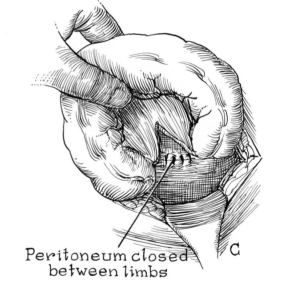

FIG. 7-15. *A,* For elective sigmoid colostomy, transverse left lower quadrant incision is preferred. *B,* Sigmoid loop is delivered through muscle-splitting incision and mesentery opened. *C,* Mesentery and serosa of colon are sutured to peritoneum with multiple interrupted sutures. (From Haller, J. A., Jr., and White, J. J.: *In* Operative Surgery: Principles and Techniques. Edited by P. F. Nora.)

rectum and produce temporary complete obstruction of the large intestine (Mikity, 1967). Typically, a small amount of meconium is passed initially by these babies and then increasing abdominal distention occurs. Varying degrees of meconium plugging occur in many babies and is not associated with systemic disease. In a few cases it may be a variant of meconium plugging of the ileum (meconium ileus), which is usually associated with mucoviscidosis and pancreatic dysfunction.

The initial step in evaluation of newborn obstipation is to examine the anus to make certain the obstruction does not result from high rectal stenosis or atresia. This can be determined by rectal examination with the little finger and verified with a barium enema.

Frequently, the digital examination and the barium enema result in expulsion of a long meconium cast and the baby is cured. Not infrequently, multiple enemas are required to empty the whole colon. A typical

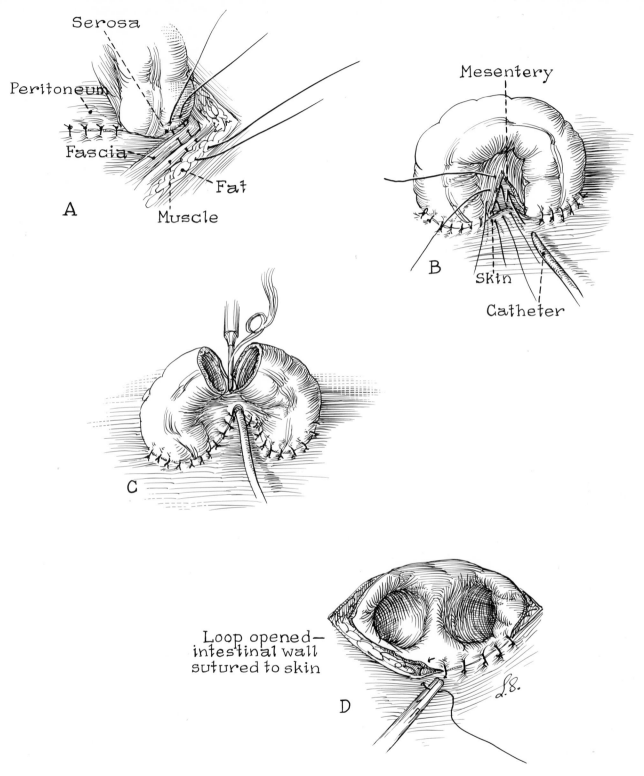

FIG. 7-16. *A*, Each layer of abdominal wall is similarly sutured to serosal coat of colon. *B*, Soft rubber catheter may be passed through mesentery to facilitate subsequent division of loop of colon with electric cautery. Serosa is also sutured to skin. *C*, Antimesenteric wall is opened on day of operation if desired and mesenteric wall 24 to 48 hours later. *D*, Many surgeons prefer to mature loop colostomy in operating room by opening bowel and suturing mucosa to skin. This is appropriate when no major obstruction factor is present in colon with pooling of toxic fecal material. (From Haller, J. A., Jr., and White, J. J.: *In* Operative Surgery: Principles and Techniques. Edited by P. F. Nora.)

roentgen finding in meconium plug syndrome is shown in Figure 7-17. Recently, the hypertonic effect of Gastrograffin (or other hypertonic contrast media) enemas has been described as highly effective in dislodging and eliminating meconium plugs. There is some evidence that babies with Hirschsprung's disease may also present with a meconium plug syndrome. All such infants should be carefully observed during their neonatal growth and development.

Atresia of the Colon. Atresia and congenital stenosis of the large bowel are rare. If the predominant etiology of atresia is a vascular catastrophe, as seems to be the case with atresia of the small bowel, it may well be that vascular injuries are much less common in the colon and of less consequence because of excellent collateral circulation.

Resection and primary anastomosis constitute the treatment of choice for this rare anomaly. If the baby is not seen until tremendous distention of the proximal

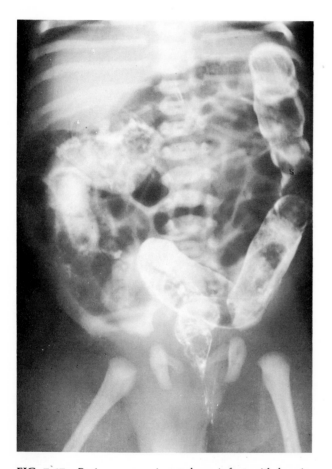

FIG. 7-17. Barium enema in newborn infant with low intestinal obstruction. Tube-like radiolucent areas represent inspissated meconium plugs which were subsequently passed by this infant, relieving his colonic obstruction.

colon has taken place, a colostomy may be necessary as an emergency measure.

Hirschsprung's Disease (Congenital Megacolon). Hirschsprung's disease is a congenital absence or agenesis of the myenteric parasympathetic nerve ganglia in the distal colon and rectum. This deficiency in the myenteric plexus results in a tonic contracted state of the involved segment and produces the major functional abnormality of Hirschsprung's disease, namely mechanical intestinal obstruction of the distal colon. This condition is, therefore, characterized by chronic constipation, dating from birth, with the attendant complications of hypertrophy of the immediately proximal bowel and ultimately of gross dilatation of the colon. Thus, the descriptive term "congenital megacolon" is appropriate.

The major pathophysiology of Hirschsprung's disease results from distorted peristaltic activity in the area of aganglionosis. The secondary intestinal obstruction produces varying degrees of dysfunction, ranging from mild constipation to marked intestinal obstruction in the newborn infant. The latter may necessitate emergency decompression.

A typical history of a patient with Hirschsprung's disease is characterized by constipation dating from birth. Since this is a congenital abnormality, it is not surprising that symptoms of constipation should begin in the immediate neonatal period, but it is often difficult to document this from the history. The time of onset of constipation is a crucial point in the differential diagnosis, since the condition that most closely mimics congenital megacolon, acquired megacolon, or pseudo-Hirschsprung's disease (Ravitch, 1958), does not begin in the neonatal period but rather after the child becomes bowel conscious. Explosive diarrhea may indicate a form of ulcerative enterocolitis, which complicates the obstruction. This may lead to early perforation and gram-negative septicemia. Characteristic punched-out ulcer lesions may be seen in the dilated colon on air contrast barium enema. Babies with enterocolitis are desperately ill and require immediate colonic decompression by emergency colostomy (Bill, 1962).

Diagnosis. As noted, a significant feature in the diagnosis of congenital megacolon is a history of the onset of troublesome constipation in the first few hours or days of life. Failure to thrive with poor weight gain may be a presenting feature of some young infants with constipation from Hirschsprung's disease (Felman, 1971). X-ray examination of the colon by a contrast technique confirms the presence of a contracted distal segment and elongation of the sigmoid colon. Most radiologists prefer to carry out their barium enema studies before enemas have been used to remove all

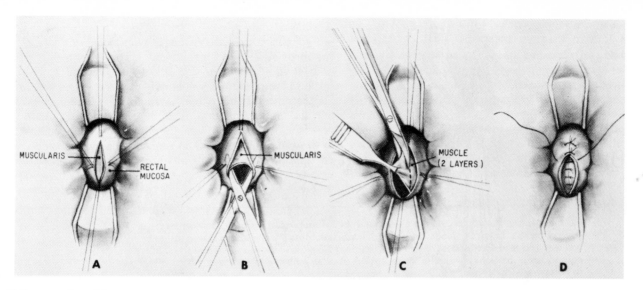

FIG. 7-18. Rectal biopsy to determine absence of myenteric parasympathetic ganglia. *A*, Retractors in anus; rectal mucosa incised. *B*, Mucosa separated from muscularis, which is being mobilized. *C*, Muscularis being excised. *D*, Mucosa and muscularis closed in layers. (From Benson, C. D., et al. (Eds.): Pediatric Surgery. Chicago, Year Book, 1962, Vol. 2.)

of the fecal material from the colon. In a classic example of Hirschsprung's disease, the contracted distal segment is seen to descend near to the anus and is best demonstrated on a lateral film. On the 24-hour follow-up film, barium is still present in the distal colon. Experienced children's radiologists usually can make a differential diagnosis of Hirschsprung's disease on the basis of a careful barium enema.

A definitive diagnosis of Hirschsprung's disease is made by a rectal biopsy through the full thickness of the muscular coat of the distal rectum just inside the anus, by removal of an ellipse of mucosa and both muscle layers from the posterior rectum (Fig. 7-18). The histologic evaluation of the excised bowel wall reveals an absence of myenteric parasympathetic ganglia. An increase in the number of myenteric nerve bundles or trunks is usually observed in association with this.

In the young infant who presents primarily with mechanical intestinal obstruction and obstipation, the procedure of choice is a proximal colostomy, which will decompress the obstructed bowel and prevent further dilatation of the colon (Shim, 1966). The technique of colostomy is no different from that of colostomy for other infants, but it should be re-emphasized that in all infants it is imperative that the colonic serosa be sutured carefully to both the peritoneum and the fascia to avoid an almost inevitable herniation of small bowel around the colostomy (Figs. 7-15 and 7-16). This propensity for herniation is probably due to an increase in intra-abdominal pressure brought about by crying and straining. Otherwise, the only significant require-

ment is that the colostomy be placed in a portion of bowel with normal ganglia, as determined by frozen section. A colostomy carried out in a portion of aganglionic colon results in an atonic colostomy, which will function no better than did the child's own anus. We prefer to place a colostomy in the most proximal normal colon because we propose to use the functional end of this colostomy for the new anus when the definitive pull-through operation is performed.

One other potential complication is the rare occurrence of skip areas of aganglionosis in the colon, which obviously complicate the decision of the operating surgeon in his selection of bowel for colostomy. Fortunately, this occurs rarely and usually can be detected on a preoperative barium enema, since other areas of stenosis are visible in the transverse colon. In a few patients total aganglionosis has been reported in the small intestine as well. Such a condition compounds the difficulties in management. Fortunately these cases are rare. Most of these children have involvement of the distal sigmoid and rectum only and respond to a standard colostomy and subsequently to resection and pull-through.

Imperforate Anus. Absence of an anal orifice is easily diagnosed, but frequently is overlooked unless the perineum is carefully inspected in a newborn infant. The diagnosis is usually made when the baby fails to pass meconium stools or when an ectopic anal orifice is noted. It is not uncommon, when the anus is absent, to find a large rectovaginal fistula, which could be overlooked because there may be no apparent functional disturbance.

There are many classifications of the anatomic types of imperforate anus (Stephens, 1963). A classification based on functional disability has proved helpful to us because it realistically defines management. In this classification (Table 7-1), patients are divided into two groups: (1) those with no anus and an adequate external fistula, and (2) those with no anus and either no opening or an inadequate opening for egress of stool.

Group 1: Imperforate Anus with Adequate External Fistula. Almost all such fistulas occur in female infants and the majority have a large rectovaginal fistula. However, a few infants, male and female, may have a large perineal fistula which, if dilated, may permit adequate evacuation, but this rarely suffices for long periods. As already noted, a large rectovaginal fistula may function so well that the absent anus is not detected until later. In such cases, gentle dilatation may be the only treatment needed until these children are 12 to 16 months of age and about to be given bowel training, at which time definitive repair can be carried out. Inasmuch as a fistula does not have true sphincteric function these children will not have real continence unless they have adequate perineal reconstructions.

Group 2: Imperforate Anus with Inadequate or No Fistula. This condition characterizes the largest group of infants with imperforate anus. All require some type of colon decompression within the first few days of life. They may be further divided into two anatomic groups, each requiring different surgical management.

The first subgroup are infants with a low-lying rectal pouch, in whom a proper anus can be constructed with a perineal operative approach. If a fistula is present, it is almost always a vaginal or perineal fistula rather than a fistula to the urinary tract, and can therefore be divided through the same perineal approach.

The second subgroup are children with a high-lying rectal pouch that lies above the puborectalis sling or urogenital diaphragm. A high rectal pouch is practically always associated with a urethral, vesical, or high vaginal fistula. The complicating fistula and distance between pouch and perineum make it impossible to reconstruct an anus via a perineal approach alone. This condition requires a combined abdominal-perineal operation. These infants are all managed best by an initial decompressing, abdominal colostomy.

Evaluation of an Infant with No Anus. The two most important aspects of evaluation in a newborn infant with no anus are ascertainment of the level of the blind rectal pouch with identification of any associated fistula, and a careful estimate of the potential function of a surgically reconstructed anus.

The level of the blind rectal pouch is best determined by radiologic examination. The classic test for a blind pouch is the Wangensteen-Rice (1930) upside-down, plain film, in which colonic air rises to the tip of the blind pouch and thus defines its most distal extent. This examination is not foolproof because inspissated meconium may give a falsely high level of the gas bubble. In addition, the test cannot be carried out within the first few hours of life as there is no air in the distal colon. However, after 36 to 48 hours a satisfactory definition of the distal pouch should be possible. Injection of an external fistula, if one is present, may further delineate the pouch.

As a general rule, a pouch lying above the puborectalis sling is too high for a perineal pull-through; one below this level lends itself to a simple perineal approach. Its location is defined by a line drawn on an upside-down, lateral film, between the pubic symphysis and the coccyx. If the air-filled rectal pouch lies on the perineal side of this line (Fig. 7-19*A*), the baby is a reasonable case for perineal anoplasty. If it lies above it (Fig. 7-19*B*), a combined abdominal-perineal approach is necessary. Recently the accuracy of a determination of the level of the puborectalis sling by x-ray measurements has been challenged, but we have found this approach to be a useful guide. In all infants in whom this pouch lies above the puborectalis sling, a colostomy is the operation of choice in the newborn period. A definitive abdominoperineal pull-through is then completed when he reaches the age of 12 to 18 months.

An estimation of the potential for normal function of a reconstructed anus is equally critical. Congenital absence of the anus is not infrequently associated with

---

TABLE 7-1. Types of Imperforate Anus

Adequate external fistula
   Vaginal
   Perineal

Inadequate opening for stool
   Low-lying pouch
      Fistula
      No fistula
   High pouch
      Fistula
      No fistula

Evaluation of level: puborectalis sling
   Above—all colostomy
   Below—perineal repair with division of fistula

Evaluation of potential function of new perineal anus
   Careful neurologic examination
   X-ray examination of sacrum
   Tests for urinary bladder function

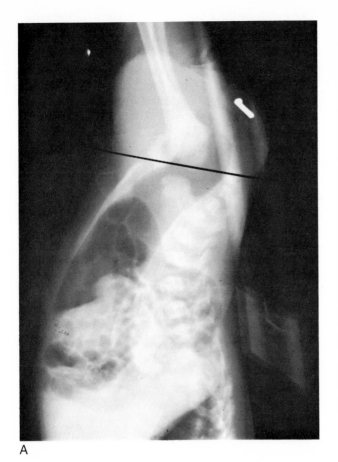

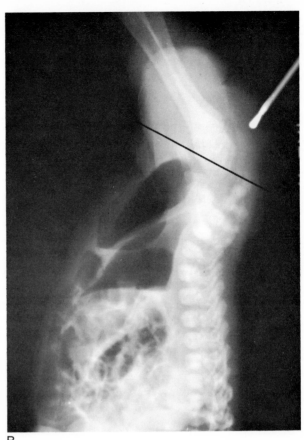

A   B

FIG. 7-19. *A,* Upside-down plain abdominal roentgenogram of newborn infant with imperforate anus and air-filled distal colon *below* puborectalis sling (identified by line). This probably represents good case for perineal anoplasty (see exceptions in text). *B,* Upside-down plain abdominal roentgenogram of newborn infant with imperforate anus and air-filled distal colon *above* puborectalis sling (identified by line). This case probably represents one in which perineal anoplasty cannot be carried out as definitive procedure (see exceptions in text.)

other perineal abnormalities (Berdon, 1966). They may be related to obvious external defects, such as meningo-myelocele, but more commonly, evidence of neurologic abnormality is more occult. Obviously, if innervation of perineal musculature and sphincters is abnormal or absent, no operation that brings the rectal pouch to a normal anal position can result in a functioning anus. Under such circumstances it is far better to have a permanent abdominal colostomy that can be managed than to have a normal-appearing anus that in reality is an uncontrollable perineal colostomy!

The first step in evaluation of potential function is a careful neurologic examination. If there is evidence of muscular malfunction of the lower extremities, or of sensory deficit over the perineum, a more detailed functional examination of the involved structures is in order. A helpful adjunct is an x-ray examination of the lower sacrum and vertebral bodies, because neurologic deficits are often associated with sacral defects.

The internal and external sphincteric mechanisms are innervated by components of the sacral plexus. As this plexus also innervates the urinary bladder, evidence of bladder neck obstruction and atony is a positive sign of abnormal pelvic innervation (Smith, 1968). Thus, a careful x-ray examination of the urinary tract is imperative. It will exclude any associated congenital anomalies and also permit evaluation of the function of the bladder. Evaluation of the urinary tract is best carried out with an initial intravenous pyelogram. If this appears abnormal, it is followed with a careful cysto-urethrogram.

Treatment. In a newborn infant with no anus who has neither an adequate fistula nor a low-lying perineal pouch, an abdominal colostomy is the treatment of choice. It should be performed within the first 24 to 48 hours of life. A colostomy is also preferred in infants with complicated associated anomalies, of which congenital heart disease and esophageal atresia are common.

Two types of colostomy have been recommended: (1) a sigmoid loop colostomy and (2) a transverse loop colostomy. Either is quite satisfactory for immediate management of the imperforate anus because either will decompress and probably bypass the fecal stream. Diverting the fecal stream is important to prevent contamination of the urinary tract if a fistula is present.

An advantage of the sigmoid colostomy is that the functioning end of the colostomy may be used for the new anus and the distal pouch can be discarded. Those who prefer a transverse colostomy usually do so because they wish to use the distal pouch for length and for its possible intrinsic sensory innervation. If a transverse colostomy is selected, it is important that it be closed within a few weeks following final reconstruction of a perineal anus. This closure ensures early function and prevents contraction of pelvic tissues around an otherwise unused segment of pulled-through rectum, which lies in a fresh operative bed.

A technique for perineal anoplasty is illustrated in Figure 7-20. The basic features of the procedure are: (1) careful identification of the external sphincter (Fig. 7-20*A*); (2) generous mobilization of the distal rectal pouch so that it comes easily to the perineal skin (Fig. 7-20*B*); and (3) two-layer closure with insertion of rectal wall into the four points of the cruciate incision (Fig. 7-20*C*).

The combined abdominoperineal pull-through procedure that we use for a high-lying rectal pouch is not carried out in newborn infants. In later infancy, when reconstruction is appropriate, we prefer a posterior subsacral approach (Kiesewetter, 1966).

Complications. The major complication of the abdominoperineal pull-through procedure for imperforate anus has been *fecal incontinence,* which should not occur in more than 10 to 15 per cent of patients, but has been reported to occur in 50 to 60 per cent of patients in some series. If there is normal innervation of the pelvic structures and if a proper reconstruction of the relationship between the rectum and the puborectalis sling can be carried out, the incidence of fecal incontinence should be low (Schnaufer, 1967).

A much less serious complication is *stenosis* or *stricture*

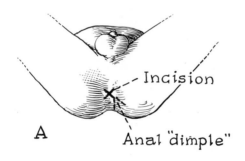

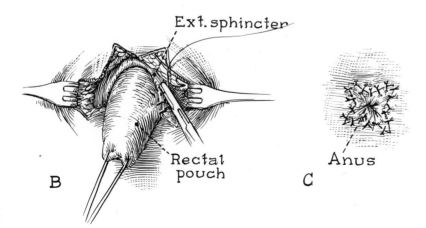

FIG. 7-20. Repair of low rectal pouch with or without perineal fistula. *A,* Cruciate incision is centered over external sphincter muscle and oriented as shown to permit maximal skin bridge for perineum. *B,* Rectal pouch is mobilized through sphincter muscle. *C,* Pouch is finally incised and mucosa interdigitated with skin incision in Z-plasty fashion to decrease chance of heavy circular scar tissue. (From Haller, J. A., Jr., and White, J. J.: *In* Operative Surgery: Principles and Techniques. Edited by P. F. Nora.)

at the mucocutaneous suture line. This will usually respond to dilatation under anesthesia, but occasionally it is necessary to carry out a type of anoplasty to release this circumferential scar.

The overall mortality for this major operative procedure is under 5 per cent if it is staged with a colostomy in the newborn period and a pull-through procedure 12 to 18 months later. A higher mortality occurs if a combined abdominoperineal procedure is carried out in the newborn infant. For this reason newborn repair has been largely abandoned in this country.

Gastrointestinal Perforation: Stomach and Small Intestine

Spontaneous perforation of the gastrointestinal tract is an unusual newborn surgical emergency, and survival is directly related to early recognition and operative correction (Lloyd, 1969). Since the fetal intestinal contents are sterile, and remain so for the first few days after birth, perforation during this time produces a reactive chemical type of peritonitis. If leakage occurs after the first three days of life, the usual bacterial peritonitis ensues.

Antepartum Perforation. Intrauterine perforation usually results from distal intestinal obstruction secondary to atresia, volvulus, strangulated hernia, or meconium ileus and cystic fibrosis of the pancreas. Meconium has progressed through the distal intestinal tract to the level of the ileocecal valve by the fourth month of gestation, and is released into the peritoneal cavity whenever subsequent perforation occurs. The sterile meconium induces a severe chemical and foreign body reaction, which creates an intense fibroplastic peritonitis. The peritoneal contents are enveloped by this adherent fibrinous membrane in which calcium is rapidly deposited. Since these events frequently antedate closure of the processus vaginalis, scrotal calcifications also may result. The point of perforation is usually sealed by the reactive process, but occasional persistence of leakage may lead to the formation of a large fibrous cyst, which can fill the entire abdominal cavity.

Intrauterine intestinal perforation and meconium peritonitis can be diagnosed prior to birth by roentgenograms of the mother, in which typical calcifications are demonstrated within the fetal abdomen. Following birth, such infants characteristically develop signs and symptoms of intestinal obstruction, either because of the original bowel lesion or as a result of the dense adhesive scar that encompasses the peritoneal contents. Intra-abdominal and scrotal calcifications confirm the diagnosis. Intraperitoneal air appears within 48 to 72 hours in cases in which intestinal leakage persists. Whenever intestinal obstruction or persistent perito-

neal soilage is suspected, immediate surgical exploration is required. In the absence of these indications, watchful waiting and supportive therapy occasionally are justified.

Postpartum Perforation. The vast majority of perforations in the newborn occur in the stomach; only a few have been reported in the small intestine. The latter is almost exclusively associated with ischemic necrosis of the small intestine secondary to volvulus or some other cause of strangulation. Perforation of the colon is the rarest of all gastrointestinal perforations and is usually associated with diagnostic manipulations, such as sigmoidoscopy, or a broken rectal thermometer (Fonkalsrud, 1966). The major condition to be considered in perforations of the gastrointestinal tract is spontaneous rupture of the stomach.

Gastric Perforation. Neonatal gastric perforation has been noted with increasing frequency in recent years (Robarts, 1968). The condition usually develops within the first week of life and often within the first three days. Prematurity is present in over 20 per cent of cases. The diagnosis may be indicated initially by bilious vomiting in association with rapidly progressive abdominal distention. The entire abdomen, including the usual area of liver dullness, becomes tympanitic to percussion. The distention is frequently so pronounced as to produce secondary respiratory distress and circulatory embarrassment. The signs and symptoms of shock ensue. Plain abdominal roentgenograms frequently demonstrate the pathognomonic signs of gastrointestinal perforation (Fig. 7-21).

Neonatal gastric perforation has been attributed to a variety of causes. Gastric distention resulting from distal intestinal obstruction, positive pressure ventilation with resuscitation at birth, or overzealous early feedings all may induce gastric rupture. Trauma to the stomach wall as a result of nasogastric intubation or birth injury also has been implicated. The relatively high gastric acidity in the first few days of life, particularly in association with prematurity, intracranial lesions, or other sources of neonatal stress, may predispose to acute peptic ulceration and perforation. Finally, "idiopathic" gastric perforation of the newborn in which none of the preceding factors are present has been recognized as a distinct entity. These cases usually present within the first five days of life, and the stomach wall characteristically ruptures along the greater curvature. Histologic examination of specimens taken from the site of perforation has suggested that a congenital deficiency of gastric musculature may be a primary or contributory factor (Herbut, 1943). More recent studies suggest that this reported abnormality of the gastric musculature may be an artifact that results from the rupture.

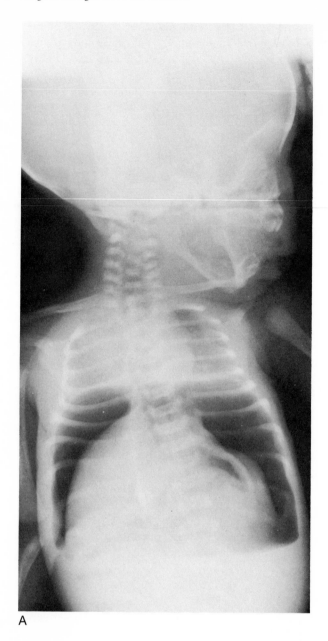

A

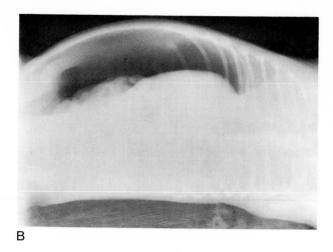

B

FIG. 7-21. *A,* Upright abdominal film in 2-day-old infant with sudden abdominal distention and vomiting. Massive pneumoperitoneum is characteristic of perforated stomach. Classic "saddlebag" finding consists of liver and remaining intestine suspended from diaphragm and surrounded by air. *B,* Lateral decubitus abdominal film of same infant showing accumulation of free air anterior to abdominal viscera.

Regardless of etiology, rapid resuscitation and early surgical intervention are imperative in all cases. Occasionally, immediate relief of massive abdominal distention by needle paracentesis may be required. The situation is comparable to that encountered in tension pneumothorax, with impairment of diaphragmatic excursion, compression of the lungs, and impingement on venous return to the heart. Under these circumstances, preoperative peritoneal decompression may prove lifesaving. If necessary, drainage may be maintained during transport of the child by attachment of a paracentesis catheter to underwater seal drainage, similar to that used for pleural drainage.

Unfortunately, most perforations go unnoticed for several hours until the baby presents with marked hypovolemia and often septic shock. The most significant clinical feature of rupture of the stomach is abdominal distention with marked tympani. The diagnosis is made unequivocally by an upright film of the abdomen, which shows a striking pneumoperitoneum with the viscera, including the liver, apparently hanging by a stalk from the diaphragm.

The exceptionally high mortality associated with spontaneous stomach perforation in the newborn is the result of (1) progressive hypovolemia, secondary to fluid loss from the chemical peritonitis, and (2) sepsis and bacteremia. The management of these babies is predicated on correction of these two threats to life. A central venous pressure line should be inserted immediately and balanced electrolyte solutions and blood administered to return the circulating blood volume to normal. Without further delay, a laparotomy should be performed and the perforation closed. At the time of surgical exploration, the possibility of an associated distal intestinal obstruction must be excluded, and the surface of the stomach must be thoroughly explored. Inspection of the posterior gastric wall may be accomplished through an opening in the gastrocolic omentum into the lesser sac. The site of perforation should be debrided of all devitalized tissue and closed with a double layer of inverting sutures. A gastrostomy is a useful adjunct in maintaining gastric decompression during the immediate postoperative period, and subsequently assists in initiating intestinal alimentation. Methicillin and kanamycin are the antibiotics of choice and should be initiated along with fluid replacement and continued throughout the postoperative course.

In assessing fluid and colloid requirements, it should be noted that the peritoneal surface is roughly equivalent to 20 per cent of the total body surface area. Accordingly, fluid losses in a patient with peritoneal inflammation may approximate those from burns of at least 20 per cent of the body surface. A monitoring routine that incorporates serial determinations of central venous pressure, total serum solids, hematocrit, and urinary output and specific gravity may prove particularly helpful under these circumstances in maintaining an optimum balance of fluid and colloids.

Neonatal Necrotizing Enterocolitis. Perforation of the colon or terminal ileum in the newborn is most often associated with an idiopathic necrotizing enterocolitis (Stevenson, 1971). Approximately 100 cases have now been documented in the American and English literature. The syndrome commonly occurs in the premature infant within the first few days of life, although it may appear in the full-term newborn and as late as two months after birth. The typical case is that of a premature infant who has experienced minor respiratory distress at birth, but subsequently appears to have recovered until the third to fifth day of life, when he develops vomiting, progressive respiratory distress, and abdominal distention. Signs of sepsis and shock, with hypothermia and poor peripheral perfusion, rapidly ensue. The passage per rectum of bloody mucus or diarrhea also may occur. Abdominal films usually demonstrate free peritoneal gas, pneumotosis intestinalis, or hepatic portal venous gas. Occasionally, the diagnosis may be confirmed roentgenographically before the clinical syndrome becomes full-blown. A history of previous umbilical artery or venous cannulation

may be significant (Corkery, 1968). A milder form of the disease appears to be characterized by gross rectal bleeding, whereas rectal bleeding plays a relatively insignificant role in the more fulminant cases, which rapidly progress to free perforation, abdominal distention, sepsis, and shock.

Although conservative treatment may be initially undertaken in the less critical cases, a need for early surgical intervention should be anticipated. Therapy should include intestinal decompression, parenteral fluids, and antibiotics. A surgeon should be consulted immediately and, with the pediatrician, should observe the patient carefully for any evidence of progression of the process. Any suggestion of intraperitoneal perforation necessitates immediate exploration. If surgery is required, the involved bowel should be resected and either an end-to-end anastomosis or temporary diverting colostomy or ileostomy should be performed. A recent report shows that adherence to these principles of management resulted in a 65 per cent survival rate in one practice.

The etiology of this unusual condition remains unclear, but the frequent association of previous umbilical artery or venous cannulation appears to be significant. Histologic sections of the involved segments of bowel frequently show ischemic changes.

Gastrointestinal Hemorrhage

Massive bleeding from the gastrointestinal tract rarely occurs in a newborn infant. It is poorly tolerated because of the relatively small blood volume of the infant, and thus must be diagnosed and managed aggressively (Spencer, 1964; Sherman, 1967). Hematemesis (vomiting of blood) is much less common than melena (passage of blood per rectum). Two common nonsurgical causes of melena in the newborn infant are *swallowed maternal blood* and *hemorrhagic disease of the newborn* (Apt, 1955). Swallowed blood results from premature separation of the placenta or, occasionally, blood in the birth canal. Hemorrhagic disease of the newborn rarely results in massive hemorrhage, and is due to hypoprothrombinemia. This condition results from inadequate vitamin K production by the mother. The passage of maternal blood per rectum is a self-limited disease, and the administration of vitamin K to the newborn infant will stop the bleeding of hypothrombinemia.

The most serious cause of newborn gastrointestinal hemorrhage is a *bleeding duodenal ulcer,* which is commonly associated with perforation as well. The combination of bleeding and perforation carries a high mortality in the newborn infant. Unfortunately, these infants often present with signs of peritonitis and near exsanguination, and the full clinical picture is not recognized until an emergency laparotomy is carried out. Not infrequently, however, these babies may vomit blood. A pyloroplasty is by far preferable to a gastric resection in the desperately ill newborn infant. It is often necessary to coagulate the bleeding vessels or oversew them at the time of pyloroplasty.

Stress ulcers of the stomach and of the duodenum may lead to rapid exsanguination of a small infant. Gastric lavage with cold saline or topical thrombin has been advocated as treatment, but frequently early exploration with exposure and direct suture ligation of the bleeding vessel in the ulcer base is necessary. There does not appear to be any predisposition for chronic peptic ulcer disease in later years following an acute stress ulcer in infancy. Therefore, extensive gastric surgery, such as resection or vagotomy and pyloroplasty, is not required. Adequate gastric drainage through a large gastrostomy tube is a useful adjunct in managing these patients, as it ensures gastric decompression and facilitates postoperative feeding.

Duplication of the intestine may result in massive bleeding in the newborn infant, if a communication exists between the duplication and the main lumen of the intestine and if there is erosion or ulceration of the mucosa of the duplication. Since these lesions are usually composed of ectopic tissue, not infrequently gastric mucosa, autodigestion of surrounding tissue leads to ulceration and bleeding.

Closely related to duplication is a *Meckel's diverticulum,* which will bleed if ectopic mucosa results in ulceration. These two lesions characteristically produce massive, painless rectal bleeding in the newborn. An emergency GI series may reveal the presence of a duplication by distortion of adjacent bowel, but is rarely helpful in a Meckel's diverticulum, which seldom fills with contrast medium. Excision is the proper treatment of both these lesions. In the duplication cyst, a wedge resection of the involved bowel is necessary because the cyst lies in its mesentery and an end-to-end anastomosis is then carried out. A Meckel's diverticulum occasionally may be resected without a wedge resection of the adjoining intestine, but usually a wedge resection and anastomosis are necessary.

Significant gastrointestinal hemorrhage may result from *colonic polyps.* Bleeding from polyps seldom occurs in the newborn infant, but has been reported. They are always juvenile retention polyps and these have no relationship to colonic adenomas. They may bleed from irritation of their mucosa or from their site of attachment if they spontaneously slough. Cessation of this bleeding is the rule, but the blood loss may on occasion be life-threatening. Unless the bleeding is massive, surgical treatment is not indicated because most of these polyps ultimately slough. In recurrent, uncontrolled hemorrhage, the polyps must be removed by either sigmoidoscopy or laparotomy.

Hernias

Inguinal hernias may present as surgical emergencies in the newborn if incarceration occurs. Umbilical hernias rarely become incarcerated in infants and are therefore of little statistical significance. The inguinal hernia or processus vaginalis frequently contains a loop of small intestine which may become incarcerated, especially in male infants.

A typical infant with an incarcerated inguinal hernia has a moderately distended abdomen, colicky abdominal pain, and a tender groin and scrotal mass. The hernial mass may be easily overlooked in a chubby newborn boy, and the signs of mechanical intestinal obstruction may not point to a hernia until a plain abdominal film reveals gas-containing bowel outside the abdominal cavity.

Most incarcerated hernias in infants can be reduced by delicate manual manipulation. If the baby is born with an incarcerated hernia, it is usually wise to proceed directly to operative repair because the period of incarceration is unknown and bowel necrosis is often present. Moderate sedation and a 30-degree head-down position will facilitate reduction. When the baby is relaxed, gentle downward traction often disengages the loop of bowel from the internal ring and allows bowel contents to run into the abdominal loop. Then with firm steady pressure the intestine usually is reduced.

Although infarcted bowel cannot be reduced, bowel with small areas of ischemia and serosal damage may be pushed into the abdominal cavity. Because of potential hazard of secondary perforation and, more importantly, because incarceration may recur, all babies with incarcerated inguinal hernia must be hospitalized and the hernia repaired during that hospitalization. We prefer to wait 48 to 72 hours after reduction to permit subsidence of edema in the inguinal canal before proceeding with repair of an incarcerated hernia. Tissues of an acutely incarcerated hernia are like wet tissue paper, and operative management is difficult.

If manual reduction is not successful after a sustained, gentle effort, immediate operative reduction and repair are mandatory to prevent strangulation and its serious consequences. The usual transverse crease incision gives satisfactory exposure. Often when the fibers of the external oblique are incised, the release of pressure causes spontaneous reduction. If this has not occurred, the incarcerated sac should be held snugly by an assistant while the internal ring is incised anteriorly. The sac should then be opened and the incarcerated bowel carefully inspected before it is returned to the abdomen. If viability is questionable, warm saline pads may facilitate return of normal color to the bowel wall. Strangulation necrosis is exceedingly rare in infants because of early diagnosis and excellent circulation of the bowel. The neck of the edematous processus vaginalis is closed with nonabsorbable sutures. The incised internal ring is repaired, and if the fascial defect is unusually large, several sutures may be used to bring the conjoined tendon over the cord to the inguinal ligament. No more formal reconstruction is necessary for infant hernias.

Long-Term Parenteral Nutrition

A recent advance in newborn surgery is the development of improved techniques for long-term parenteral nutrition (Dudrick, 1968; Filler, 1969). Not infrequently the newborn infant who has had corrective surgery for a gastrointestinal anomaly requires a protracted period before normal gastrointestinal function is achieved. In the past, the surgeon and pediatrician faced a potential race for survival in all such instances, with a constant threat of exhausting the baby's limited metabolic reserves before a satisfactory mechanism for restoring them could be established. With the new techniques of parenteral feeding, this critical time period has been significantly extended, and in some instances, progression of normal growth has continued uninterrupted. (See Chapter 4.)

REFERENCES

Apt, L., and Downey, W. S., Jr.: "Melena" neonatorum: swallowed blood syndrome: simple test for differentiation of adult and fetal hemoglobin in bloody stools. J. Pediat., 47:6, 1955.

Berdon, W. E., et al.: The association of lumbosacral spine and genitourinary anomalies with imperforate anus. Amer. J. Roentgenol., 98:181, 1966.

Bill, A. H., Jr., and Chapman, N. D.: Enterocolitis of Hirschsprung's disease. Amer. J. Surg., 103:70, 1962.

Bishop, H. E., and Koop, C. E.: Management of meconium ileus. Ann. Surg., 145:410, 1957.

Clatworthy, H. W., et al.: Extensive small bowel resection in young dogs. Surgery, 32:341, 1952.

Corkery, J. J., Dubowitz, V., Lister, J., and Moosa, A.: Colonic perforation after exchange transfusion. Brit. Med. J., 4:345, 1968.

Donnison, A. B., Shwachman, H., and Gross, R. E.: A review of 164 children with meconium ileus seen at the Children's Hospital Medical Center, Boston. Pediatrics, 37:833, 1966.

Dorst, J.: Personal communication. 1970.

Dudrick, S. J., et al.: Long-term total parenteral nutrition with growth, development, and positive nitrogen balance. Surgery, 64:134, 1968.

Esterly, J., and Talbert, J. L.: Jejunal atresia in twins with presumed congenital rubella. Lancet, 1:1028, 1969.

Felman, A. H., and Talbert, J. L.: Failure to thrive. How about Hirschsprung's disease? Clin. Pediat., 10:125, 1971.

Filler, R. M., Eraklis, A. J., Rubin, V. G., and Das, J. B.: Long-term total parenteral nutrition in infants. New. Eng. J. Med., 281:589, 1969.

Fonkalsrud, E. W., et al.: Neonatal peritonitis. J. Pediat. Surg., 1:227, 1966.

Gross, R. E.: The Surgery of Infancy and Childhood. Philadelphia, W. B. Saunders Co., 1953.

Haller, J. A., Jr.: Atresia of the small intestine. Clin. Pediat., 3:257, 1964.

Haller, J. A., Jr., and Cahill, J. L.: Combined congenital gastric and duodenal obstruction: pitfalls in diagnosis and treatment. Surgery, 63:503, 1968.

Herbut, P. A.: Congenital defect in the musculature of the stomach with rupture in the newborn infant. Arch. Path., 36:91, 1943.

Holder, T. M., and Gross, R. E.: Temporary gastrostomy in pediatric surgery: experience with 187 cases. Pediatrics, 26:36, 1960.

Kalayoglu, M., Sieber, W. K., Rodnan, J. B., and Kiesewetter, W. B.: Meconium ileus: a critical review of treatment and eventual prognosis. J. Pediat. Surg., 6:290, 1971.

Kiesewetter, W. B.: Imperforate anus. Ann. Surg., 164:655, 1966.

Ladd, W. E., and Gross, R. E.: Abdominal Surgery of Infancy and Childhood. Philadelphia, W. B. Saunders, 1941.

Lloyd, J. R.: Gastrointestinal perforations in the newborn: etiology and management. J. Pediat. Surg., 4:77, 1969.

Lloyd, J. R., and Clatworthy, H. W.: Hydramnios as an aid to the early diagnosis of congenital obstruction of the alimentary tract: a study of the maternal fetal factors. Pediatrics, 21:903, 1958.

Louw, J. H.: Congenital intestinal atresia and stenosis in the newborn. Observation on its pathogenesis and treatment, Ann. Roy. Coll. Surg. England, 25:209, 1959.

Louw, J. H., and Barnard, C. N.: Congenital intestinal atresia: observations on its origin. Lancet, 2:1065, 1955.

Lynn, H. B., and Espinas, E. E.: Intestinal atresia. Arch. Surg., 79:357, 1959.

Meeker, I. A., Jr., and Kincannon, W. N.: Acetylcysteine used to liquefy inspissated meconium causing intestinal obstruction in the newborn. Surgery, 56:419, 1964.

Mikity, V. G., Hodgman, J. W., and Paciulli, J.: Meconium blockage syndrome. Radiology, 88:740, 1967.

Nixon, H. H.: Intestinal obstruction in the newborn. Arch. Dis. Child., 30:13, 1955.

Parkkulainen, K. V.: Intrauterine intussusception as a cause of intestinal atresia. Surgery, 44:1106, 1958.

Randolph, J. G., Zollinger, R. M., and Gross, R. E.: Mikulicz resection in infants and children. Ann. Surg., 158:481, 1963.

Ravitch, M. M.: Pseudo Hirschsprung's disease. Ann. Surg., 147:781, 1958.

Robarts, F. H.: Neonatal perforation of the stomach. Z. Kinderchir., Suppl., 5:62, 1968.

Rowe, M. I., Buchner, D., and Clatworthy, H. W.: Wind sock web of the duodenum. Amer. J. Surg., 116:444, 1968.

Schnaufer, L., et al.: Differential sphincteric studies in the diagnosis of anorectal disorders of childhood. J. Pediat. Surg., 2:538, 1967.

Sherman, N. J., and Clatworthy, H. W., Jr.: Gastrointestinal bleeding in neonates. Surgery, 2:164, 1967.

Shim, W. K. T., and Swenson, O.: Treatment of congenital megacolon in 50 infants. Pediatrics, 38:185, 1966.

Smith, E. D.: Urinary anomalies and complications in imperforate anus and rectum. J. Pediat. Surg., 3:337, 1968.

Spencer, R.: Gastrointestinal hemorrhage in infancy and childhood: 467 cases. Surgery, 55:718, 1964.

Stephens, F. D.: Congenital malformations of the rectum, anus and genitourinary tracts. Edinburgh, E. and S. Livingstone, 1963.

Stevenson, J. K., Oliver, T. K., Jr., Graham, C. B., Bell, R., and Gould, V.: Aggressive treatment of neonatal necrotizing enterocolitis. J. Pediat. Surg., 6:28, 1971.

Talbert, J. L., and Haller, J. A., Jr.: Recent advances in the postoperative management of infants. J. Surg. Res., 6:502, 1966.

Talbert, J. L., Felman, A. H., and DeBusk, F. L.: Gastrointestinal surgical emergencies in the newborn. J. Pediat., *76*:783, 1970.

Tandler, J.: Zür entwick-lung Seschichte des menschlichen Duodenum in frühen Embryonalstudien. Morphol. Jahrb., *29*:187, 1902.

Wangensteen, C. H., and Rice, C. O.: Imperforate anus. Ann. Surg., *92*:77, 1930.

Zimmerman, L. M., and Laufman, H.: Intra-abdominal hernias due to developmental and rotational anomalies. Ann. Surg., *138*:82, 1953.

8

Birth Trauma and Neonatal Accidents

Trauma constitutes a leading cause of death in the first 48 hours of life, and follows prematurity and asphyxia in order of frequency (Potter, 1962). In some instances, seemingly insignificant trauma may be magnified in its injury potential by the relatively immature physiologic response of the newborn. In general, the large, full-term or postmature baby appears most susceptible to such injuries, with the incidence of serious trauma in infants weighing over 2500 Gm. twice that in infants weighing under 1000 Gm. Fetal position and birth presentation, the size of the fetus with relationship to the maternal pelvic outlet, and the association of fetal anomalies are also important determinants of susceptibility to injury. Any factor that renders delivery more difficult increases the relative hazard of birth and the potential for fetal trauma. The incidence of birth injuries is accordingly highest in breech extraction and lowest in cesarean section.

Traumatic Birth Injury

In general, birth injuries can be classified according to the three general anatomic areas affected: (1) head and neck; (2) extremities; and (3) thoracoabdominal region.

HEAD AND NECK INJURIES

The most frequent site of traumatic birth injury in the neonate is the head. Superficial damage to the skin and subcutaneous tissues is seen with relative frequency, and the chief threat of this type of injury is secondary infection or persistent extravasation of blood into the tissues as a result of an underlying bleeding diathesis. Forceps application can lead to superficial abrasions or contusions, although infrequently more serious deep tissue trauma may result with fat necrosis of the subcutaneous tissues produced by prolonged pressure. Vacuum extractors may also lead to excessive tissue edema and even to underlying tissue necrosis when applied for inordinate periods with excessive suction.

The scalp is composed of five potential layers, each of which may respond differently to the effects of trauma. In order of depth these layers are: (1) skin, (2) subcutaneous tissue, (3) aponeurotic layer, (4) loose connective tissue, and (5) periosteum.

Caput Succedaneum. This common manifestation of scalp trauma is a diffuse edema involving the superficial tissues over the presenting area of the scalp, which regresses spontaneously within a few days. This condition must be differentiated from more extensive and serious hemorrhage into the subaponeurotic layer. The latter process usually is noted some time between the first one-half hour and the fourth day after birth and may be signaled by the sudden onset of hypovolemic shock as a result of sequestration of large quantities of blood into the potential space. This unusual condition has been likened to a hemorrhagic caput succedaneum and can involve the entire scalp, obscuring the suture lines and fontanelles, producing pitting edema, and imparting a bluish discoloration to the overlying tissues (Barrow, 1968; Robinson, 1968).

Subaponeurotic hemorrhage must be differentiated from cephalohematoma, in which bleeding occurs beneath the periosteum, and accordingly is limited in extent by the periosteal attachment at the suture lines.

Massive Subaponeurotic Hemorrhage. Noted most frequently in babies of Negro parentage, this hemorrhage is probably associated with clotting abnormalities characterized by deficiences in vitamin K-dependent clotting factors. Total blood loss may approximate one-quarter to one-half of the total blood volume in these infants and may be associated with bleeding sites elsewhere in the body. A useful rule for estimating the volume of blood sequestered in the hematoma is to allow 50 ml. for each centimeter increase in head circumference over the normal range for an infant of comparable size and weight. Successful management of these patients requires correction of the associated clotting deficits as well as adequate restoration of circulating blood volume. Surgical drainage is rarely required and is usually contraindicated because of the danger of introducing secondary infection.

Cephalohematoma. Characteristically, this subperiosteal collection of blood is limited in extent by the periosteal attachments of the suture lines. The condition usually presents as a localized soft tissue swelling one to two days following birth, and regresses spontaneously over the subsequent two to three weeks. Occasionally, calcification of the lesion may be observed when resorption is incomplete. Aspiration or an incision and drainage procedure is usually contraindicated because of the danger of secondary infection. An underlying skull fracture may be identified in as many as 25 per cent of cases.

Skull Fractures. In spite of the considerable molding of the head required in the normal birth process, skull fractures are relatively unusual because of the low calcium content and malleability of the fetal bones. Excessive molding or mechanical pressures resulting from rapid or difficult delivery, however, particularly when forceps extraction is required in a contracted pelvis, may cause displacement or localized depression of one of the cranial bones. Because of its cartilaginous nature and extreme malleability, a scooped out indentation in the bone may occur in the absence of a demonstrable break, a lesion comparable to the typical greenstick fracture of the extremity. Neonatal skull fractures may even occur prior to birth as a result of in utero pressure on the fetal skull by the mother's prominent sacral promontory, by protruding fragments of a severe comminuted fracture of the maternal pelvis, by fibroid tumors of the uterus, or by tumors or deformities in the maternal pelvis (Alexander, 1969). There is a high incidence of associated cephalohematomas in all cases of neonatal skull fractures and evidence of accom-

panying intracranial bleeding should always be sought. Surgical elevation of a depressed skull fracture is indicated when the fragment is depressed more than 5 mm. below the level of the adjacent bone, in order to prevent continuing pressure on the underlying cortex.

It is difficult to interpret skull roentgenograms of newborn infants, and on palpation, it is easy to confuse suture lines with depressed fractures. Routine needle aspirations should be avoided and, in the absence of a depressed fracture or localized neurologic signs, close observation is the best treatment.

Intracranial Bleeding. A major cause of death in the newborn infant, intracranial bleeding may result from the trauma of a prolonged or difficult delivery, from neonatal anoxia, or from an underlying bleeding diathesis. Overriding of the sutures may lead to tearing of small veins or sinuses on the tentorium, producing subarachnoid or subdural bleeding. In some instances, bleeding that is initiated by trauma may be potentiated by deficits in the newborn's clotting mechanisms. Abnormalities in vitamin K-dependent clotting factors must be identified and corrected. Splenectomy may be required when neonatal idiopathic thrombocytopenic purpura leads to progressive, life-threatening central nervous system bleeding (Grosfeld, 1970).

Nasal Trauma. Trauma may produce dislocation of the cartilaginous septum with resultant airway obstruction. Immediate correction is required.

Facial Nerve Palsy. The most likely cause of facial nerve palsy in the newborn is direct pressure on the nerve by the forceps blade or by protrusion of the shoulder of the fetus into the lateral aspect of the face when the head is maintained in a position of sharp lateral flexion for prolonged periods during the birth process. In general, the prognosis for spontaneous recovery from this injury has appeared favorable, but recent reports have suggested that residual deficits may persist longer than had been previously appreciated (Gerber, 1969). Initial treatment should be directed toward protection of the cornea from drying and ulceration until eyelid function is regained and adequate closing of the eye during sleep is achieved.

Acute Torticollis. In this condition hemorrhage into the torn sternocleidomastoid muscle produces an inflammatory tumor, which may subsequently contract and lead to abnormal positioning of the head (Fig. 8-1). If this condition persists severe facial and skull distortion may ensue unless the scarred muscle is resected.

Spinal Injuries. In the newborn, spinal injuries most frequently involve the lower cervical and upper thoracic vertebrae and may result from traction or forced movements of the neck during delivery, producing compression or laceration of the vertebral arteries; tears

FIG. 8-1. Acute torticollis. Inflammatory tumor produced by traumatic hemorrhage into sternocleidomastoid muscle.

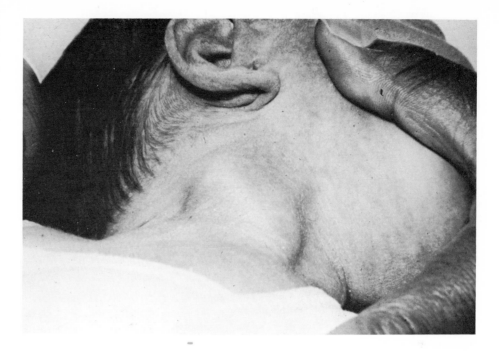

in the cervical joint capsules, dura, or nerve roots; or compression of the spinal cord. The premature infant (or firstborn) is particularly susceptible to such damage. Injuries of this type may be more common than realized, since the signs are usually obscured by associated cerebral damage. Serious damage to the spinal cord may occur in the absence of demonstrable skeletal abnormalities because of the flexibility of the newborn's spine. Severe injuries are manifested by paraplegia, paradoxical breathing, and loss of sensation below the level of the injury. Lesser degrees of injury may produce localized nerve root damage, with accompanying deficits in peripheral nerve function.

Phrenic Nerve Palsy. Cervical spine damage or traction on the cervical nerves may cause phrenic nerve palsy. Although the resulting diaphragmatic paralysis is well tolerated in older infants and children, it may produce serious respiratory embarrassment at this age because of a lack of fixation of mediastinal structures. Paradoxical movement of the paralyzed diaphragm results in a pendulum-like motion of the mediastinum, with serious restriction of ventilatory exchange. The resultant respiratory insufficiency may require emergency imbrication of the diaphragm in order to stabilize intrathoracic volume and ensure adequate vital capacity (see Chapter 5).

Horner's Syndrome. Damage to the cervical nerve roots may cause miosis, ptosis of the eyelid, and facial anhidrosis.

Brachial Plexus Palsy. This condition is described in the next section.

INJURIES TO THE EXTREMITIES

In general, birth trauma affects the extremities either through peripheral nerve damage or through fractures of the long bones.

Total Brachial Plexus Palsy. Rarely is this condition observed in newborn infants, but partial damage producing characteristic deficits in motor function occurs more frequently. Involvement of the fifth and sixth cervical nerves leads to paralysis of the deltoid and upper arm muscles, so-called Erb's palsy, whereas less frequently, involvement of the seventh and eighth cervical and first thoracic nerves produces the characteristic lower arm and hand paralysis of Klumpke's palsy. Spontaneous recovery from these conditions usually occurs in approximately ten days. As interim treatment of Erb's palsy, the sleeve of the infant's gown can be pinned to the bed or pillow and the arm maintained in abduction and flexion at the elbow. Treatment of Klumpke's palsy requires immobilization of the hand and forearm in a cock-up splint to prevent the typical claw-like deformity of the hand. Physical therapy is an important adjunct to clinical care. Neuroplasty may be considered if paralysis persists for longer than two to three months, suggesting a disruption of the nerve fibers.

Fractures of the Extremities. Such fractures may result from forceful traction at the time of delivery or from neurologic and developmental anomalies, such as meningomyelocele or arthrogryposis multiplex congenita, which impair the normal passage of the fetus through the maternal birth canal. Fractures of the extremities usually involve the shaft of the femur or humerus and can be readily managed by simple immobilization in the corrected position. The diagnosis is suggested by a failure of the baby to spontaneously move the affected extremity and by an absence of the Moro reflex. Treatment must be initiated quickly, since callus formation occurs rapidly at this age. Even with inadequate correction of the fracture, a good long-term result can be anticipated, since callus formation and growth eventually produce spontaneous molding of the extremity with satisfactory alignment and no significant residual deformity. Fractures of the forearm and leg are encountered less frequently, and are more likely to be accompanied by injuries to the brachial or lumbosacral plexus.

Epiphyseal Separation. Found in the femur most frequently following breech extraction, epiphyseal separation is associated with considerable subperiosteal hemorrhage and subsequent callus formation. Significant bony displacement may require reduction and immobilization of the limb to achieve adequate healing.

THORACOABDOMINAL INJURIES

Because of the resiliency of the rib cage of the newborn infant, serious intrathoracic and intra-abdominal trauma may be sustained without roentgenographic evidence of skeletal deformity. If the observer is unaware of these unique aspects of injury in the newborn infant, apparent discrepancies in findings may lead to serious errors in diagnosis.

Clavicular Fractures. The most frequent form of skeletal injury in the newborn infant, these fractures usually result when there is difficulty in delivery of the shoulder. The lesion should always alert the physician to the possibility of an associated brachial plexus, pulmonary or phrenic nerve injury. A common manifestation of these last two complications is respiratory distress, induced either by pneumothorax or diaphragmatic paralysis.

The infant with a clavicular fracture characteristically fails to move, or to freely move, the arm on the affected side, and crepitus may be elicited. Although figure-of-eight shoulder bandages are useful in treating clavicular fractures in older children, it is extremely difficult, and probably unnecessary, to employ this technique in newborns. In tiny infants there is a tendency for such bandages to exert maximum pressure immediately over the fracture site rather than at an optimal point on the distal shoulder. Certainly, Velpeau dressings and arm slings are contraindicated for treatment of this problem in any age group. In the neonate

the easiest, and safest, treatment is to avoid lifting the affected extremity. Maintaining the infant in the usual prone position achieves a result comparable to splinting with a figure-of-eight dressing and permits excellent healing (Haller and Talbert, 1968).

Pneumothorax. Another common injury in the newborn, pneumothorax may result from trauma, overly zealous resuscitation, or accentuation of the normal physiologic process of pulmonary inflation at birth. The etiology and management of this condition are discussed in detail in Chapter 5. Hemothorax and chylothorax are other potential complications of thoracic trauma and are also discussed in detail in Chapter 5.

Injuries to Intra-abdominal Organs. Such injuries may be signified by the clinical signs of perforation or bleeding. Intestinal perforation in the newborn, which is discussed at length in Chapter 7, may result from trauma to the stomach or rectum. Since the small intestine and colon are collapsed and do not contain air at birth, traumatic rupture of this portion of the bowel does not usually present a potential hazard.

Although intra-abdominal bleeding is diagnosed infrequently in the newborn infant, Potter (1962) noted 28 deaths from laceration of intra-abdominal organs and associated hemorrhage in a series of 2000 neonatal autopsies. The most complete analysis of this problem has been reported by Cywes (1967) from the Red Cross War Memorial Children's Hospital in Cape Town, South Africa, where 52 occurrences were noted in a ten-year period. Thirty-two of these cases involved bleeding from the liver, eight from the adrenal, five from the spleen, four from the kidney, one from both the liver and spleen, and two from intramural hemorrhage into the duodenum. This distribution of lesions agrees generally with the relative incidence noted by previous reports. Approximately three-quarters of the cases presented clinically between the second and fifth day of life, with the greatest incidence on the second day. Half of those cases occurring in the first day of life affected premature infants.

The characteristic clinical picture of intra-abdominal hemorrhage is that of a newborn infant who appears well at birth, but between one and six days following birth (usually about 48 hours), suddenly develops pallor, grunting respirations, listlessness, cyanosis, and shock. Tachycardia, tachypnea, and hypothermia also may occur with some frequency. Significant abdominal distention is apparent in most cases and may be accompanied by evidence of free peritoneal fluid or a palpable mass. In some instances, bluish discoloration of the umbilicus or the scrotum may be observed in association with a patent processus vaginalis. There may also be clinical evidence of bleeding elsewhere in the body. Anemia is apparent if blood loss is sufficiently slow to allow intravascular equilibration. Abnormalities in bleeding and clotting factors are identifiable in most patients. Paracentesis provides confirmatory proof of intra-abdominal bleeding in obscure cases, but is usually not required for diagnosis when the classic clinical picture is evident.

The site of intra-abdominal bleeding can be identified roentgenographically in the majority of cases; supine and erect films show a generalized abdominal haziness and separation of the air-filled intestinal loops by fluid. The presence of an opaque mass displacing air-filled bowel also may indicate which organ is the source of bleeding. An enlarged liver displaces the transverse colon downward, perirenal or adrenal hemorrhage produces a retroperitoneal flank mass, which displaces the intestines medialward, and an enlarged spleen indents the greater curvature of the stomach. Intramural hemorrhage of the duodenum produces partial or complete intestinal obstruction, as evidenced by air-fluid levels in the duodenum and stomach.

Although birth trauma provides the initiating factor in most cases, progression of the process appears to be related to a deficiency of vitamin K-dependent clotting factors. In all instances in which studies have been obtained prior to treatment, prolongation of the prothrombin index has been identified. Although the deficits in clotting factors may not be as marked as those ordinarily anticipated in hemorrhagic disease of the newborn, a potential for this disease appears to be present in such cases and is activated by subsequent traumatic injury. Accordingly, proper treatment and care entail correction of the clotting deficits by administration of vitamin K (restoring the prothrombin index to 60 per cent or higher), replacement of blood volume by administration of *fresh* whole blood, correction of acid-base disturbances, and administration of fresh frozen plasma as required. If the infant's condition is sufficiently stable, correction of the clotting abnormalities is ideally achieved prior to surgical exploration, since continued or uncontrollable bleeding may ensue during or following operation if impairment of coagulation processes persists.

In some instances, bleeding may be contained within an organ or surrounding tissues, as occurs in subcapsular splenic or hepatic hematomas, or periadrenal or renal hemorrhage. In these cases the resulting intra-abdominal mass must be differentiated from other tumors of the newborn infant. Progressive expansion of the hematoma usually proceeds to perforation and free intraperitoneal bleeding.

The liver is affected most frequently by trauma at this age and may be involved by a laceration of the capsule, a subcapsular hematoma, or an actual rupture of a lobe (Monson and Raffensperger, 1967). Massive congenital hemangiomas of the liver appear particularly susceptible to traumatic rupture and may present as massive intra-abdominal hemorrhage at birth (Graivier et al., 1967).

The adrenal glands are involved next in frequency, probably as a result of their relatively large size and rich blood supply at this age (Gross, 1967). The resultant bleeding may be contained within the retroperitoneal space and may mimic neuroblastoma in clinical presentation. This latter diagnosis often can be excluded on the basis of screening examinations of the urine for products of catecholamine metabolism (i.e., negative VMA and HVA tests). The process is usually unilateral, involving the right adrenal in 70 per cent of cases, but is bilateral in 5 to 10 per cent. Secondary infection, intra-abdominal perforation and hemorrhage, and adrenal insufficiency are potential complications. When blood volume has been restored and clotting deficits corrected, surgical exploration should be undertaken. The hematoma should be evacuated and bleeding points ligated. Adrenalectomy may be required and is well tolerated if the lesion is unilateral, since adrenal function is decreased by only 30 per cent when a single adrenal gland is removed.

Splenic rupture is relatively rare at this age, but may be encountered in association with hepatic injury or with erythroblastosis fetalis (Sirola, 1967). This latter condition may predispose to splenic rupture because of (1) increased size of the spleen, (2) weakening of supporting structures, and (3) a hemorrhagic tendency that may accompany erythroblastosis fetalis—a tendency that may be accentuated by the use of heparinized donor blood for exchange transfusions (Sirola, 1967). Splenic bleeding probably results from a traumatic subcapsular hematoma which progresses to rupture between two and four days of life and requires treatment by emergency laparotomy and splenectomy—so-called "delayed rupture of the spleen" (Fig. 8-2).

Renal injury occasionally may be the source of significant retroperitoneal bleeding and can be differentiated by a urinalysis, infusion pyelography, and aortogram via the umbilical artery. Birth injuries to other retroperitoneal structures, such as pancreas and bladder, are extremely rare. Cywes has reported two instances of typical intramural hematoma of the duodenum, which produced intestinal obstruction and required evacuation of the subserosal thrombus for relief. These cases appear to be clinically comparable to the traumatic intramural duodenal hematomas characteristically encountered in older infants and small children, although correction of the associated clotting deficits presents a unique requirement for successful treatment at this age.

A

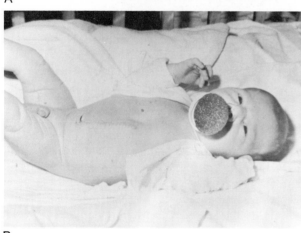

B

FIG. 8-2. Traumatic splenic rupture in the newborn infant. A 4-day-old baby boy was referred to The Johns Hopkins Hospital with the unusual history of sudden development of abdominal distention and drop in hematocrit after uneventful, full-term pregnancy and uncomplicated vaginal delivery. An indwelling catheter had been placed in the abdomen because of respiratory difficulty and whole blood was aspirated from the abdominal cavity through the catheter. This occurred on the third day of life, after entirely normal first 72 hours. He rapidly developed a shock-like state, was given 400 cc. whole blood at his primary hospital through an umbilical vein catheter, and then transferred by ambulance in Isolette for further evaluation. He required another 300 cc. of whole blood, which represented a total of 2½ times his theoretic blood volume, before his central venous pressure was normal and he was taken to the operating room. A left paramedian incision was made, abdominal cavity entered, and 400 cc. of fresh and clotted blood removed.

A, Small spleen was noted to have rupture of its capsule with continuing fresh bleeding. Denuded surface of splenic pulp can be seen with fragments of remaining splenic capsule. Spleen was removed uneventfully; patient had smooth postoperative course and was discharged on his sixth postoperative day. *B,* child is shown just prior to discharge. Because of dangers of overwhelming streptococcal and pneumococcal infections in child with splenectomy at this early age, he is being managed on prophylactic penicillin for first year of life. He continues to thrive and develop normally.

where vitamin K_1 is not administered to newborn infants prophylactically. With proper recognition and management, the majority of these patients can be salvaged by an alert and informed physician.

Finally, intraperitoneal bleeding may occur from a large congenital intra-abdominal tumor as a result of traumatic rupture at birth. Cases of congenital hemangiomas of the liver have been noted previously. Wilms' tumor of the kidney also may form a similar source of bleeding and cases of ruptured ovarian cysts have been reported. Mainolfi has reported successful treatment of a ruptured ovarian cyst in a newborn infant at three hours of age (1968).

Successful management of intra-abdominal hemorrhage in the newborn infant demands prompt recognition of the clinical picture, restoration of blood volume, correction of clotting deficits, and judicious surgical exploration as soon as the patient's condition permits. This problem appears to occur with greater frequency than generally appreciated, especially in localities

Neonatal Accidents

Immediately following birth the newborn infant is exposed to a whole new spectrum of hazards, including those of the environment. Neonaticide may result when a mother attacks her infant during the first 24 hours after birth, sometimes on hearing its first cry. These mothers are usually immature, passive women who apparently are attempting to deny their pregnancy rather than showing any evidence of premeditation of murder. They are characteristically young—often unmarried—and are infrequently psychotic, as contrasted to those mothers who inflict injuries on their children at an older age. Smothering by bed clothes or pillows or aspiration and choking on food or vomitus are also potential threats to the newborn. Suffocation accounts for 30 per cent of deaths in the first year of life and is particularly common in the first month.

A further environmental threat to the newborn infant is that of iatrogenic injury. Just as medical and surgical management of the seriously ill baby has increased in sophistication and complexity, so have the opportunities for accidents and adverse reactions to the various treatment modalities that are required. The hazards of accidental perforation of the pharynx by an endo-

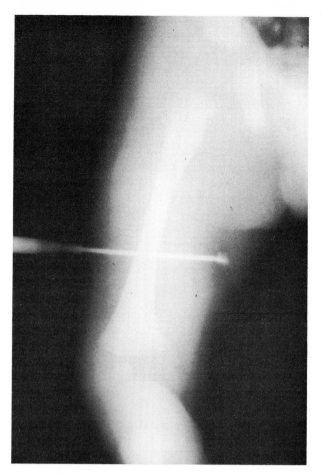

FIG. 8-4. Demonstration (autopsy case) of ease with which standard 1½-inch, 20 gauge needle may pierce entire width of lower thigh of full-term infant. (From Talbert, J. L. et al.: Gangrene of the foot following intramuscular injection in the lateral thigh. J. Pediat., *70:*110, 1967.)

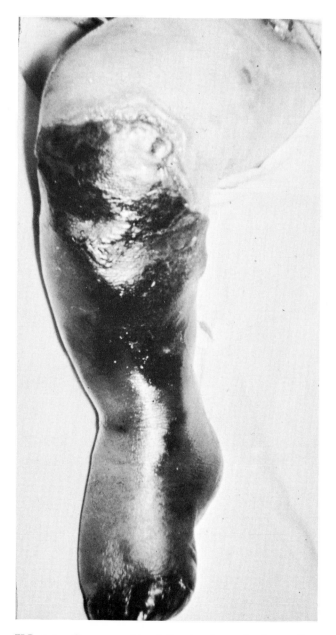

FIG. 8-3. Gangrene of leg following femoral artery catheterization in newborn infant.

tracheal tube, the stomach by a Levin tube, or the rectum by a thermometer have been emphasized (Chapter 7). A further source of complications which has been encountered with increasing frequency is that related to vascular accidents. Catheterization of the arterial or central venous system poses a threat of perforation of the heart or great vessels if the position of the catheter tip is not monitored carefully roentgenographically. Prolonged peripheral venous or arterial catheterization also may produce local vascular thrombosis and gangrene (Fig. 8-3). Even intramuscular administration of medications may lead to vascular injury if the needle size or technique of injection is inappropriate (Fig. 8-4) (Talbert, 1967). *Caution must be exercised at all times in the treatment of these tiny patients.*

9

REFERENCES

Alexander, E., Jr., and Davis, C. H., Jr.: Intra-uterine fracture of the infant's skull. J. Neurosurg., *30:*446, 1969.

Barrow, E., and Peters, R. L.: Exsanguinating hemorrhage into the scalp in newborn infants. S. Afr. Med. J., *42:*265, 1968.

Cywes, S.: Haemoperitoneum in the newborn. S. Afr. Med. J., *41:*1063, 1967.

Gerber, C. T., Bepko, F. J., Jr., Gerber, A. H., and Cohen, O.: Facial nerve paralysis in the newborn. Med. Ann. D.C., *38:663,* 1969.

Graivier, L., Vatteler, T. P., and Dorman, G. W.: Hepatic hemangiomas in newborn infants. J. Pediat. Surg., *2:*229, 1967.

Grosfeld, J. L., Naffis, D., Boles, E. T., and Newton, W. A.: The role of splenectomy in neonatal idiopathic thrombocytopenic purpura. J. Pediat. Surg., *5:*166, 1970.

Gross, M., Kottmeier, P. K., and Waterhouse, K.: Diagnosis and treatment of neonatal adrenal hemorrhage. J. Pediat. Surg., *2:*308, 1967.

Haller, J. A., Jr., and Talbert, J. L.: Trauma and the child. *In* Management of Trauma. Edited by W. F. Ballinger, II. Philadelphia, W. B. Saunders Co., 1968.

Mainolfi, F. G., Standiford, J. W. E., and Hubbard, T. B., Jr.: Ruptured ovarian cyst in the newborn. J. Pediat. Surg., *3:*612, 1968.

Monson, D. O., and Raffensperger, J. G.: Intraperitoneal hemorrhage secondary to liver laceration in a newborn. J. Pediat. Surg., *2:*464, 1967.

Potter, E. I.: Pathology of the Fetus and the Infant. Chicago, Yearbook Medical Publishers, Inc., 1962.

Robinson, R. J., and Rossiter, M. A.: Massive subaponeurotic hemorrhage in babies of African origin. Arch. Dis. Child., *43:*648, 1968.

Sirola, K.: Subcapsular bleeding of the spleen with rupture in a newborn infant with erythroblastosis fetalis. J. Pediat. Surg., *2:*155, 1967.

Talbert, J. L., Haslam, R. H. A., and Haller, J. A., Jr.: Gangrene of the foot following intramuscular injection in the lateral thigh: A case report with recommendations for prevention. J. Pediat., *70:*110, 1967.

9

Skin Defects

Major skin defects in newborn infants represent a primary lethal threat because of bacterial invasion and septicemia. Because infection is not an immediate danger to a baby with *extrophy of the bladder,* this condition is not included in our discussion of skin defects. In addition, extrophy of the bladder does not constitute a life-endangering emergency in a newborn infant. Although very careful evaluation of the genitourinary tract should be done in the first few days of life, the necessary, extensive reconstructive procedures are probably best carried out when the infant is older.

Omphalocele and Gastroschisis

An omphalocele is a large, periumbilical, abdominal wall defect, which is covered only by fetal amniotic membrane. In a newborn infant this amniotic sac is an extension of the parietal peritoneum at the umbilicus. These umbilical defects vary greatly in size and may contain the entire liver and spleen in addition to large portions of the intestinal tract (Duhamel, 1963). They may be associated with more complicated abdominal and thoracic defects (Haller, 1966; Cantrell, 1958). At the other extreme it may be no more than an umbilical hernia with an extension of peritoneum into the cord.

The major pathophysiology of an omphalocele relates to its lack of skin coverage. The exposed amniotic membrane is easily perforated and becomes a potential site for the entry of lethal pathogenic bacteria. The two acute complications of an omphalocele are intrauterine rupture and rupture during birth with evisceration. The exposed abdominal organs are immediately contaminated at birth. They rapidly become edematous and

9a

matted together and convert a reparable congenital anomaly into a serious emergency. Intrauterine and extrauterine rupture of an omphalocele result in a very high mortality. The only satisfactory treatment is to replace the viscera within the abdomen and close the defect or to cover it with surrounding abdominal skin or plastic membrane.

Under normal conditions an unruptured omphalocele presents an immediate challenge of providing adequate coverage by skin to prevent sepsis and death. In a small omphalocele, primary repair may be carried out in much the same way that a large umbilical hernia is handled. The relatively small volume of the omphalocele contents can be returned to the abdomen, the amniotic membrane can be excised, and the fascial defect closed directly with skin closure as a second layer.

The only other congenital anomaly that can be confused with a ruptured omphalocele is gastroschisis (Swenson, 1969). This is a rare defect of fusion of the anterior abdominal wall, which is associated with varying degrees of intestinal evisceration. The differential feature is that gastroschisis occurs below and separate from the umbilical cord, whereas an omphalocele defect is intimately associated with the umbilicus. A gastroschisis defect can often be closed primarily; sepsis and possible bowel damage and perforation are its complications.

Treatment. Two forms of treatment are available for a large omphalocele. The oldest form of management and one that is currently being re-evaluated is a non-operative approach (Grob, 1957; Wollenweber, 1959). The omphalocele sac is carefully protected and usually covered with a mild antiseptic solution, such as aqueous mercurochrome or dilute silver nitrate. A natural formation of granulation tissue and skin overgrowth is allowed to occur. This treatment requires careful nursing care and prolonged hospitalization, but if infection is prevented, large omphalocele sacs ultimately are covered by normal skin and close by contracture. Any fascial defect that remains can be repaired by a secondary operative procedure (Grob, 1963).

In this country a more common treatment for large omphaloceles is based on the surgical management first outlined by Gross (1948). This treatment consists essentially of mobilizing all available abdominal and flank skin on each side to cover the extra-abdominal mass with an envelope of viable skin. With a large omphalocele, this may require the undermining of skin flaps for the complete circumference of the baby to the vertebral spines. A second stage in this repair is carried out after further development of the abdominal cavity takes place and it becomes possible to return the extra-abdominal mass of viscera to its normal posi-

tion. At this time, excess skin is removed, the fascia is approximated in the midline, and a total reconstruction is accomplished (Fig. 9-1).

In the past, attempts at primary closure of big omphaloceles often met with failure because forceful replacement of the viscera into an adequate abdominal cavity resulted in intolerable elevation of the diaphragm and acute respiratory distress. The staged procedure of Gross has proved satisfactory for the handling of large omphaloceles. It requires tedious dissection, careful postoperative management, and eventually a second operative procedure.

In the past few years, plastic sheeting has been employed to facilitate immediate coverage of large omphaloceles (Schuster, 1967). Basically this technique consists of the suturing of a plastic bag to the fascial defect and then serially pushing the contents into the baby's enlarging abdominal cavity by staged exclusion of more and more of the bag (Fig. 9-2). Silastic sheeting with knitted Teflon backing produces an artificial

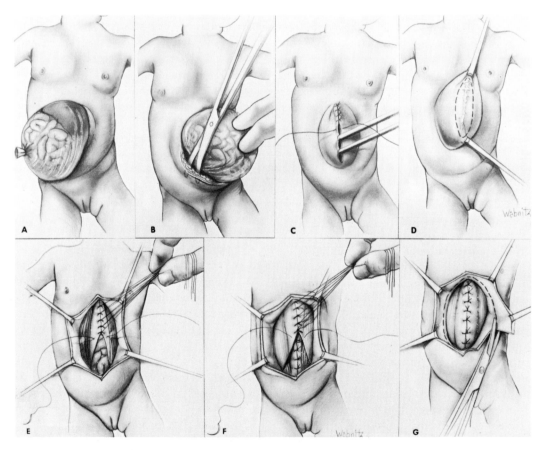

FIG. 9-1. Repair of large omphalocele. *A,* Large omphalocele with intestine showing through peritoneum. *B,* Undermining of skin. *C,* Closure of skin over omphalocele. Second stage: *D,* Excision of old scar. *E,* Development of skin flaps and closure of posterior rectus sheath. *F,* Closure of anterior rectus sheath. *G,* Removal of redundant skin, to be followed by skin closure. (From Schwartz, S. I.: Principles of Surgery. New York, McGraw-Hill, 1969.)

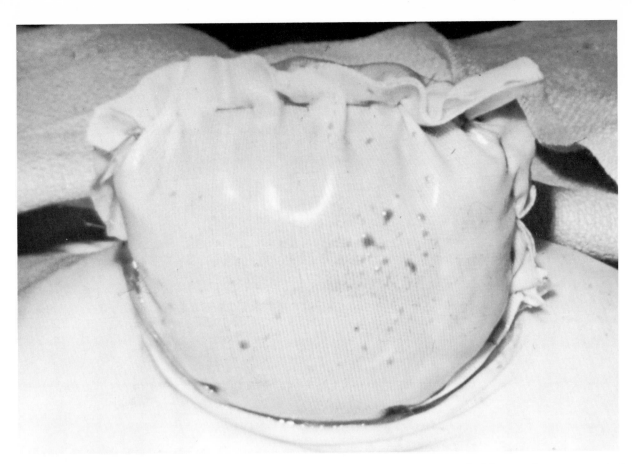

FIG. 9-2. Operative photograph of Silon pouch used for initial coverage of large omphalocele. Silon pouch was progressively decreased in size and ultimately removed with secondary closure of abdominal fascia.

"amnion," which is remarkably well tolerated with a low incidence of sepsis. The plastic bag is serially excised as rapidly as possible and secondary fascial and skin closures are carried out. Recent favorable reports suggest wider application of this treatment for giant omphaloceles (Gilbert, 1968).

Meningoceles and Meningomyeloceles

Both meningoceles and meningomyeloceles appear in the newborn infant as an obvious cystic mass usually overlying the lower back. They may occur anywhere along the vertebral axis, but 80 to 85 per cent occur in the lumbosacral area. Both are epithelium-lined sacs with free communication to the spinal subarachnoid space. The dynamics of this communication are easily verified by noting the increased turgidity of the mass when the baby cries. If nerve roots are attached to the wall of the arachnoid diverticulum or are contained within the sac, outside the spinal canal, the term meningomyelocele is applied; if the sac communicates with the arachnoid space but contains no neural elements, it is the less complicated meningocele.

The only lesions that constitute true newborn emergencies are those that lack skin coverage. The indication for operative repair is the threat of lethal infection and ascending meningitis. Gross neurologic deficits are rare with meningoceles, but are characteristic of meningomyeloceles. There may be marked loss of motor and sensory functions at birth. As pointed out by McQueen (1962), this major dysfunction is probably related to the trauma of the birth process. Substantial improvement may occur over the ensuing one to two weeks. The following findings greatly increase hospital mortality and the incidence of severe mental retardation and paralysis: (1) extensive paralysis, (2) a head circumference greater than 2 cm. above the 90th percentile, (3) extensive kyphosis, (4) associated major heart anomalies or birth injuries, such as intracranial hemorrhage. Unless there are severe neurologic complications, such as marked hydrocephalus (which unfortunately occurs in a high percentage of patients), obvious impairment of urethral, vesical, and rectal sphincters,

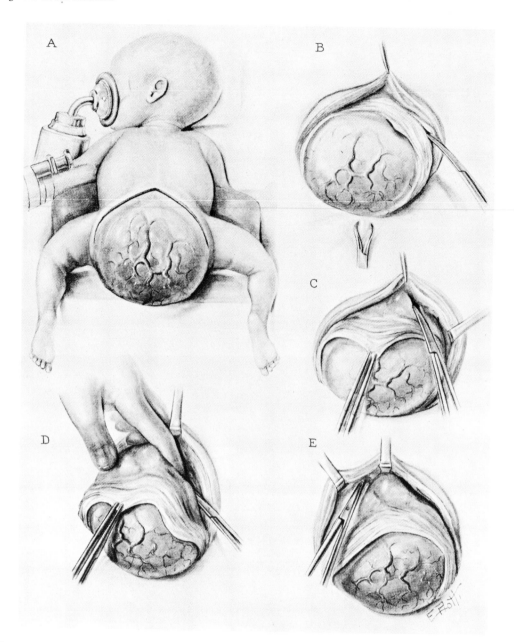

FIG. 9-3. Operative steps in removal of a sacrococcygeal teratoma. *A,* Position on table. Abdomen supported over a roll, to raise lower half of body from table. V-shaped cutaneous incision at upper border of mass. *B,* Incision being developed through subcutaneous tissues and superficial fascia. *C,* Beginning dissection over superior portion of mass. *D,* Carrying dissection as far as possible along a cleavage plane. *E,* Sharp dissection is at times necessary to free the mass from surrounding structures.

or profoundly areflexic and deformed legs, most neurologists and neurosurgeons feel that the sacs should be excised and the associated defects covered with skin flaps.

The characteristic radiographic finding with these anomalies is a widening of the spinal canal, centered over the posterior mass. Commonly associated with the sacral mass is disordered vertebral segmentation.

Since rupture of the thin-walled sacs and infection are constant dangers, immediate repair is indicated. Even in those defects with complete skin coverage, repair at birth has the important advantage of decreasing the incidence of syncytial adhesions between the spinal cord and the arachnoid. With early repairs, there is reported to be a decreased rate of hydrocephalus of the Arnold-Chiari type.

The baby should be positioned with its head slightly tilted downward to decrease the loss of cerebrospinal fluid when the sac is opened. The sac and surrounding skin are carefully cleansed with an appropriate antiseptic. Dissection is carried down through the subcutaneous tissues to the deep sacral fascia. Here the narrow fascial neck is incised to free the whole sac and to allow for identification and careful freeing of contained nerve roots or other neural elements. If there are no nerve components, the sac is amputated at its base and the arachnoid defect repaired with multiple fine sutures. The whole sac of a meningomyelocele may not be resectable and portions of it may be returned to the space beneath the spinal membranes to preserve the adherent neural filaments. Exact repair of the defect in the lumbosacral fascia is then completed. Skin closure is imperative and may be difficult in large defects. Skin flaps may be undermined to facilitate primary midline closure and skin grafts used to repair the lateral clefts. Healing without infection prevents major tissue breakdown and serious ascending sepsis.

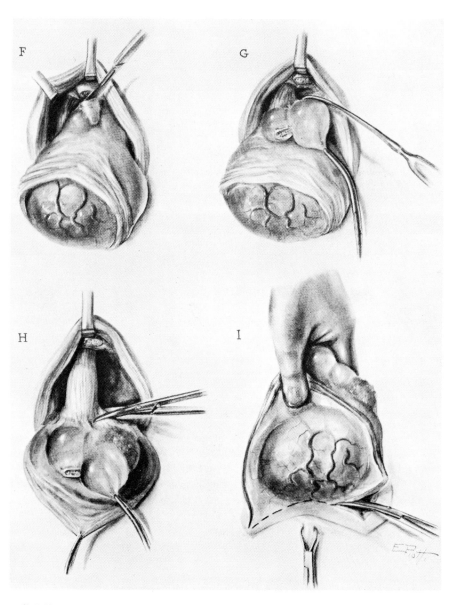

FIG. 9-3. (Continued) *F,* Entire coccyx cut away with teratoma, a most important step. *G,* Dissection being carried up into hollow of the sacrum. Rectum coming into view. *H,* Entire posterior wall of rectum exposed, the teratoma having been dissected away from it. *I,* Cutting cutaneous edge inferiorly, the last remaining attachment on the mass. (The towel clip is just superior to the anus and keeps this out of the field.)

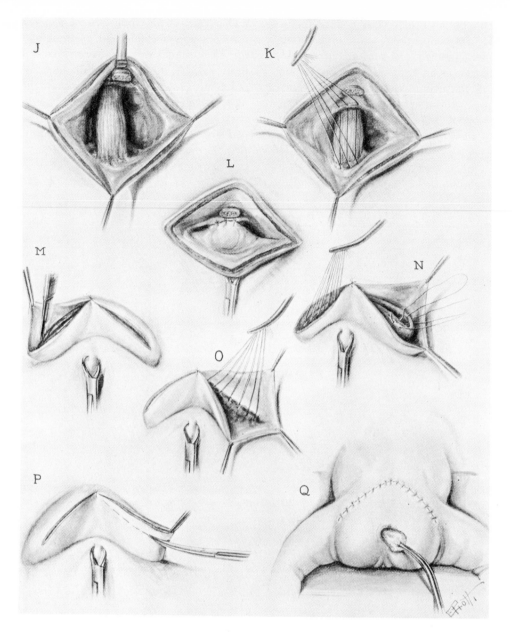

FIG. 9-3. (Continued) *J,* After removal of the teratoma, the rectum remains widely exposed throughout its entire length. *K,* To bring the anal area up to a normal position, the perianal tissues (base of the levator ani muscles) are brought to the presacral fascia with several silk sutures. *L,* Supporting sutures tied. *M,* Apex of skin sutured into an inverted V. *N,* Excess skin being dissected away from underlying gluteus muscles. (All muscle is saved no matter how much it is frayed out.) *O,* Suture of muscles being completed. *P,* Excess skin being trimmed away. *Q,* Skin closure completed. Petrolatum gauze pack being removed from the rectum. (From Gross, R. E., Clatworthy, H. W., Jr., and Meeker, I. A., Jr.: Sacrococcygeal teratomas in infants and children. Surg. Gynec. Obstet., *92:*341, 1951.)

Sacrococcygeal Teratoma

There is rarely any question about the presence of a sacrococcygeal teratoma because it presents as a large exophytic, fungating mass attached to the coccygeal area of the newborn infant. It should be excised at birth because of the immediate hazards of erosion and hemorrhage and the potential threat of malignant tissue components. If it is carefully and completely removed, the long-term results are excellent.

Grossly the teratoma appears to arise from the coccyx. Histologically any and all tissue elements may be present. Neurologic deficits are rarely present (which helps to differentiate a small teratoma from a large meningomyelocele). Since presacral extension is possible, a barium enema should be carried out as well as an intravenous pyelogram.

Gross (1951) has championed a transverse or chevron buttock incision. It is vitally important that the attached coccyx be included with block excision of the entire tumor. This incision protects the rectum and keeps the wound away from the anus. Endotracheal anesthesia is used. It is important to suspend the chest to permit adequate respiratory excursions during elevation of the buttocks (Izant, 1962). Blood loss is usually relatively large; therefore, a central venous pressure catheter should be inserted at the outset of the procedure. The mortality is in the range of 15 to 20 per cent for operations performed soon after birth and almost three times this figure for those performed one month or more after birth (Ravitch, 1951). The increased mortality associated with delay in excision is due to rupture and hemorrhage and to malignant extension. These figures underline the necessity for operative intervention in the early newborn period. The long-term results are excellent and significant associated anomalies are rare. The operative approach is illustrated in Figure 9-3.

REFERENCES

Cantrell, J. R., Haller, J. A., Jr., and Ravitch, M. M.: A syndrome of congenital defects involving the abdominal wall, sternum, diaphragm, pericardium, and heart. Surg. Gynec. Obstet., *107*:602, 1958.

Duhamel, B.: Embryology of exomphalos. Arch. Dis. Child., *38*:142, 1963.

Gilbert, M. G., et al.: Staged surgical repair of large omphaloceles and gastroschisis. J. Pediat. Surg., *3*:702, 1968.

Grob, M.: Lehrbuch der Kinderchirurgie. Stuttgart, George Thieme Verlag, 1957.

Grob, M.: Conservative treatment of exomphalos. Arch. Dis. Child., *38*:148, 1963.

Gross, R. E.: A new method for surgical treatment of large omphaloceles. Surgery, *24*:277, 1948.

Gross, R. E., Clatworthy, H. W., Jr., and Mecker, I. A.: Sacrococcygeal teratomas in infants and children. Surg. Gynec. Obstet., *92*:341, 1951.

Haller, J. A., Jr., and Cantrell, J. R.: Diagnosis and surgical correction of combined congenital defects of supra-umbilical abdominal wall, lower sternum, and diaphragm. J. Thorac. Cardiovasc. Surg., *51*:286, 1966.

Izant, R. J.: *In* Pediatric Surgery. Edited by Benson, C. D., et al., Chicago, Year Book, 1962.

McQueen, J. D.: *In* Pediatric Surgery. Edited by Benson, C. D., et al. Chicago, Year Book, 1962.

Ravitch, M. M., and Smith, E. I.: Sacrococcygeal teratomas in infants and children. Surgery, *30*:733, 1951.

Schuster, S. R.: A new method for staged repair of large omphaloceles. Surg. Gynec. Obstet., *125*:837, 1967.

Schwartz, S. I.: Principles of Surgery. New York, McGraw-Hill, 1969.

Swenson, O., et al.: Gastroschisis. Arch. Surg., *98*:742, 1969.

Wollenweber, E. J., and Coe, H. E.: Conservative management of eventration in the newborn. Amer. J. Surg., *97*:769, 1959.

10

Abdominal Masses

Although the majority of abdominal masses in newborn infants eventually prove to be benign lesions, early diagnosis and treatment remain essential components of optimum care in all cases. In some instances, immediate surgical intervention is necessitated by bleeding, perforation, or ischemic necrosis of an intra-abdominal tumor. In the absence of these indications of catastrophe, however, judicious haste is warranted in establishing an accurate diagnosis and instituting appropriate treatment. This approach will minimize complications resulting from adverse local effects of benign lesions and enhance the potential for total extirpation and permanent cure of malignant neoplasms.

In most instances, the newborn infant presents with asymptomatic swelling of the abdomen (Hendren, 1963; Schaffer, 1968). Palpation defines the size, location, consistency, and mobility of the lesion. Bimanual palpation through the rectum and abdominal wall documents the extent of pelvic involvement and the relationship to pelvic structures. Inspection of the perineum and genitalia confirms the adequacy of vaginal, urethral, and anal orifices. Transillumination assists in distinguishing air- or fluid-filled cystic lesions from solid tumors (Mofenson and Greensher, 1968). Auscultation may identify a bruit in a vascular neoplasm. A peritoneal tap can aid in differentiation of ascites, peritonitis, and intraperitoneal hemorrhage.

Hematuria suggests renal vein thrombosis or renal trauma. Increased levels of urinary catecholamines (VMA and HVA) are associated with neuroblastoma. Shock and anemia suggest hematoma formation, bleeding into a tumor or organ, or free bleeding into the peritoneal cavity. Elevation of blood urea nitrogen results from impairment of renal function and/or dehydration. Bone marrow aspiration can ascertain the presence of metastatic cells, particularly neuroblastoma.

Plain roentgenograms of the abdomen and chest assist in defining the exact location of the mass on the basis of displacement of air-filled intestine. Radiographic visualization of identifiable bone or teeth within this mass may indicate a teratoma. Investigation of the lung and skeleton is essential for total evaluation of these infants in order to identify or exclude the presence of metastic lesions.

Since the majority of intra-abdominal masses at this age arise from the kidney, an intravenous pyelogram is an essential component of investigation. Infusion pyelography, as described by Rowe and associates, is especially helpful in that it provides an inferior venacavogram, nephrogram, and voiding cystourethrogram as a single study (Rowe et al., 1967) (Fig. 10-1). For this technique, a dosage of 50 per cent sodium diatrizoate (Hypaque), calculated on the basis of 2.5 ml. per pound for infants under 8 pounds, is administered with an equal volume of 5 per cent dextrose in 0.2 normal saline. In order to obtain an inferior venacavogram, venous tourniquets are applied to the legs bilaterally. One-fourth of the calculated dose of contrast material is then rapidly injected into one ankle vein. When three-quarters of this material has been administered, the ipsilateral venous tourniquet is released and the remaining portion of the undiluted contrast medium injected. An anteroposterior abdominal film obtained at this time delineates the inferior vena cava. Final injection is then immediately completed by infusion of the remaining three-quarter dose of contrast

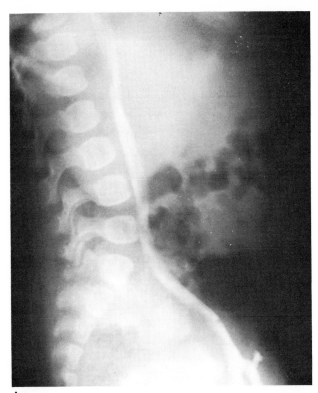

A

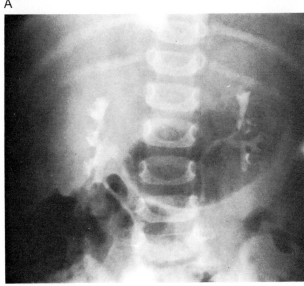

B

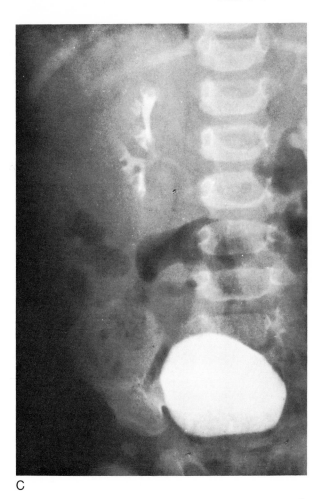

C

FIG. 10-1. Infusion pyelography includes within a single study *A,* inferior venacavogram, *B,* nephrogram, and *C,* excretory urogram.

medium plus an equal volume of 5 per cent dextrose and 0.2 normal saline. An anteroposterior abdominal film is obtained as soon as the total dosage has been administered, usually within two minutes of the injection. X-ray studies are repeated at 10, 20, and 30 minutes, with additional follow-up films indicated if renal function is impaired. At 30 minutes, oblique films of the pelvis are obtained while voiding is induced by suprapubic pressure. In addition to the inferior venacavogram, early anteroposterior films of the abdomen demonstrate a nephrogram. Because of the brisk diuresis induced by administration of a relatively large volume of dilute contrast material in a short time, maximum visualization of the collecting system is achieved.

Caution must be exercised in interpreting inferior venacavograms, since extrinsic pressure by intra-abdominal mass, crying and straining, or intestinal distention may simulate complete obstruction of the vena cava. This finding can be erroneously interpreted as a sign of inoperability in the presence of an intra-abdominal tumor (Berdon, 1967). Such studies, however, are helpful in localizing intra-abdominal masses and in defining the presence of thrombus propagation into the vena cava in cases of renal vein thrombosis.

Liver scans are useful in defining tumors arising from this organ (Fig. 10-2). Arteriograms also can be performed at this age through the umbilical artery. This last technique provides a unique means of studying intra-abdominal tumors in the newborn (Salerno et al.,

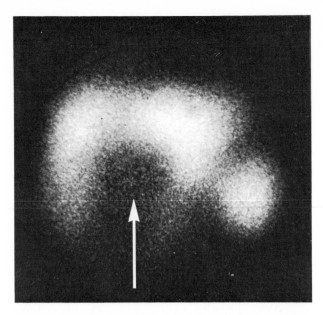

FIG. 10-2. Liver scan of infant with hepatoblastoma arising in medial aspect of right lobe. Large central filling defect (arrow) indicates location of tumor (same case as presented in Fig. 10-13).

1970). During the first few days of life, the umbilical arteries can be readily exposed at the base of the umbilical stump. Later, when the cord has degenerated, exposure of the vessels can only be achieved through a semilunar skin incision just inferior to the umbilicus. The abdominal wall fascia is then incised in the midline, and the underlying arteries are identified and isolated, with care exerted to avoid tearing the adjacent peritoneum. A soft plastic catheter can be inserted into the aorta via these umbilical arteries as late as ten days after birth. Complete obliteration of the umbilical artery reportedly does not occur until the age of three to five weeks.

Renal Masses

Masses of renal origin include benign cysts, hydronephrosis, renal vein thrombosis, and neoplasms.

Cysts. Solitary or multilocular cysts and polycystic disease of the kidney are rare in the newborn infant. The latter condition is a hereditary disorder in which both kidneys are diffusely cystic. The disease occurs in two general types, an *adult* and an *infantile* form, a distinction based on differences in (1) patterns of inheritance, (2) clinical manifestation, and (3) structural character.

The *adult* form of polycystic disease of the kidney has a strong familial incidence. Although rapid progression of the process can occur in an affected infant,

the symptoms of hypertension, bilateral kidney enlargement, and progressive renal insufficiency are usually delayed until adulthood. Bilateral renal involvement is confirmed on intravenous pyelography by elongation and distortion of the renal pelvis. This form of polycystic kidney has islands of normal parenchyma interspersed among the numerous cysts.

The *infantile* variety of polycystic disease of the kidney is manifested shortly after birth and usually results in early death (Osathanondh and Potter, 1964). Although siblings may be affected, this form has not been reported to occur in more than one generation of any family. Both kidneys invariably have radially arranged, fusiform cystic clefts in which no normal renal parenchyma can be identified. Multiple epithelial cysts or extensive bile duct proliferation occurs in the liver of every patient with infantile polycystic disease. Occasional cysts occur in the lungs and pancreas, but congenital malformations elsewhere in the body are rare.

A congenital multicystic kidney is the single most common intra-abdominal mass found in the newborn (Flanagan and Kozah, 1968). This process, usually unilateral (in contrast to polycystic disease of the kidney), is almost invariably associated with complete absence of renal function in the affected kidney. Ureteral anomalies with obstruction or stenosis are usually present and the renal parenchyma on the affected side is almost always completely destroyed by the cystic process (Fig. 10-3). In contradistinction to patients with polycystic disease of the kidney, the prognosis in multicystic disease following nephrectomy is usually excellent, since the remaining kidney is ordinarily

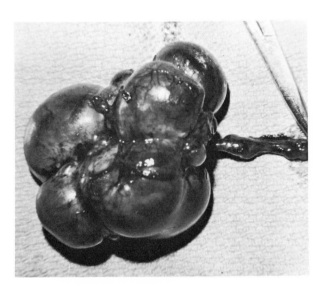

FIG. 10-3. Unilateral multicystic kidney removed from newborn infant. Ureteral atresia was also present.

unaffected. A diagnosis of a congenital multicystic kidney is suggested by normal urinalysis, the presence of a unilateral mass in the newborn (sometimes ectopic in location), and absence of function in the involved kidney on intravenous pyelography.

Hydronephrosis. Obstruction of the drainage system of the kidney may result from congenital stenosis of the ureteropelvic junction or extrinsic compression by an aberrant vessel. Distal ureteral stenosis and uretero-vesical obstruction are less commonly encountered in the newborn infant. Rarely, in cases of a double collecting system, one ureter (usually that supplying the upper pole of the kidney) is obstructed while the other drains normally (Fig. 10-4). This last condition may be accompanied by a ureterocele (an aneurysmal ballooning of the most distal part of the ureter beneath the bladder mucosa at the ureteral oriffice). In all cases in which renal parenchyma is still identifiable, every effort should be exerted by the surgeon to preserve functioning tissue. Successful implementation of this dictum may require division of aberrant vessels, pyeloplasty, resection of a ureteral stenosis with re-anastomosis to the renal pelvis or bladder, or subtotal nephrectomy with resection of an associated hydro-ureter in the presence of a double collecting system (Fraley and Paulson, 1969; Hendren, 1970). If both kidneys are hydronephrotic, obstruction of the urethra or bladder neck should be suspected. In such cases, a complete evaluation of the genitourinary system is required.

Renal Vein Thrombosis. Acute renal vein thrombosis in the newborn infant occurs most often in association with maternal diabetes and dehydration. This diagnosis should be suggested by the presence of a flank mass in a newborn infant in association with hematuria and thrombocytopenia. The thrombocytopenia probably results from consumption of platelets within the thrombus. The affected kidney is not visualized on an intravenous pyelogram (Fig. 10-5). The left kidney is involved more frequently than the right, but the condition can occur bilaterally. An inferior venacavogram is helpful in documenting the extent of thrombus propagation. Transumbilical aortography can also provide an accurate index of the degree of vascular involvement and may assist in ruling out a diagnosis of renal trauma.

Emergency nephrectomy usually has been advocated for treatment of unilateral renal vein thrombosis because of the threat of secondary hypertension and because of possible thrombus extension into the adjacent vena cava and opposite renal vein. Recent reports, however, have emphasized the role of conservative therapy in management of this lesion (Belman et al., 1970). Maintenance of hydration and correction of

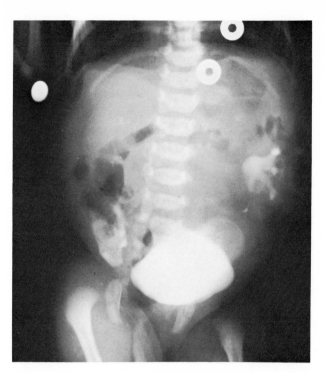

FIG. 10-4. Double collecting system of left kidney presenting as intra-abdominal mass secondary to hydronephrosis and obstruction of ureter draining upper pole. On intravenous pyelogram, the lower pole collecting system and ureter are displaced inferiorly and laterally by upper pole mass, producing characteristic "drooping lily" effect.

electrolyte imbalance and hypoglycemia are essential to the success of this approach. Heparin has been administered in some cases, but difficulties in achieving adequate control of anticoagulation in small infants may interfere with its routine use. Adoption of non-operative treatment is followed by a spontaneous return of renal function in some cases. At the same time, personal experience has indicated that unilateral renal vein thrombosis may indeed progress to involvement of the entire vena cava and the opposite renal vein (Fig. 10-5). Because of this potential, great caution must be exercised in pursuing nonoperative treatment, particularly in the presence of persistent hematuria and anemia. Arteriography may provide assistance in defining the potential for survival of the affected kidney in selected cases. When surgical exploration and nephrectomy are undertaken, successful extraction of thrombus from the vena cava and opposite renal vein can be achieved by use of a small Fogarty catheter.

Neonatal Renal Tumors. The characteristic Wilms' tumor of infancy presents as a unicentric, encapsulated embryoma arising from mesodermal cell rests within the kidney. Most renal neoplasms of the newborn infant, however, are not typical Wilms' tumors but are

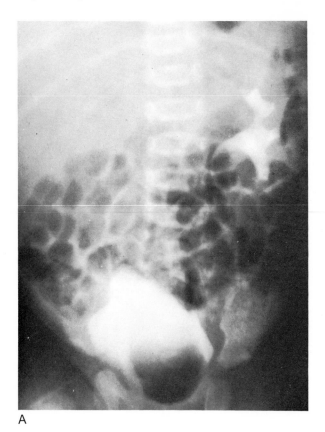

A

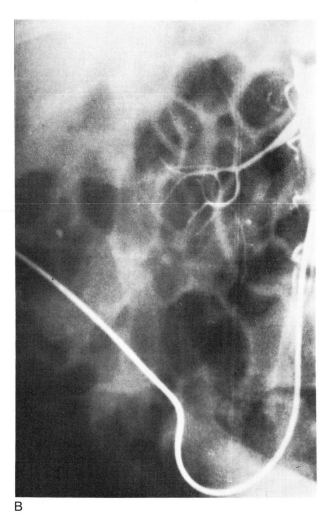

B

C

FIG. 10-5. *A,* Intravenous pyelogram obtained in newborn infant who presented with right flank mass, hematuria, and history of maternal diabetes. Right kidney is not visualized. *B,* Right renal arteriogram obtained by umbilical artery catheterization also failed to demonstrate functioning of right kidney or filling of right renal vein. *C,* Infarcted right kidney was removed subsequently at operation. Extensive thrombectomy was performed, with extraction of clot (arrow) from inferior vena cava, both iliac veins, and left renal vein by use of small Fogarty catheter. Venous drainage from left kidney had been maintained through left spermatic vein prior to thrombectomy.

diffuse, nonencapsulated, mesenchymal proliferations, which envelop islands of normal or dysplastic renal parenchyma (Richmond and Dougall, 1970; Waisman and Cooper, 1970). These unusual tumors present a bulging, pale, whorled cut surface. Histologically, the predominant cells are either fibroblasts or smooth muscle cells, which are conjoined into woven bundles of spindle-shaped cells containing elongated nuclei. Mitotic figures are relatively uncommon.

These unique neoplasms usually appear as asymptomatic abdominal masses shortly following birth, although they occasionally may be associated with maternal hydramnios. An intravenous pyelogram demonstrates typical distortion of the renal pelvis and calyces by an intrinsic mass (Fig. 10-6). The most important clinical feature of these distinctive "mesoblastic nephromas" is their benign behavior as contrasted to that of the usual Wilms' tumor occurring later in life

(Bolande et al., 1970). These neoplasms have been called "Wilms' tumors" in most reported series and, therefore, the literature is confusing on this point of histologic differentiation. There have been no documented instances of local recurrence or metastasis of these tumors following nephrectomy. On the other hand, addition of other modalities of therapy, including chemotherapy and radiation, often has resulted in a significant increase in mortality and morbidity (Hamanaka et al., 1969). Whether or not these unique neoplasms represent a more differentiated variety of nephroblastoma (Wilms' tumor) is unclear, but clinical data are inescapable: nephrectomy is probably curative and the addition of radiation and chemotherapy may present a greater hazard to the patient than the lesion itself.

Nonrenal Retroperitoneal Masses

The diagnosis and treatment of traumatic hematoma of the adrenal gland and kidney have been discussed

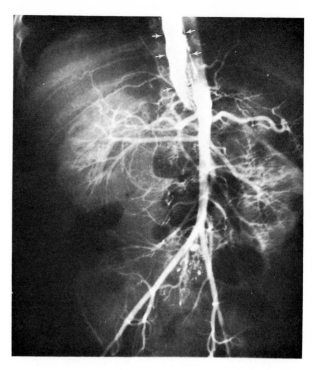

FIG. 10-7. Myelogram and arteriogram in infant presenting with right flank mass and paraplegia. Right kidney is displaced laterally by mass just inferior to right renal artery. Myelogram (arrows) confirms intraspinal extension of tumor with obstruction of subarachnoid space. Following laminectomy and removal of intraspinal neuroblastoma, this infant was treated with chemotherapy and radiation. She has subsequently regained normal motor activity in her legs and has no evidence of residual tumor, three years later.

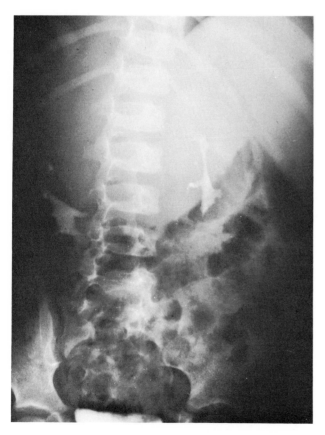

FIG. 10-6. Demonstration by intravenous pyelography of characteristic distortion and displacement of collecting system of right kidney by intrarenal mass. In infants this picture is typically associated with Wilms' tumor.

in Chapter 8. Nonrenal neoplasms arising from the retroperitoneal space in newborn infants include neuroblastoma, teratoma, and soft tissue sarcomas.

Neuroblastoma. This congenital tumor can originate anywhere that derivatives of the neural crest ectoderm exist (Koop, 1964). Accordingly, neuroblastomas may arise in the embryo at any point along the sympathetic chain of ganglia extending from the neck to the pelvis or within the adrenal medulla. Histologically, the neoplasm varies from an undifferentiated, highly malignant form, to a more mature lesion. Occasionally, a highly differentiated, obviously malignant, neuroblastoma spontaneously matures into a benign ganglioneuroma, a unique phenomenon first documented by Cushing in 1927 (Bill, 1968).

Approximately 40 per cent of neuroblastomas arise from the adrenal, 55 per cent from the retroperitoneal, paravertebral sympathetic chain, and 5 per cent within the pelvis. Occasionally, the tumor extends through an adjacent intervertebral foramen in a dumbbell-like manner, compressing the spinal cord and producing paraplegia (Fig. 10-7). Because of their origin from neural crest tissue, these tumors frequently produce catecholamines, and the metabolites VMA and HVA are identifiable in the urine. Screening of the urine for these substances in suspected patients not only assists in initial diagnosis, but also provides a continuing assessment of response to therapy and may reveal late recurrences.

Neuroblastoma is a nonencapsulated tumor that spreads by direct extension into adjacent organs and by metastases through lymphatic channels and blood stream, to the skeleton, retro-orbital area, liver, and lymph nodes. Metastatic involvement of the pulmonary parenchyma is rare. Skeletal metastases may be evident on roentgenogram or may be identifiable microscopically in bone marrow. Bone involvement implies a poor prognosis, whereas lymph node and liver me-

tastases in the young infant often prove compatible with eventual cure. Total surgical extirpation is the ideal treatment, but partial excision followed by radiation therapy and chemotherapy also can achieve an excellent survival rate, especially in a young infant. Accordingly, as contrasted to the philosophy usually adopted for the treatment of cancer in older children and adults, less aggressive measures are recommended in young infants with neuroblastoma with the surgeon exercising particular care not to damage major organs or produce an undue degree of postoperative morbidity and mortality while striving to excise the tumor completely.

Neuroblastomas can be differentiated from primary renal neoplasms by their tendency to involve midline structures, by their firm, finely nodular consistency, by

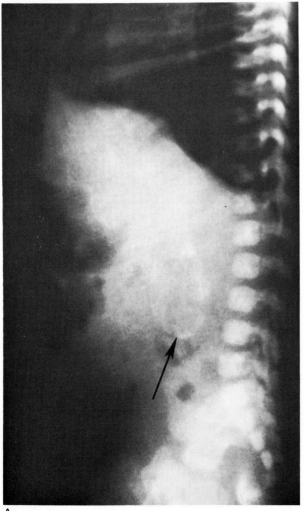

A

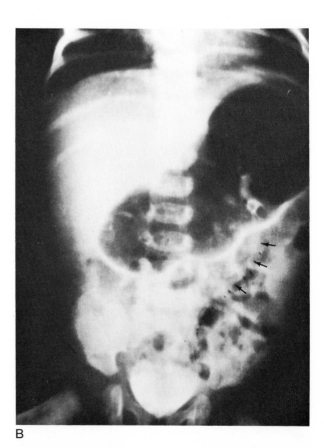

B

FIG. 10-8. *A,* Calcified intra-abdominal neuroblastoma (arrow) producing *B,* lateral displacement of left kidney and ureter (arrows).

the presence of calcification on roentgenogram, by their characteristic metastatic spread to the skeleton and liver, and by the excretion of catecholamines (VMA and HVA) in the urine. Finally, since the tumor arises outside the kidney, frequently from the adrenal medulla, an intravenous pyelogram often demonstrates extrinsic compression and/or displacement of the urinary collecting system, as contrasted to the characteristic calyceal and pelvic distortion which results from an intrinsic renal tumor (Fig. 10-8).

The improved survival rate in young infants afflicted by this tumor, even in the presence of extensive hepatic metastasis, deserves emphasis. Even paraplegia may be reversible through the judicious use of a combined therapeutic approach incorporating surgery, chemotherapy, and radiation. The chemotherapeutic agents employed most frequently in management of these patients are vincristine and cyclophosphamide.

Teratoma. This is a rare neoplasm that probably results from an abnormal sequestration of cells early in fetal development. The resulting tumor contains derivatives of all three germinal layers—ectoderm, mesoderm, and endoderm (Berry et al., 1969). The degree of histologic differentiation and malignant potential of the resulting tumor varies widely. These masses are usually situated near the midline, and most commonly present as sacrococcygeal growths in newborn infants (Fig. 10-9) (see Chapter 9) (Hendren and Henderson, 1970). The next most common location at this age is the retroperitoneal area, but teratomas can also arise in the ovary, testicle, anterior mediastinum, thyroid gland, and nasopharynx. Intra-abdominal teratomas are most frequently located in the upper midline and may be characterized on roentgenogram by the presence of discernible bone elements or teeth. This tumor is usually diagnosed earlier in life than are neuroblastomas, which characteristically appear later in infancy. An intravenous pyelogram often demonstrates displacement and compression of the whole kidney, characteristics of an extrinsic rather an intrinsic neoplasm. X-ray studies of the gastrointestinal tract may provide further assistance in delineating the tumor. Teratomas occur more frequently in females than in males and there may be an associated family history of twinning.

Although teratomas may achieve enormous size, they are usually encapsulated and can be separated from adjacent structures by careful surgical dissection. When the tumor arises from the stomach, it is necessary to remove a section of contiguous, involved gastric wall.

As in the case of all large intra-abdominal tumors, provision must be made for intraoperative administration of fluid and blood through the superior vena cava, since potential compression and/or operative damage to the inferior vena cava may impede blood flow

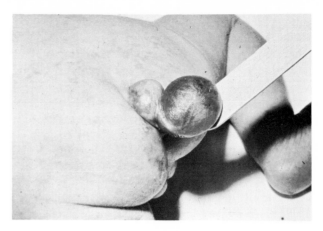

FIG. 10-9. Small sacrococcygeal teratoma in newborn infant.

from the lower extremities. The importance of early removal of sacrococcygeal teratomas in newborn infants has been emphasized (Chapter 9). Such tumors can originate in the presacral area and be identifiable only on rectal examination or by palpation of the lower abdomen. The older the patient at the time of surgical excision, the poorer the prognosis, since there appears to be an increased propensity for malignant degeneration with aging.

Sarcoma. A variety of sarcomas arising from the soft tissues of the retroperitoneal area may appear either at birth or later in infancy. Unlike the documented experience with renal neoplasms, neuroblastoma, and teratoma, the prognosis for young infants affected by sarcomas does not appear to be any better than that of older children. Unfortunately, sarcomas arising in the flank are not as readily apparent as are similar tumors occurring in the extremities and superficial tissues of the trunk and head. Accordingly, the goal of complete surgical excision is less often possible in tumors of retroperitoneal origin. Response of such tumors to chemotherapy and radiation therapy is also less predictable and frequently less gratifying than that observed following treatment of neuroblastoma (Hays et al., 1970; Sulamaa and Moller, 1969).

Pelvic Masses Arising from the Genitourinary System

Distended Bladder. Bladder distention may be confused with a pelvic tumor and can result from any type of outlet or urethral obstruction. The condition is more likely to occur in male infants; urinary catheterization is an essential component of differential diagnosis. Severe degrees of lower urinary tract obstruction, originating early in fetal development, are likely to produce advanced hydronephrosis and extensive, irreversible renal damage. In the young fetus, the collecting tubules of the kidney are short and relatively straight, so that a maximum pressure is transmitted to the ampullary ends when severe obstruction is present. Later in fetal development, the elongated collecting system provides some degree of protection through its buffering effect.

The most common causes of obstruction of the distal urinary system are urethral meatal stenosis, posterior urethral valves, and urethral strictures. Primary bladder-neck obstruction occurs infrequently.

Hydrometrocolpos. As contrasted to the newborn male infant who is more likely to present with urinary tract obstruction, the female can develop a unique pelvic mass as a result of an imperforate hymen or vaginal atresia. Identification of a bulging perineum and absent

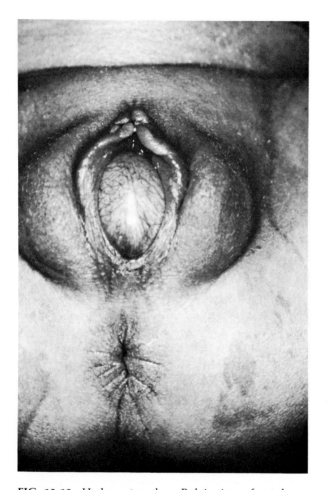

FIG. 10-10. Hydrometrocolpos. Bulging imperforate hymen is apparent in this newborn, female infant who presented with large, lower abdominal mass. Simple incision of obstructing membrane drained vagina and obliterated palpable tumor.

vaginal orifice is diagnostic in such cases (Fig. 10-10). Failure to identify this lesion can lead to an unnecessary exploratory laparotomy and even disastrous excision of the mass. Diagnostic evaluation of this mass should include an intravenous pyelogram, for which a delayed lateral film is used to demonstrate the opacified bladder. Any mass that originates between the rectum and the displaced bladder in a female infant most likely represents hydrometrocolpos. Direct needle injection of sterile contrast media through the perineum can provide final proof of diagnosis. Occasionally the diagnosis may be obscured by gastrointestinal symptoms resulting from aplastic peritonitis and adhesions produced by in utero spillage of genital secretions into the peritoneal cavity through the open ends of the Fallopian tubes (Ceballos and Hicks, 1970). Extrinsic compression of the distal urinary tract also may produce secondary hydronephrosis.

Hydrometrocolpos usually presents after menarche as a result of blockage of menstrual flow. The few cases that develop in the newborn infant result from accumulation of vaginal and cervical secretions stimulated by maternal estrogen effect.

In achieving surgical correction of this lesion, care must be taken to avoid injury to the adjacent, and frequently distorted, urethra. Rarely, a combined abdominovaginal approach may be required for correction of vaginal atresia (Fig. 10-11). Incision of the obstructing membrane ordinarily provides adequate drainage when hydrometrocolpos is associated with an imperforate hyman (Ramenofsky and Raffensperger, 1971).

Ovarian Tumors. In reviewing collected cases of ovarian tumors in the newborn infants, Mainolfi noted that 28 of the 30 ovarian tumors reported in the first 36 days of life represented simple cysts of graafian or germinal epithelial origin (Mainolfi et al., 1968). This experience contrasts with those cases of ovarian tumors reported in older infants between the ages of 36 days and one year, only eight of which proved to be benign follicular cysts. Since 50 per cent of newborn female fetuses have cystic ovaries at autopsy, it is presumed that this early predilection for cyst formation results from increased follicular activity induced by circulating placental and maternal hormones.

In most instances, ovarian cysts in newborn infants are asymptomatic masses, although an occasional association with maternal hydramnios has been noted. In rare cases, these tumors precipitate an abdominal emergency as a result of traumatic rupture and hemorrhage or ischemic infarction secondary to twisting of its pedicle.

Preoperative diagnosis is facilitated by bimanual palpation through the rectum. Inspection of the peri-

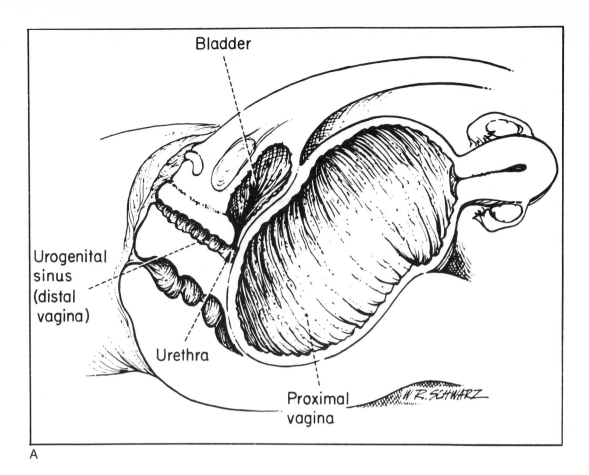

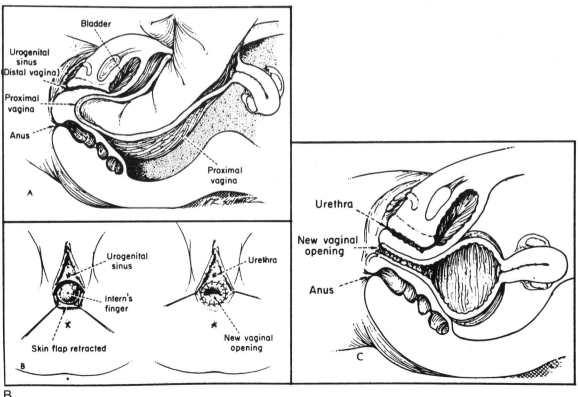

FIG. 10-11. *A*, Diagram of basic anatomy of hydrometrocolpos in infant, resulting from vaginal atresia. *B*, Combined abdomino-perineal-vaginal pull-through operation for correction of vaginal atresia and hydrometrocolpos in newborn infant. (From Ramenofsky, M. L., and Raffensperger, J. G.: An abdomino-perineal-vaginal pull-through for definitive treatment of hydrometrocolpos. J. Pediat. Surg., *6*:381, 1971.)

neum excludes a diagnosis of hydrometrocolpos, and intravenous pyelography and abdominal roentgenograms rule out urinary tract obstruction.

The preponderance of benign cystic lesions at this age encourages a conservative approach to surgical management.

Hepatic Tumors

Cysts. Extensive intrahepatic cystic disease of the bile ducts frequently accompanies the infantile form of polycystic disease of the kidney. Otherwise, most congenital hepatic cysts are solitary and may attain enormous size. Differential diagnosis is achieved by (1) plain lateral and AP abdominal films that demonstrate a characteristic downward displacement of air-filled intestine by an enlarged liver, (2) an intravenous pyelogram that demonstrates a normal urinary tract, and (3) a hepatic scan that confirms a filling defect in the liver parenchyma. Arteriography confirms the absence of vascularity and excludes the diagnosis of a solid neoplasm. In smaller isolated cysts, total surgical extirpation may prove feasible. Massive lesions, however, may require marsupialization with stripping of the lining and external tube drainage. The collapsed cyst can be excised at a later date (Fig. 10-12).

Neoplasms. Benign tumors of the liver that may appear in the newborn period include hamartomas, hemangiomas, adenomas, and lymphangiomas. Hemangiomas of the liver, as noted previously, may rupture and produce free bleeding into the peritoneal cavity (Graivier et al., 1967). Isolated tumors usually can be excised, but multiple or extensive lesions may require other forms of therapy. Hemangiomas of the liver have been noted to respond to steroid administration as well as radiation therapy. Intra-abdominal neuroblastoma at this age may present primarily as an enlarged liver containing extensive metastases. Differential diagnosis is based on increased urinary levels of catecholamines (VMA and VHA).

The primary malignant tumor that occurs at this age, hepatoblastoma, is usually unicentric in origin and surrounded by a pseudocapsule. A radioactive hepatic scan and arteriography are especially helpful in achieving a preoperative diagnosis and in assessing potential resectability of the tumor (Fig. 10-13). Some hepatoblastomas also have been noted to be associated with hemi-hypertrophy of the body and the presence of cystathioninuria (Geiser et al., 1970). Total extirpation by radical hepatic lobectomy is more likely to be effective in the cure of this lesion in infants than in the cure of the multicentric hepatomas that develop in older children and adults.

Tumors of the Biliary System. The major tumor arising from the biliary tract of newborn infants is congenital choledochal cyst (Scharli and Bettex, 1968). This lesion usually develops as a ballooning of the distal common bile duct and presents as a retroperitoneal swelling associated with intermittent jaundice. Intravenous pyelography demonstrates a downward and posterior displacement of the right kidney. Plain AP and lateral films of the abdomen and contrast studies of the upper gastrointestinal system are particularly helpful in establishing a preoperative diagnosis. The duodenum is characteristically displaced anteriorly and medially by the large retroperitoneal cyst, while the colon is displaced anteriorly and inferiorly (Fig. 10-14). The condition occurs more frequently in female infants (4:1). Some form of internal drainage of the cyst or common bile duct into the gastrointestinal tract is preferred. Roux-en-Y anastomosis to a jejunal loop is appropriate for drainage of a large choledochal cyst presenting through the transverse mesocolon, whereas direct anastomosis and drainage into the duodenum have been used for correction of smaller cysts. Because of the occurrence of recurrent attacks of ascending cholangitis following either of the above procedures, however, recent reports have advocated excision of the cyst and re-establishment of biliary drainage through a Roux-en-Y choledochojejunostomy (Jones et al., 1971).

Masses of Gastrointestinal Origin

Intra-abdominal masses representing intestinal distention in newborn infants should be readily distinguished by accompanying signs and symptoms of gastrointestinal obstruction. The rarity of solid neoplasms of the GI tract is emphasized by only five case reports of gastric teratoma (Atwell et al., 1967). The most frequent tumors arising from the gastrointestinal tract are cysts.

Duplication Cysts. Duplication cysts of the gastrointestinal tract can occur anywhere between the mouth and the rectum, but are most commonly associated with the terminal ileum and cecum (Fig. 10-15). They may present clinically as asymptomatic palpable masses, as gastrointestinal obstruction resulting from extrinsic compression of the adjacent intestine, or as intestinal bleeding resulting from peptic ulceration from ectopic gastric mucosa. The lesions may be isolated or may involve extensive segments of the intestine or colon. Duodenal duplication cysts may extend to the thoracic cavity and may be associated with vertebral anomalies. Duplication cysts of the colon may be associated with anomalies of the external genitalia (Cohen, 1968).

Differential diagnosis is made on the basis of a cystic

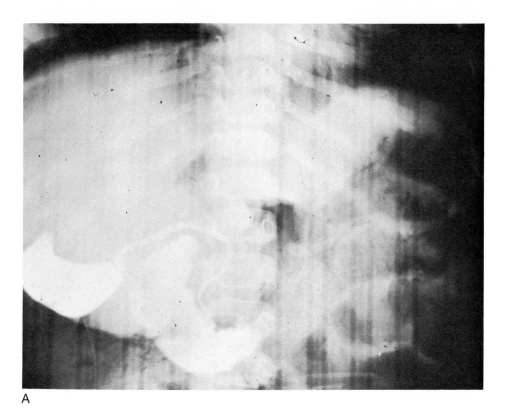

A

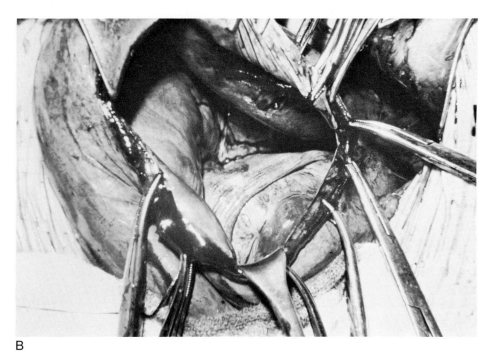

B

FIG. 10-12. *A,* Cholangiogram demonstrating displacement of gallbladder and cystic duct by large mass within right lobe of the liver. *B,* Large, unilocular hepatic cyst was found at operation. In this photograph of the liver, cyst has been unroofed and clamps are attached to its margin. Retractors are within cyst cavity, demonstrating its extensive expansion within right lobe of liver.

10

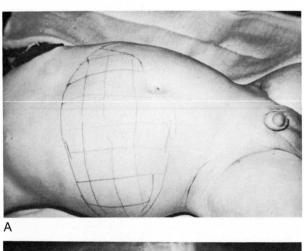

A

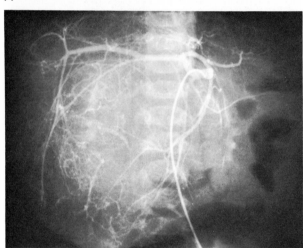

B

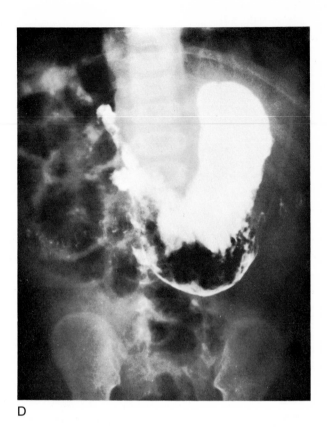

D

C

FIG. 10-13. Infant with large right upper quadrant abdominal mass, *A,* which on arteriogram, *B,* and hepatic scan (see Fig. 10-2) was demonstrated to arise from the medial aspect of right lobe of liver. *C,* Surgical specimen, consisting of entire right lobe and medial segment of left lobe of liver, contained pseudoencapsulated hepatoblastoma. *D,* Postoperative upper gastrointestinal x-ray series outlines small, residual triangle of normal left lobe of liver. For over one year since operation this patient has been observed to have normal liver function and no evidence of recurrent tumor.

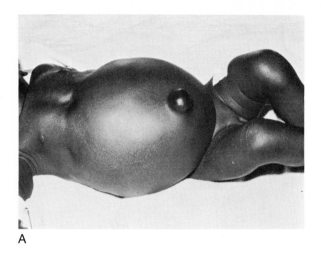

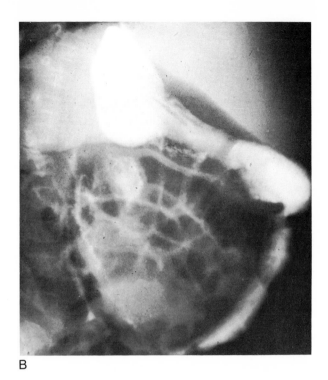

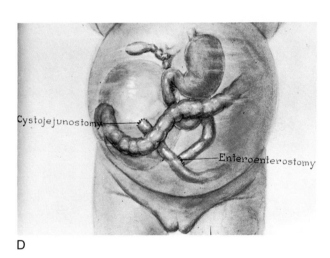

FIG. 10-14. *A,* This female infant presented with jaundice and large, palpable abdominal mass. *B,* Upper gastrointestinal x-ray series demonstrated anterior displacement and distortion of stomach and duodenum on lateral view. Large choledochal cyst containing over 500 ml. of fluid (depicted diagramatically in *C*) was corrected by Roux-en-Y anastomosis of jejunum to inferior margin of cyst wall, *D.*

abdominal mass, which is freely movable and may be associated with gastrointestinal obstruction and/or bleeding. Contrast studies of the upper gastrointestinal tract and colon are especially helpful in making a correct preoperative diagnosis. Treatment in cases of localized, readily accessible cysts is resection of both the lesion and the contiguous bowel. In the case of extensive or inaccessible lesions, marsupialization of

the tumor by windowing into the adjacent bowel wall may be preferable. Twenty per cent of duplication cysts are found to have a previously existing communication into the contiguous bowel. Any attempt at operative dissection of the cysts from adjacent intestinal wall is particularly hazardous and may result in perforation of the bowel or compromise of the shared blood supply.

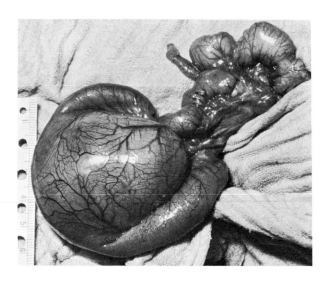

FIG. 10-15. Duplication cyst of ileum which produced partial intestinal obstruction by extrinsic compression of intestinal lumen.

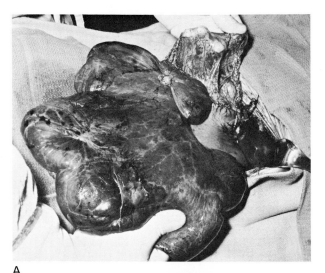

A

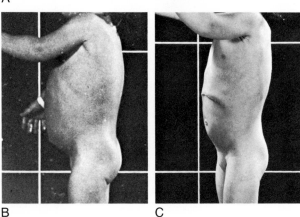

B   C

FIG. 10-16. *A*, Massive omental cyst, which had produced abdominal distention since birth. Mass was totally removed by excision of omental apron from transverse colon. *B*, Preoperative and, *C*, postoperative photographs of patient demonstrate dramatic change in configuration of abdominal wall.

Omental and Mesenteric Cysts. These tumors probably result from anomalous lymphatic development and can contain either serous or chylous fluid. They can be either unilocular or multicompartmentalized and usually present as an asymptomatic mass in a young infant (Fig. 10-16). Ischemia resulting from twisting of the mass, perforation, or intestinal obstruction can cause symptoms in rare instances (Oliver, 1964). Omental cysts are usually extensive multilocular tumors that involve most of the omental apron and are readily distinguished on lateral films of the abdomen by their anterior location. In many instances, attachment of the cyst to the adjacent bowel is so intimate as to require intestinal resection in order to achieve removal (Handelsman and Ravitch, 1954).

Vitelline Duct Cyst. Persistence of fetal omphalomesenteric duct remnants can produce, proximally, a Meckel's diverticulum; distally, a draining umbilical sinus; and centrally, an isolated cyst. Patency of the entire duct permits free egress of intestinal contents through the umbilicus (Fig. 10-17). A cystic remnant may present as a palpable abdominal mass that produces umbilical indentation on movement. Injection of contrast media into an umbilical sinus may identify a communicating vitelline cyst.

Pancreatic Cyst. Congenital cysts of the pancreas are extremely rare and may be excised by caudal pancreatectomy when the lesion is isolated in the tail of the pancreas. In more proximal locations, drainage of the cyst into a Roux-en-Y loop of jejunum or cystogastrostomy may be preferable.

Meconium Cyst. As noted in Chapter 6, perforation of the fetal intestine in utero may result in meconium cyst formation. The lesion usually results in intra-abdominal calcifications and produces intestinal obstruction following birth (Fig. 10-18).

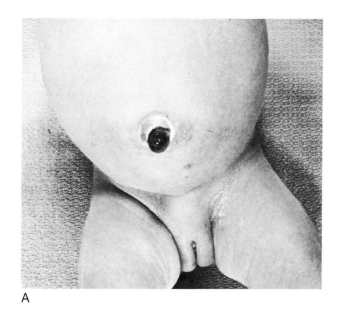

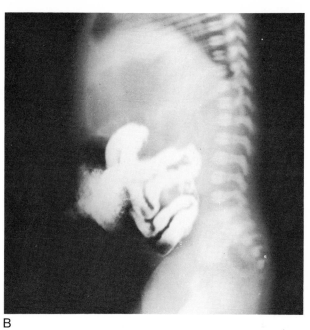

FIG. 10-17 *A,* Newborn infant with draining umbilical stump which, *B,* proved to be a persistent omphalomesenteric duct and cyst on injection of sinus tract with constrast medium. (Note opacification of small intestine via umbilical sinus.)

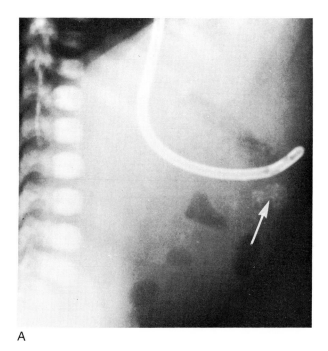

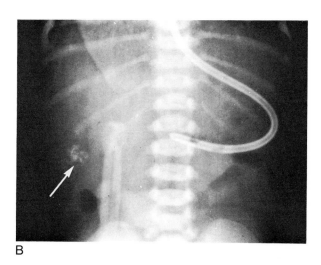

FIG. 10-18. Roentgenograms of newborn infant with a calcified meconium cyst (arrows) producing intestinal obstruction.

REFERENCES

Atwell, J. D., Claireaux, A. E., and Nixon, H. H.: Teratoma of the stomach in the newborn. J. Pediat. Surg., 2:197, 1967.

Belman, A. B., Susmano, D. F., Burden, J. J., and Kaplan, G. W.: Nonoperative treatment of unilateral renal vein thrombosis in the newborn. J.A.M.A., 211:1165, 1970.

Berdon, W. E., Baker, D. H., and Santulli, T. V.: Factors producing spurious obstruction of the inferior vena cava in infants and children with abdominal tumors. Radiology, 88:111, 1967.

Berry, C. L., Keeling, J., and Hilton, C.: Teratoma in infancy and childhood: a review of 91 cases. J. Path., 98:241, 1969.

Bill, A. H.: Studies of the mechanism of regression of human neuroblastoma. J. Pediat. Surg., 3:727, 1968.

Bolande, R. P., Brough, A. J., and Izant, R. J.: Mesenchymal renal neoplasms of infancy. J. Pediat. Surg., 5:405, 1970.

Ceballos, R., and Hicks, G. M.: Plastic peritonitis due to neonatal hydrometrocolpos: radiologic and pathologic observations. J. Pediat. Surg., 5:63, 1970.

Cohen, S. J.: Diphallus with duplication of colon and bladder. Proc. Roy. Soc. Med., 61:305, 1968.

Flanagan, M. J., and Kozah, J. A.: Congenital unilateral multicystic disease of the kidney. Arch. Surg., 96:983, 1968.

Fraley, E. E., and Paulson, D. F.: Urologic surgery. New Eng. J. Med., 281:355, 1969.

Geiser, C. F., Baez, A., Schindler, A. M., and Shih, V. E.: Epithelial hepatoblastoma associated with congenital hemihypertrophy and cystathioninuria: presentation of a case. Pediatrics, 46:66, 1970.

Graivier, L., Votteler, T. P., and Dorman, G. W.: Hepatic hemangiomas in newborn infants. J. Pediat. Surg., 2:299, 1967.

Hamanaka, Y., Okamoto, E., and Ueda, T.: Fibroma of the kidney in the newborn. J. Pediat. Surg., 4:250, 1969.

Handelsman, J. C., and Ravitch, M. M.: Chylous cysts of the mesentery in children. Ann. Surg., 140:185, 1954.

Hays, D. M., et al.: Fibrosarcomas in infants and children. J. Pediat. Surg., 5:176, 1970.

Hendren, W. H.: Neonatal surgery. In Surgery. Edited by R. Warren. Philadelphia, W. B. Saunders, 1963.

Hendren, W. H.: A new approach to infants with severe obstructive uropathy: early complete reconstruction. J. Pediat. Surg., 5:184, 1970.

Hendren, W. H., and Henderson, B. M.: The surgical management of sacrococcygeal teratomas with intrapelvic extension. Ann. Surg., 171:77, 1970.

Jones, P. G., Smith, E. D., Clarke, A. M., and Kent, M.: Choledochal cysts: experience with radical excision. J. Pediat. Surg., 6:112, 1971.

Koop, C. E.: Current management of nephroblastoma and neuroblastoma. Amer. J. Surg., 107:497, 1964.

Mainolfi, F. G., Standiford, W. E., and Hubbard, T. B., Jr.: Ruptured ovarian cyst in the newborn. J. Pediat. Surg., 3:612, 1968.

Mofenson, H. C., and Greensher, J.: Transillumination of the abdomen in infants. Amer. J. Dis. Child., 115:428, 1968.

Oliver, G. A.: The omental cyst: a rare cause of the acute abdominal crisis. Surgery, 56:588, 1964.

Osathanondh, V., and Potter, E. L.: Pathogenesis of polycystic kidneys: type I due to hyperplasia of interstitial portion of collecting tubules. Arch. Path., 77:466, 1964.

Ramenofsky, M. L., and Raffensperger, J. G.: An abdominoperineal-vaginal pull-through for definitive treatment of hydrometrocolpos. J. Pediat. Surg., 6:381, 1971.

Richmond, H., and Dougall, A. J.: Neonatal renal tumors. J. Pediat. Surg., 5:413, 1970.

Rowe, M. I., Morse, I. S., and Frye, T. R.: Infusion pyelography in infancy and childhood. J. Pediat. Surg., 2:215, 1967.

Salerno, F. G., Collins, O. D., Redmond, D., and Rice, J.: Transumbilical abdominal aortography in the newborn. J. Pediat. Surg., 5:40, 1970.

Schaffer, A. J.: Surgical diagnosis in the newborn. In Diagnosis of Surgical Disease. Edited by R. G. Shackelford. Philadelphia, W. B. Saunders, 1968.

Scharli, A., and Bettex, M.: Congenital choledochal cyst: reconstruction of the normal anatomy. J. Pediat. Surg., 3:604, 1968.

Sulamaa, M., and Moller, C.: Soft tissue sarcoma in children. J. Pediat. Surg., 4:520, 1969.

Waisman, J., and Cooper, P. H.: Renal neoplasms of the newborn. J. Pediat. Surg., 5:407, 1970.

Index

Page numbers in *italics* indicate illustrations; those followed by t indicate tables.